LLE...
2006
SUN SIGN
BOOK

Forecasts by
Terry Lamb

Book Editing and Design: K. M. Brielmaier
Cover Design: Kevin R. Brown

Copyright 2005 Llewellyn Publications
A Division of Llewellyn Worldwide, Ltd.
Llewellyn is a registered trademark of Llewellyn Worldwide, Ltd.
P.O. Box 64383 Dept. 0-7387-0149-1 St. Paul, MN 55164-0383
Astrological charts produced with Kepler software
by permission of Cosmic Patterns Software, Inc.

2005

JANUARY
```
S  M  T  W  T  F  S
               1
 2  3  4  5  6  7  8
 9 10 11 12 13 14 15
16 17 18 19 20 21 22
23 24 25 26 27 28 29
30 31
```

FEBRUARY
```
S  M  T  W  T  F  S
       1  2  3  4  5
 6  7  8  9 10 11 12
13 14 15 16 17 18 19
20 21 22 23 24 25 26
27 28
```

MARCH
```
S  M  T  W  T  F  S
          1  2  3  4  5
 6  7  8  9 10 11 12
13 14 15 16 17 18 19
20 21 22 23 24 25 26
27 28 29 30 31
```

APRIL
```
S  M  T  W  T  F  S
                  1  2
 3  4  5  6  7  8  9
10 11 12 13 14 15 16
17 18 19 20 21 22 23
24 25 26 27 28 29 30
```

MAY
```
S  M  T  W  T  F  S
 1  2  3  4  5  6  7
 8  9 10 11 12 13 14
15 16 17 18 19 20 21
22 23 24 25 26 27 28
29 30 31
```

JUNE
```
S  M  T  W  T  F  S
          1  2  3  4
 5  6  7  8  9 10 11
12 13 14 15 16 17 18
19 20 21 22 23 24 25
26 27 28 29 30
```

JULY
```
S  M  T  W  T  F  S
               1  2
 3  4  5  6  7  8  9
10 11 12 13 14 15 16
17 18 19 20 21 22 23
24 25 26 27 28 29 30
31
```

AUGUST
```
S  M  T  W  T  F  S
    1  2  3  4  5  6
 7  8  9 10 11 12 13
14 15 16 17 18 19 20
21 22 23 24 25 26 27
28 29 30 31
```

SEPTEMBER
```
S  M  T  W  T  F  S
             1  2  3
 4  5  6  7  8  9 10
11 12 13 14 15 16 17
18 19 20 21 22 23 24
25 26 27 28 29 30
```

OCTOBER
```
S  M  T  W  T  F  S
                   1
 2  3  4  5  6  7  8
 9 10 11 12 13 14 15
16 17 18 19 20 21 22
23 24 25 26 27 28 29
30 31
```

NOVEMBER
```
S  M  T  W  T  F  S
       1  2  3  4  5
 6  7  8  9 10 11 12
13 14 15 16 17 18 19
20 21 22 23 24 25 26
27 28 29 30
```

DECEMBER
```
S  M  T  W  T  F  S
             1  2  3
 4  5  6  7  8  9 10
11 12 13 14 15 16 17
18 19 20 21 22 23 24
25 26 27 28 29 30 31
```

2006

JANUARY
```
S  M  T  W  T  F  S
 1  2  3  4  5  6  7
 8  9 10 11 12 13 14
15 16 17 18 19 20 21
22 23 24 25 26 27 28
29 30 31
```

FEBRUARY
```
S  M  T  W  T  F  S
          1  2  3  4
 5  6  7  8  9 10 11
12 13 14 15 16 17 18
19 20 21 22 23 24 25
26 27 28
```

MARCH
```
S  M  T  W  T  F  S
          1  2  3  4
 5  6  7  8  9 10 11
12 13 14 15 16 17 18
19 20 21 22 23 24 25
26 27 28 29 30 31
```

APRIL
```
S  M  T  W  T  F  S
                   1
 2  3  4  5  6  7  8
 9 10 11 12 13 14 15
16 17 18 19 20 21 22
23 24 25 26 27 28 29
30
```

MAY
```
S  M  T  W  T  F  S
    1  2  3  4  5  6
 7  8  9 10 11 12 13
14 15 16 17 18 19 20
21 22 23 24 25 26 27
28 29 30 31
```

JUNE
```
S  M  T  W  T  F  S
             1  2  3
 4  5  6  7  8  9 10
11 12 13 14 15 16 17
18 19 20 21 22 23 24
25 26 27 28 29 30
```

JULY
```
S  M  T  W  T  F  S
                   1
 2  3  4  5  6  7  8
 9 10 11 12 13 14 15
16 17 18 19 20 21 22
23 24 25 26 27 28 29
30 31
```

AUGUST
```
S  M  T  W  T  F  S
       1  2  3  4  5
 6  7  8  9 10 11 12
13 14 15 16 17 18 19
20 21 22 23 24 25 26
27 28 29 30 31
```

SEPTEMBER
```
S  M  T  W  T  F  S
                1  2
 3  4  5  6  7  8  9
10 11 12 13 14 15 16
17 18 19 20 21 22 23
24 25 26 27 28 29 30
```

OCTOBER
```
S  M  T  W  T  F  S
 1  2  3  4  5  6  7
 8  9 10 11 12 13 14
15 16 17 18 19 20 21
22 23 24 25 26 27 28
29 30 31
```

NOVEMBER
```
S  M  T  W  T  F  S
          1  2  3  4
 5  6  7  8  9 10 11
12 13 14 15 16 17 18
19 20 21 22 23 24 25
26 27 28 29 30
```

DECEMBER
```
S  M  T  W  T  F  S
                1  2
 3  4  5  6  7  8  9
10 11 12 13 14 15 16
17 18 19 20 21 22 23
24 25 26 27 28 29 30
31
```

2007

JANUARY
```
S  M  T  W  T  F  S
    1  2  3  4  5  6
 7  8  9 10 11 12 13
14 15 16 17 18 19 20
21 22 23 24 25 26 27
28 29 30 31
```

FEBRUARY
```
S  M  T  W  T  F  S
             1  2  3
 4  5  6  7  8  9 10
11 12 13 14 15 16 17
18 19 20 21 22 23 24
25 26 27 28
```

MARCH
```
S  M  T  W  T  F  S
             1  2  3
 4  5  6  7  8  9 10
11 12 13 14 15 16 17
18 19 20 21 22 23 24
25 26 27 28 29 30 31
```

APRIL
```
S  M  T  W  T  F  S
 1  2  3  4  5  6  7
 8  9 10 11 12 13 14
15 16 17 18 19 20 21
22 23 24 25 26 27 28
29 30
```

MAY
```
S  M  T  W  T  F  S
       1  2  3  4  5
 6  7  8  9 10 11 12
13 14 15 16 17 18 19
20 21 22 23 24 25 26
27 28 29 30 31
```

JUNE
```
S  M  T  W  T  F  S
                1  2
 3  4  5  6  7  8  9
10 11 12 13 14 15 16
17 18 19 20 21 22 23
24 25 26 27 28 29 30
```

JULY
```
S  M  T  W  T  F  S
 1  2  3  4  5  6  7
 8  9 10 11 12 13 14
15 16 17 18 19 20 21
22 23 24 25 26 27 28
29 30 31
```

AUGUST
```
S  M  T  W  T  F  S
          1  2  3  4
 5  6  7  8  9 10 11
12 13 14 15 16 17 18
19 20 21 22 23 24 25
26 27 28 29 30 31
```

SEPTEMBER
```
S  M  T  W  T  F  S
                   1
 2  3  4  5  6  7  8
 9 10 11 12 13 14 15
16 17 18 19 20 21 22
23 24 25 26 27 28 29
30
```

OCTOBER
```
S  M  T  W  T  F  S
    1  2  3  4  5  6
 7  8  9 10 11 12 13
14 15 16 17 18 19 20
21 22 23 24 25 26 27
28 29 30 31
```

NOVEMBER
```
S  M  T  W  T  F  S
             1  2  3
 4  5  6  7  8  9 10
11 12 13 14 15 16 17
18 19 20 21 22 23 24
25 26 27 28 29 30
```

DECEMBER
```
S  M  T  W  T  F  S
                   1
 2  3  4  5  6  7  8
 9 10 11 12 13 14 15
16 17 18 19 20 21 22
23 24 25 26 27 28 29
30 31
```

Table of Contents

2006 Sun Sign Articles

Meet Terry Lamb

All horoscopes and sign descriptions for this book were written by Terry Lamb. A counselor, instructor, and healer using a spiritually oriented approach to astrology and healing, Terry specializes in electional astrology (choosing the right day for an event according to planetary influences), as well as family and relationship matters. She is the author of *Born To Be Together: Love Rela-*

tionships, Astrology, and the Soul, and is a contributing author to Llewellyn's *Moon Sign Book. The Beginning Math Workbook* was released by the National Council for Geocosmic Research in 2003, and she has also been published in *Cosmos*, the *NCGR Journal*, and the *Mountain Astrologer*, and has written a monograph on her research into planetary cycles and childhood called *The Cycles of Childhood*. In addition, her publications have appeared on various websites, including StarIQ.com, and her own site, www.terrylamb.net.

Terry is also director of the Astrological Certification Program, a two-year online and home study course, which may be used to gain certification and success in an astrological career. Fourth-level certified by the National Council for Geocosmic Research (NCGR), she is an instructor in the NCGR Online College, and serves on their Board of Examiners. She is also NCGR's executive director, the president of the San Diego chapter of NCGR, and a past board member of the San Diego Astrological Society. Terry is a faculty member of the United Astrology Congress and is a featured speaker at the State of the Art Astrology Conference and NCGR Education conferences, and regional conferences and seminars. She currently resides in Spring Valley, California.

New Concepts for Signs of the Zodiac

The signs of the zodiac represent characteristics and traits that indicate how energy operates within our lives. The signs tell the story of human evolution and development, and all are necessary to form the continuum of whole life experience. In fact, all twelve signs are represented within your astrological chart.

Although the traditional metaphors for the twelve signs (such as Aries, the Ram) are always functional, these alternative concepts for each of the twelve signs also describe the gradual unfolding of the human spirit.

Aries: The Initiator is the first sign of the zodiac and encompasses the primary concept of getting things started. This fiery ignition and bright beginning can prove to be the thrust necessary for new life, but the Initiator also can appear before a situation is ready for change and create disruption.

Taurus: The Maintainer sustains what Aries has begun and brings stability and focus into the picture, yet there also can be a tendency to try to maintain something in its current state without allowing for new growth.

Gemini: The Questioner seeks to determine whether alternatives are possible and offers diversity to the processes Taurus has brought into stability. Yet questioning can also lead to distraction, subsequently scattering energy and diffusing focus.

Cancer: The Nurturer provides the qualities necessary for growth and security, and encourages a deepening awareness of emotional needs. Yet this same nurturing can stifle individuation if it becomes too smothering.

Leo: The Loyalist directs and centralizes the experiences Cancer feeds. This quality is powerfully targeted toward self-awareness, but can be shortsighted. Hence, the Loyalist can hold steadfastly to viewpoints or feelings that inhibit new experiences.

Virgo: The Modifier analyzes the situations Leo brings to light and determines possibilities for change. Even though this change may be in the name of improvement, it can lead to dissatisfaction with the self if not directed in harmony with higher needs.

Libra: The Judge is constantly comparing everything to be sure that a certain level of rightness and perfection is presented. However, the Judge can also present possibilities that are harsh and seem to be cold or without feeling.

Scorpio: The Catalyst steps into the play of life to provide the quality of alchemical transformation. The Catalyst can stir the brew just enough to create a healing potion, or may get things going to such a powerful extent that they boil out of control.

Sagittarius: The Adventurer moves away from Scorpio's dimension to seek what lies beyond the horizon. The Adventurer continually looks for possibilities that answer the ultimate questions, but may forget the pathway back home.

Capricorn: The Pragmatist attempts to put everything into its rightful place and find ways to make life work out right. The Pragmatist can teach lessons of practicality and determination, but can become highly self-righteous when shortsighted.

Aquarius: The Reformer looks for ways to take what Capricorn has built and bring it up to date. Yet there is also a tendency to scrap the original in favor of a new plan that may not have the stable foundation necessary to operate effectively.

Pisces: The Visionary brings mysticism and imagination, and challenges the soul to move beyond the physical plane, into the realm of what might be. The Visionary can pierce the veil, returning enlightened to the physical world. The challenge is to avoid getting lost within the illusion of an alternate reality.

Understanding the Basics of Astrology

A strology is an ancient and continually evolving system used to clarify your identity and your needs. An astrological chart—which is calculated using the date, time, and place of birth—contains many factors which symbolically represent the needs, expressions, and experiences that make up the whole person. A professional astrologer interprets this symbolic picture, offering you an accurate portrait of your personality.

The chart itself—the horoscope—is a portrait of an individual. Generally, a natal (or birth) horoscope is drawn on a circular wheel. The wheel is divided into twelve segments, called houses. Each of the twelve houses represents a different aspect of the individual, much like the facets of a brilliantly cut stone. The houses depict different environments, such as home, school, and work. The houses also represent roles and relationships: parents, friends, lovers, children, partners. In each environment, individuals show a different side of their personality. At home, you may represent yourself quite differently than you do on the job. Additionally, in each relationship you will project a different image of yourself. Your parents rarely see the side you show to intimate friends.

Symbols for the planets, the Sun, and the Moon are drawn inside the houses. Each planet represents a separate kind of energy. You experience and express that energy in specific ways. (For a complete list, refer to the table on the next page.) The way you use each of these energies is up to you. The planets in your chart do not make you do anything!

The twelve signs of the zodiac indicate characteristics and traits that further define your personality. Each sign can be expressed in positive and negative ways. (The basic meaning of each of the signs is explained in the corresponding sections ahead.) What's more, you have all twelve signs somewhere in your chart. Signs that are strongly emphasized by the planets have greater force. The Sun, Moon, and planets are placed on the chart according to their position at the time of birth. The qualities of a sign, combined with the

Signs of the Zodiac

Aries	♈	The Initiator
Taurus	♉	The Maintainer
Gemini	♊	The Questioner
Cancer	♋	The Nurturer
Leo	♌	The Loyalist
Virgo	♍	The Modifier
Libra	♎	The Judge
Scorpio	♏	The Catalyst
Sagittarius	♐	The Adventurer
Capricorn	♑	The Pragmatist
Aquarius	♒	The Reformer
Pisces	♓	The Visionary

energy of a planet, indicate how you might be most likely to use that energy and the best ways to develop that energy. The signs add color, emphasis, and dimension to the personality.

Signs are also placed at the cusps, or dividing lines, of each of the houses. The influence of the signs on the houses is much the same as their influence on the Sun, Moon, and planets. Each house is shaped by the sign on its cusp.

When you view a horoscope, you will notice that there appear to be four distinctive angles dividing the wheel of the chart. The line that divides the chart into a top and bottom half represents the horizon. In most cases, the left side of the horizon is called the Ascendant. The zodiac sign on the Ascendant is your rising sign. The Ascendant indicates the way others are likely to view you.

The Sun, Moon, or planet can be compared to an actor in a play. The sign shows how the energy works, like the role the actor plays in a drama. The house indicates where the energy operates, like the setting of a play. On a psychological level, the Sun represents who

The Planets

Sun	☉	The ego, self, willpower
Moon	☽	The subconscious self, habits
Mercury	☿	Communication, the intellect
Venus	♀	Emotional expression, love, appreciation, artistry
Mars	♂	Physical drive, assertiveness, anger
Jupiter	♃	Philosophy, ethics, generosity
Saturn	♄	Discipline, focus, responsibility
Uranus	♅	Individuality, rebelliousness
Neptune	♆	Imagination, sensitivity, compassion
Pluto	♇	Transformation, healing, regeneration

you think you are. The Ascendant describes who others think you are, and the Moon reflects your inner self.

Astrologers also study the geometric relationships between the Sun, Moon, and planets. These geometric angles are called aspects. Aspects further define the strengths, weaknesses, and challenges within your physical, mental, emotional, and spiritual self. Sometimes, patterns also appear in an astrological chart. These patterns have meaning.

To understand cycles for any given point in time, astrologers study several factors. Many use transits, which refer to the movement and positions of the planets. When astrologers compare those positions to the birth horoscope, the transits indicate activity in particular areas of the chart. The *Sun Sign Book* uses transits.

As you can see, your Sun sign is just one of many factors that describes who you are—but it is a powerful one! As the symbol of the ego, the Sun in your chart reflects your drive to be noticed. Most people can easily relate to the concepts associated with their Sun sign, since it is tied to their sense of personal identity.

Using this Book

This book contains what is called "Sun sign astrology," that is, astrology based on the sign that your Sun was in at the time of your birth. The technique has its foundation in ancient Greek astrology, in which the Sun was one of five points in the chart that was used as a focal point for delineation.

The most effective way to use astrology, however, is through one-on-one work with a professional astrologer, who can integrate the eight or so other astrological bodies into his or her interpretation to provide you with guidance. There are factors related to the year and time of day you were born that are highly significant in the way you approach life and vital to making wise choices. In addition, there are ways of using astrology that aren't addressed here, such as compatibility between two specific individuals, discovering family patterns, or picking a day for a wedding or grand opening.

To best use the information in the monthly forecasts, you'll want to determine your Ascendant, or rising sign. If you don't know your Ascendant, the tables following this description will help you determine your rising sign. They are most accurate for those born in the continental United States. They're only an approximation, but they can be used as a good rule of thumb. Your exact Ascendant may vary from the tables according to your time and place of birth. Once you've approximated your ascending sign using the tables or determined your Ascendant by having your chart calculated, you'll know two significant factors in your chart. Read the monthly forecast sections for both your Sun and Ascendant to gain the most useful information. In addition, you can read the section about the sign your Moon is in. The Sun is the true, inner you; the Ascendant is your shell or appearance and the person you are becoming; the Moon is the person you were—or still are based on habits and memories.

I've also included information about the planets' retrogrades this year. Most people have heard of "Mercury retrograde." In fact, all the planets except the Sun and Moon appear to travel backward (retrograde) in their path periodically. This only appears to happen because we on the Earth are not seeing the other planets from the middle of the solar system. Rather, we are watching them from our own moving object. We are like a train that moves past cars on the freeway that are going at a slower speed. To us on the train, the cars look like they're going backward. Mercury turns retrograde about every four months for three weeks; Venus every eighteen months for six weeks; Mars every two years for two to three months. The rest of the planets each retrograde once a year for four to five months. During each retrograde, we have the opportunity to try something new, something we conceived of at the beginning of the planet's yearly cycle. The times when the planets change direction are significant, as are the beginning and midpoint (peak or culmination) of each cycle. These are noted in your forecast each month.

Your "Rewarding and Challenging Days" sections indicate times when you'll feel either more centered or more out of balance. The rewarding days are not the only times you can perform well, but the times you're likely to feel better integrated! During challenging days, take extra time to center yourself by meditating or using other techniques that help you feel more objective.

The Action Table found at the end of each sign's section offers general guidelines for the best time to take a particular action. Please note, however, that your whole chart will provide more accurate guidelines for the best time to do something. Therefore, use this table with a grain of salt, and never let it stop you from taking an action you feel compelled to take.

You can use this information for an objective awareness about the way the current cycles are affecting you. Realize that the power of astrology is even more useful when you have a complete chart and professional guidance.

2006 at a Glance

It's time to hold steady on our course as the planets maintain their sign position throughout the year, with most of the slow movers in the fixed signs of Taurus, Leo, Scorpio, and Aquarius. We will be challenged to know what to keep and what to change—to know what we really value. This is related to the ongoing opposition of Saturn and Chiron. Their opposition began in autumn 2003 and will continue through this year. Jupiter and Neptune interact with them as well, creating a strident T-square, which "heats up" in February, May through July, and November. However, this pattern is eased by soothing Saturn-Pluto and Jupiter-Uranus trines, which suggest that solutions to burning questions will be found through technological advances and a new willingness of powerful factions to come to the bargaining table.

The year opens with expansive Jupiter in transformative Scorpio, where it will stay until November 23. Through its contacts with Saturn and Chiron, Jupiter will bring to us new awareness of dilemmas such as global warming and pollution, and will have a dampening effect on the world economy. However, Jupiter's trine to Uranus bodes well for technological advances that solve these problems. Saturn will continue its course through Leo, and its trine to Pluto suggests that delayed structural changes will finally be able to occur, leading to increased quality of life.

Chiron remains in Aquarius, teaching us how much we have to learn about getting along in groups, showing us that only by coming together can we overcome the problems we face. Uranus travels through another four degrees of Pisces this year, drawing closer to the square it will form with Pluto starting in 2009. Even now, we notice this interaction taking shape through the increasing crisis in oil supplies. On a larger scale, Uranus is breaking up systems that have been established on the basis of blind faith, especially religious factions.

Neptune has been in Aquarius since 1998, where it remains this year, through which we revere technology and independence. As Jupiter, Saturn, and Chiron increase their involvement with Neptune over the year, we will see the gap between these ideals and reality, motivating us to improve our uses of technology.

Pluto also continues in Sagittarius, pointing out more ways that the truth is still hidden from us. With a harmonious trine from Saturn, we will be able to make sweeping changes in our understanding of the truth and how it is presented.

The eclipses begin to activate Virgo and Pisces in March. The theme becomes integration of what we know into techniques that we can use in practical ways. It's not enough to be spiritual now—we have to use our good intentions to help others.

Ascendant Table

Your Time of Birth

Your Sun Sign	6–8 am	8–10 am	10 am–Noon	Noon–2 pm	2–4 pm	4–6 pm
Aries	Taurus	Gemini	Cancer	Leo	Virgo	Libra
Taurus	Gemini	Cancer	Leo	Virgo	Libra	Scorpio
Gemini	Cancer	Leo	Virgo	Libra	Scorpio	Sagittarius
Cancer	Leo	Virgo	Libra	Scorpio	Sagittarius	Capricorn
Leo	Virgo	Libra	Scorpio	Sagittarius	Capricorn	Aquarius
Virgo	Libra	Scorpio	Sagittarius	Capricorn	Aquarius	Pisces
Libra	Scorpio	Sagittarius	Capricorn	Aquarius	Pisces	Aries
Scorpio	Sagittarius	Capricorn	Aquarius	Pisces	Aries	Taurus
Sagittarius	Capricorn	Aquarius	Pisces	Aries	Taurus	Gemini
Capricorn	Aquarius	Pisces	Aries	Taurus	Gemini	Cancer
Aquarius	Pisces	Aries	Taurus	Gemini	Cancer	Leo
Pisces	Aries	Taurus	Gemini	Cancer	Leo	Virgo

Your Time of Birth

Your Sun Sign	6–8 pm	8–10 pm	10 pm–Midnight	Midnight–2 am	2–4 am	4–6 am
Aries	Scorpio	Sagittarius	Capricorn	Aquarius	Pisces	Aries
Taurus	Sagittarius	Capricorn	Aquarius	Pisces	Aries	Taurus
Gemini	Capricorn	Aquarius	Pisces	Aries	Taurus	Gemini
Cancer	Aquarius	Pisces	Aries	Taurus	Gemini	Cancer
Leo	Pisces	Aries	Taurus	Gemini	Cancer	Leo
Virgo	Aries	Taurus	Gemini	Cancer	Leo	Virgo
Libra	Taurus	Gemini	Cancer	Leo	Virgo	Libra
Scorpio	Gemini	Cancer	Leo	Virgo	Libra	Scorpio
Sagittarius	Cancer	Leo	Virgo	Libra	Scorpio	Sagittarius
Capricorn	Leo	Virgo	Libra	Scorpio	Sagittarius	Capricorn
Aquarius	Virgo	Libra	Scorpio	Sagittarius	Capricorn	Aquarius
Pisces	Libra	Scorpio	Sagittarius	Capricorn	Aquarius	Pisces

How to use this table: 1. Find your Sun sign in the left column.
2. Find your approximate birth time in a vertical column.
3. Line up your Sun sign and birth time to find your Ascendant.

This table will give you an approximation of your Ascendant. If you feel that the sign listed as your Ascendant is incorrect, try the one either before or after the listed sign. It is difficult to determine your exact Ascendant without a complete natal chart.

Astrological Glossary

Air: One of the four basic elements. The air signs are Gemini, Libra, and Aquarius.

Angles: The four points of the chart that divide it into quadrants. The angles are sensitive areas that lend emphasis to planets located near them. These points are located on the cusps of the First, Fourth, Seventh, and Tenth Houses in a chart.

Ascendant: Rising sign. The degree of the zodiac on the eastern horizon at the time and place for which the horoscope is calculated. It can indicate the image or physical appearance you project to the world. The cusp of the First House.

Aspect: The angular relationship between planets, sensitive points, or house cusps in a horoscope. Lines drawn between the two points and the center of the chart, representing the Earth, form the angle of the aspect. Astrological aspects include conjunction (two points that are 0 degrees apart), opposition (two points, 180 degrees apart), square (two points, 90 degrees apart), sextile (two points, 60 degrees apart), and trine (two points, 120 degrees apart). Aspects can indicate harmony or challenge.

Cardinal Sign: One of the three qualities, or categories, that describe how a sign expresses itself. Aries, Cancer, Libra, and Capricorn are the cardinal signs, believed to initiate activity.

Chiron: Chiron is a comet traveling in orbit between Saturn and Uranus. Although research on its effect on natal charts is not yet complete, it is believed to represent a key or doorway, healing, ecology, and a bridge between traditional and modern methods.

Conjunction: An aspect or angle between two points in a chart where the two points are close enough so that the energies join. Can be considered either harmonious or challenging, depending on the planets involved and their placement.

Cusp: A dividing line between signs or houses in a chart.

Degree: Degree of arc. One of 360 divisions of a circle. The circle of the zodiac is divided into twelve astrological signs of 30 degrees each. Each degree is made up of 60 minutes, and each minute is made up of 60 seconds of zodiacal longitude.

Earth: One of the four basic elements. The earth signs are Taurus, Virgo, and Capricorn.

Eclipse: A solar eclipse is the full or partial covering of the Sun by the Moon (as viewed from Earth), and a lunar eclipse is the full or partial covering of the Moon by the Earth's own shadow.

Ecliptic: The Sun's apparent path around the Earth, which is actually the plane of the Earth's orbit extended out into space. The ecliptic forms the center of the zodiac.

Electional Astrology: A branch of astrology concerned with choosing the best time to initiate an activity.

Elements: The signs of the zodiac are divided into four groups of three zodiacal signs, each symbolized by one of the four elements of the ancients: fire, earth, air, and water. The element of a sign is said to express its essential nature.

Ephemeris: A listing of the Sun, Moon, and planets' positions and related information for astrological purposes.

Equinox: Equal night. The point in the Earth's orbit around the Sun at which the day and night are equal in length.

Feminine Signs: Each zodiac sign is either masculine or feminine. Earth signs (Taurus, Virgo, and Capricorn) and water signs (Cancer, Scorpio, and Pisces) are feminine.

Fire: One of the four basic elements. The fire signs are Aries, Leo, and Sagittarius.

Fixed Signs: Fixed is one of the three qualities, or categories, that describe how a sign expresses itself. The fixed signs are Taurus, Leo, Scorpio, and Aquarius. Fixed signs are said to be predisposed to existing patterns and somewhat resistant to change.

Hard Aspects: Hard aspects are those aspects in a chart that astrologers believe to represent difficulty or challenges. Among the hard aspects are the square, the opposition, and the conjunction (depending on which planets are conjunct).

Horizon: The word "horizon" is used in astrology in a manner similar to its common usage, except that only the eastern and western horizons are considered useful. The eastern horizon at the point of birth is the Ascendant, or First House cusp, of a natal chart, and the western horizon at the point of birth is the Descendant, or Seventh House cusp.

Houses: Division of the horoscope into twelve segments, beginning with the Ascendant. The dividing line between the houses are called house cusps. Each house corresponds to certain aspects of daily living, and is ruled by the astrological sign that governs the cusp, or dividing line between the house and the one previous.

Ingress: The point of entry of a planet into a sign.

Lagna: A term used in Hindu or Vedic astrology for Ascendant, the degree of the zodiac on the eastern horizon at the time of birth.

Masculine Signs: Each of the twelve signs of the zodiac is either "masculine" or "feminine." The fire signs (Aries, Leo, and Sagittarius) and the air signs (Gemini, Libra, and Aquarius) are masculine.

Midheaven: The highest point on the ecliptic, where it intersects the meridian that passes directly above the place for which the horoscope is cast; the southern point of the horoscope.

Midpoint: A point equally distant to two planets or house cusps. Midpoints are considered by some astrologers to be sensitive points in a person's chart.

Mundane Astrology: Mundane astrology is the branch of astrology generally concerned with political and economic events, and the nations involved in these events.

Mutable Signs: Mutable is one of the three qualities, or categories, that describe how a sign expresses itself. Mutable signs are Gemini, Virgo, Sagittarius, and Pisces. Mutable signs are said to be very adaptable and sometimes changeable.

Natal Chart: A person's birth chart. A natal chart is essentially a "snapshot" showing the placement of each of the planets at the exact time of a person's birth.

Node: The point where the planets cross the ecliptic, or the Earth's apparent path around the Sun. The North Node is the point where a planet moves northward, from the Earth's perspective, as it crosses the ecliptic; the South Node is where it moves south.

Opposition: Two points in a chart that are 180 degrees apart.

Orb: A small degree of margin used when calculating aspects in a chart. For example, although 180 degrees form an exact opposition, an astrologer might consider an aspect within 3 or 4 degrees on either side of 180 degrees to be an opposition, as the impact of the aspect can still be felt within this range. The less orb on an aspect, the stronger the aspect. Astrologers' opinions vary on how many degrees of orb to allow for each aspect.

Outer Planets: Uranus, Neptune, and Pluto are known as the outer planets. Because of their distance from the Sun, they take a long time to complete a single rotation. Everyone born within a few years on either side of a given date will have similar placements of these planets.

Planets: The planets used in astrology are Mercury, Venus, Mars, Jupiter, Saturn, Uranus, Neptune, and Pluto. For astrological purposes, the Sun and Moon are also considered planets. A natal or birth chart lists planetary placement at the moment of birth.

Planetary Rulership: The sign in which a planet is most harmoniously placed. Examples are the Sun in Leo, Jupiter in Sagittarius, and the Moon in Cancer.

Precession of Equinoxes: The gradual movement of the point of the Spring Equinox, located at 0 degrees Aries. This point marks the beginning of the tropical zodiac. The point moves slowly backward through the constellations of the zodiac, so that about every 2,000 years the equinox begins in an earlier constellation

Qualities: In addition to categorizing the signs by element, astrologers place the twelve signs of the zodiac into three additional categories, or qualities: cardinal, mutable, or fixed. Each sign is considered to be a combination of its element and quality. Where the element of a sign describes its basic nature, the quality describes its mode of expression.

Retrograde Motion: Apparent backward motion of a planet. This is an illusion caused by the relative motion of the Earth and other planets in their elliptical orbits.

Sextile: Two points in a chart that are 60 degrees apart.

Sidereal Zodiac: Generally used by Hindu or Vedic astrologers. The sidereal zodiac is located where the constellations are actually positioned in the sky.

Soft Aspects: Soft aspects indicate good fortune or an easy relationship in the chart. Among the soft aspects are the trine, the sextile, and the conjunction (depending on which planets are conjunct each other).

Square: Two points in a chart that are 90 degrees apart.

Sun Sign: The sign of the zodiac in which the Sun is located at any given time.

Synodic Cycle: The time between conjunctions of two planets.

Trine: Two points in a chart that are 120 degrees apart.

Tropical Zodiac: The tropical zodiac begins at 0 degrees Aries, where the Sun is located during the Spring Equinox. This system is used by most Western astrologers and throughout this book.

Void-of-Course: A planet is void-of-course after it has made its last aspect within a sign, but before it has entered a new sign.

Water: One of the four basic elements. Water signs are Cancer, Scorpio, and Pisces.

Meanings of the Planets

The Sun

The Sun indicates the psychological bias that will dominate your actions. What you see, and why, is told in the reading for your Sun. The Sun also shows the basic energy patterns of your body and psyche. In many ways, the Sun is the dominant force in your horoscope and your life. Other influences, especially that of the Moon, may modify the Sun's influence, but nothing will cause you to depart very far from the basic solar pattern. Always keep in mind the basic influence of the Sun and remember all other influences must be interpreted in terms of it, especially insofar as they play a visible role in your life. You may think, dream, imagine, and hope a thousand things, according to your Moon and your other planets, but the Sun is what you are. To be your best self in terms of your Sun is to cause your energies to work along the path in which they will have maximum help from planetary vibrations.

The Moon

The Moon tells the desire of your life. When you know what you mean but can't verbalize it, it is your Moon that knows it and your Sun that can't say it. The wordless ecstasy, the mute sorrow, the secret dream, the esoteric picture of yourself that you can't get across to the world, or that the world doesn't comprehend or value—these are the products of the Moon. When you are misunderstood, it is your Moon nature, expressed imperfectly through the Sun sign, that feels betrayed. Things you know without thought—intuitions, hunches, instincts—are the products of the Moon. Modes of expression that you feel truly reflect your deepest self belong to the Moon: art, letters, creative work of any kind; sometimes love; sometimes business. Whatever you feel to be most deeply yourself is the product of your Moon and of the sign your Moon occupies at birth.

Mercury

Mercury is the sensory antenna of your horoscope. Its position by sign indicates your reactions to sights, sounds, odors, tastes, and touch impressions, affording a key to the attitude you have toward the physical world around you. Mercury is the messenger through which your physical body and brain (ruled by the Sun) and your inner nature (ruled by the Moon) are kept in contact with the outer world, which will appear to you according to the index of Mercury's position by sign in the horoscope. Mercury rules your rational mind.

Venus

Venus is the emotional antenna of your horoscope. Through Venus, impressions come to you from the outer world, to which you react emotionally. The position of Venus by sign at the time of your birth determines your attitude toward these experiences. As Mercury is the messenger linking sense impressions (sight, smell, etc.) to the basic nature of your Sun and Moon, so Venus is the messenger linking emotional impressions. If Venus is found in the same sign as the Sun, emotions gain importance in your life, and have a direct bearing on your actions. If Venus is in the same sign as the Moon, emotions bear directly on your inner nature, add self-confidence, make you sensitive to emotional impressions, and frequently indicate that you have more love in your heart than you are able to express. If Venus is in the same sign as Mercury, emotional impressions and sense impressions work together; you tend to idealize the world of the senses and sensualize the world of the emotions to interpret emotionally what you see and hear.

Mars

Mars is the energy principle in the horoscope. Its position indicates the channels into which energy will most easily be directed. It is the planet through which the activities of the Sun and the desires of the Moon express themselves in action. In the same sign as the Sun, Mars gives abundant energy, sometimes misdirected in temper, temperament, and quarrels. In the same sign as the Moon, it gives a great capacity to make use of the innermost aims, and to make the inner desires articulate and practical. In the same sign as Venus, it quickens emotional reactions and causes you to act on them, makes for ardor and passion in love, and fosters an earthly awareness of emotional realities.

Jupiter

Jupiter is the feeler for opportunity that you have out in the world. It passes along chances of a lifetime for consideration according to the basic nature of your Sun and Moon. Jupiter's sign position indicates the places where you will look for opportunity, the uses to which you wish to put it, and the capacity you have to react and profit by it. Jupiter is ordinarily, and erroneously, called the planet of luck. It is "luck" insofar as it is the index of opportunity, but your luck depends less on what comes to you than on what you do with what comes to you. In the same sign as the Sun or Moon, Jupiter gives a direct, and generally effective, response to opportunity and is likely to show forth at its "luckiest." If Jupiter is in the same sign as Mercury, sense impressions are interpreted opportunistically. If Jupiter is in the same sign as Venus, you interpret emotions in such a way as to turn them to your advantage; your feelings work harmoniously with the chances for progress that the world has to offer. If Jupiter is in the same sign as Mars, you follow opportunity with energy, dash, enthusiasm, and courage; take long chances; and play your cards wide open.

Saturn

Saturn indicates the direction that will be taken in life by the self-preservative principle that, in its highest manifestation, ceases to be purely defensive and becomes ambitious and aspiring. Your defense or attack against the world is shown by the sign position of Saturn in the horoscope of birth. If Saturn is in the same sign as the Sun or Moon, defense predominates, and there is danger of introversion. The farther Saturn is from the Sun, Moon, and Ascendant, the better for objectivity and extroversion. If Saturn is in the same sign as Mercury, there is a profound and serious reaction to sense impressions; this position generally accompanies a deep and efficient mind. If Saturn is in the same sign as Venus, a defensive attitude toward emotional experience makes for apparent coolness in love and difficulty with the emotions and human relations. If Saturn is in the same sign as Mars, confusion between defensive and aggressive urges can make an indecisive person—or, if the Sun and Moon are strong and the total personality well developed, a balanced, peaceful, and calm individual of sober judgment and moderate actions may be indicated. If Saturn is in the same sign as Jupiter, the reaction to opportunity is sober and balanced.

Uranus

Uranus in a general way relates to creativity, originality, or individuality, and its position by sign in the horoscope tells the direction in which you will seek to express yourself. In the same sign as Mercury or the Moon, Uranus suggests acute awareness, a quick reaction to sense impressions and experiences, or a hair-trigger mind. In the same sign as the Sun, it points to great nervous activity, a high-strung nature, and an original, creative, or eccentric personality. In the same sign as Mars, Uranus indicates high-speed activity, love of swift motion, and perhaps love of danger. In the same sign as Venus, it suggests an unusual reaction to emotional experience, idealism, sensuality, and original ideas about love and human relations. In the same sign as Saturn, Uranus points to good sense; this can be a practical, creative position, but, more often than not, it sets up a destructive conflict between practicality and originality that can result in a stalemate. In the same sign as Jupiter, Uranus makes opportunity, creates wealth and the means of getting it, and is conducive to the inventive, executive, and daring.

Neptune

Neptune relates to the deepest wells of the subconscious, inherited mentality, and spirituality, indicating what you take for granted in life. Neptune in the same sign as the Sun or Moon indicates that intuitions and hunches—or delusions—dominate; there is a need for rigidly holding to reality. In the same sign as Mercury, Neptune indicates sharp sensory perceptions, a sensitive and perhaps creative mind, and a quivering intensity of reaction to sensory experience. In the same sign as Venus, it reveals idealistic and romantic (or sentimental) reaction to emotional experience, as well as the danger of sensationalism and a love of strange pleasures. In the same sign as Mars, Neptune indicates energy and intuition that work together to make mastery of life—one of the signs of having angels (or devils) on your side. In the same sign as Jupiter, Neptune describes intuitive response to opportunity generally along practical and money-making lines; one of the signs of security if not indeed of wealth. In the same sign as Saturn, Neptune indicates intuitive defense and attack on the world, generally successful unless Saturn is polarized on the negative side; then there is danger of unhappiness.

Pluto

Pluto is a planet of extremes—from the lowest criminal and violent level of our society to the heights people can attain when they realize their significance in the collectivity of humanity. Pluto also rules three important mysteries of life—sex, death, and rebirth—and links them to each other. One level of death symbolized by Pluto is the physical death of an individual, which occurs so that a person can be reborn into another body to further his or her spiritual development. On another level, individuals can experience a "death" of their old self when they realize the deeper significance of life; thus they become one of the "second born." In a natal horoscope, Pluto signifies our perspective on the world, our conscious and subconscious. Since so many of Pluto's qualities are centered on the deeper mysteries of life, the house position of Pluto, and aspects to it, can show you how to attain a deeper understanding of the importance of the spiritual in your life.

2006 SUN SIGN BOOK

Forecasts

By Terry Lamb

ARIES

The Ram
March 19 to April 21

♈

Element:	Fire
Quality:	Cardinal
Polarity:	Yang/Masculine
Planetary Ruler:	Mars
Meditation:	I build upon my strengths
Gemstone:	Diamond
Power Stones:	Bloodstone, carnelian, ruby
Key Phrase:	I am
Glyph:	Ram's head
Anatomy:	Head, face, throat
Color:	Red, white
Animal:	Ram
Myths/Legends:	Artemis, Jason and the Golden Fleece
House:	First
Opposite Sign:	Libra
Flower:	Geranium
Key Word:	Initiative

Your Ego's Strengths and Weaknesses

You're at the starting line and ready to go, ever ready to launch a new plan or explore a new frontier. This is because you are a cardinal fire sign. Cardinal means "first," and you are first because you respond quickly and eagerly. You are at your best when your reflexes are called into play, whether they are physical, mental, or spiritual. You have a "take charge" attitude, not because you want to be the boss but because your inspiration about what to do in a crunch is automatic. You don't have to think to know how to act. In an emergency you can show genius, because your natural instincts are geared to preserving life without thought or hesitation. However, in a situation where planning is involved, you may have little patience, especially when others put forth their ideas. You have difficulty with process, and you prefer to work on your own, because then your own initiative is unhampered. Little wonder that you don't like to operate in a group unless it is absolutely necessary. Others may perceive you as abrasive, even obstructive, because your manner is more focused on getting things done than on soothing the social environment.

The speed with which you initiate action is only enhanced by the fact that Aries is a fire sign. Because fire's movement is upward, you aspire to new heights. You move as quickly as your element does, burning through projects and ideas with the speed of light. The down side of both the cardinal and the fire is a tendency to act impetuously. Impulsive actions are often misunderstood by others and bruise the sensitivities of the watery types around you. When emotion is added to your orientation, it can add up to joy and enthusiasm—or anger. Learning to inject a pause between impulse and action will give you the time you need to redirect your inner forces.

Shining Your Love Light

Your outlook on love is fresh, eager, and even naive. Each new relationship is full of hope; it's as if you've never had a broken heart each time you fall in love again. Unfortunately, you may find it hard to stay in balance in a relationship, to develop a true partnership where each of you plays an equal role. As long as you have a partner who is willing to let you stand in center stage and call most of the shots, you'll be successful in love.

With a fellow Aries, a competitive edge may emerge. Try to channel that into fun activities—sports or horseplay—rather than through career, family, social ties, or a power struggle between you. Taurus signs give you the foundation you need, and the consistency to go on flights of fancy. Don't forget to appreciate their practical side when they're scrutinizing your schemes. You get along with Gemini, chattering away, mind and body moving quickly in tandem. You're the best of friends, but you have to remember to draw upon qualities that don't come naturally to make your life together a success: practicality, responsibility, and sensitivity. Cancer is just as active as you are, but you have different motives and desire different results; it's conquest versus security. Honoring each other's needs will go far to create harmony. You and Leo will set the house on fire with your shared enthusiasm for life. This is sure to be a playful, humor-filled bond. Virgo supplements your pro-active approach with analysis. You each supply a quality the other would do well to incorporate. Libra reveals your shadow (reminding you that we are all equals), and brings a gift of self-awareness, if you will listen. Scorpio presents another side of your own nature, a will- and emotion-driven call to action that supplements your competitive approach. Sagittarius keeps up with your every step, sharing your taste for adventure and maybe even exceeding it. You'll be poetry in motion, with the emphasis on motion. Capricorns may seem too serious to you, but they can give structure that enables you to succeed beyond your wildest dreams. Aquarius signs share your gregarious nature, but you'll have to be willing to accept their more political side. Pisces can teach you about the inner world that gives you inspiration, nudging you gently toward your spiritual center.

Making Your Place in the World

Your high energy and ingenuity will serve you well in the world as you travel your road to success. You can work hard, although you're better producing short, intense bursts of activity than long endurance runs; however, you can do either, especially when you're enthralled with a project. Careers that will feel natural to you include entrepreneurship, team leadership, sports and athletics, acting, emergency services, medicine (especially surgery), metal-working, jewelry-making, hairdressing, and sales. You thrive in environments where you work for or by yourself, but you are more successful where you feel a competitive edge with others. You can succeed in any environment in which you are given the reins, but you are brilliant in new situations, e.g., business start-ups, pioneer ventures, and think tanks. Ideas flow abundantly from your mind when you are allowed to take the lead without hindrance. An obstacle to success could arise if you fail to listen adequately to others (a common Aries weakness).

Putting Your Best Foot Forward

To put our best foot forward, we have to overcome our weaknesses. Aries tends to trip itself up with its single-minded focus. Single-mindedness is a great quality. It gives you the ability to take on pioneering roles, because you are not daunted by others' doubts, negativity, and criticisms. Your ability to focus without distraction keeps you on track. However, there are times when others' input and feedback are important. It's important to be open to suggestion, to have a truly open ear and open mind to others' ideas. There are always different ideas of how something can be done, and sometimes your ideas won't be the best. You need not fear that your ideas will be lost, because the more you listen, the more your ideas will become attuned to the needs of those around you. Listening can prevent serious mistakes and stop you from taking the impulsive actions that are another effect of your singular focus. It always helps that your actions are taken with sincerity and the best of intentions. If you can learn to broaden your focus to let in other people's ideas and incorporate the best into your plans, you'll be a winner every time!

Tools for Change

Sometimes, to be at our best, we have to shore up our weak areas in order to be truly strong. There are several things you can do to add to your gifts and make your efforts more effective. With your single-minded approach to life, anything you can do to diffuse your attention or see things from a perspective other than your own will help ensure that this approach operates as true genius. At the core, it will help if you cultivate long-term relationships. Any consistent pattern that you establish where you listen to people you trust will develop the habit of taking in other points of view.

To truly understand your partner and friends, you may want to study psychology. This will give you insight into the nature of people who do not share your fiery personality. You'll come to understand the more watery types and how to work with their sensitivities. You'll see that the airy and earthy types' lack of passion is an asset—that objectivity and logic are beneficial characteristics. If it's not your style or you just can't settle down with one person, you can develop a relationship with a pet. You can choose to match your personality, and this will help you cultivate the same qualities in yourself. Education is the process of examining alternate viewpoints, and higher education (taking any education seriously) prepares you for a more mature leadership style in the workaday world. Withdrawing from the "battlefield" of daily events through meditation reduces stress and aggression and gives you the distant perspective needed to get fresh ideas. Yoga is a more active form of meditation that induces flexibility of mind through the mind-body union. Postures that focus on forward bending develop receptivity, while those that bend backward develop the will and assertiveness. Finally, keeping a written journal will give you a reflection of yourself that can be invaluable when monitoring and catalyzing your personal growth. You need not scatter your forces in all these directions at once—rather, adopting just one or two new tools and techniques can tip the scales in your favor.

Affirmation for the Year

I enjoy working with others
to create greater abundance in my life.

The Year Ahead for Aries

A fter six years of working behind the scenes and another acquainting others with your new efforts, you're ready to begin reaping the rewards of all your hard work. With Jupiter in Scorpio and your solar Eighth House of other people's resources until November 23, you'll find money flows a little more easily. You could even get some unexpected windfall profits, from an insurance payment to an inheritance. You may be required to make an investment in order to ensure future returns, but that is to be expected. If you build the right way this year, you'll enter a three-year pinnacle of success once Jupiter enters Sagittarius on November 23. This is your Ninth House, so don't be surprised if you manage to squeeze in a trip to far-flung places as well.

From its position in Leo, your solar Fifth House, Saturn continues to draw your attention to creative efforts. It's time to look at your artistic endeavors, but it's also time to look at how and what you want your life to be. If you feel that it lacks meaning, now is the time to recast your direction so that it aligns with your deepest motivations. You may also find that children are more important to you this year. Romance takes on a more serious tinge as well.

Chiron spends its second year in Aquarius and your Eleventh House of groups and organizations, continuing to reflect the need for adjustment and growth in your interactions with others. You may feel an urge to get to know your extended family, change your role in groups, or even leave a group behind. On the whole, however, you'll have the opportunity to gently change old habits that no longer work in social situations.

Uranus remains in Pisces, working quietly in the background of your solar Twelfth House. Its whispering prompts you to inject more meaning into your life. You may be called upon to make sacrifices for others—sacrifices that you have a hard time justifying to those outside the situation. You may also be drawn to spiritual pursuits and a quieter life.

Neptune is in Aquarius and your solar Eleventh House for another year. Since 1998, it has been lifting your sense of what is possible in group situations. Whether you feel inspired to start a group of your own or pour your efforts into an organization promoting the welfare of others, the emphasis is on service. It is possible to lose yourself in a cause, or to sacrifice too much. However, the key for you is that you are committed to it, and nothing can stop you when you believe in something.

Pluto continues its transformative course through Sagittarius and your solar Ninth House of travel, foreign places, and higher education. You have been undergoing deep changes since 1995 that have broadened your horizons. You will continue to be drawn to far-flung places and stretches of the imagination. Chances are that you have decided to follow a new path in life, and more education may be required. No matter what form your transformation is taking, you are finding yourself in an entirely new arena, a new world, than the one you inhabited ten years ago, much to your betterment.

The eclipses of Sun and Moon have been moving through Aries and Libra, creating many unexpected, but not necessarily unwelcome, changes in your life. Although one last solar eclipse falls in Aries on March 29, the remainder fall in Virgo and Pisces, your Sixth and Twelfth Houses. Your life will calm down as changes occur internally. Just as likely, you could be inspired by the spirit of contribution to share your endless optimism with others.

If you were born between March 24 and April 16, Saturn will be contacting your Sun from your solar Fifth House. Over the past five years, you've been in a private phase of your life. However, since last July, when Saturn first entered Leo, you've been applying the inspiration you received over that private time to infuse more productivity and meaning into your life. Now you are actively involved in creating a happier life for yourself. This may involve taking less time to play or engage in habitual leisure activities. You may be engaged in turning a hobby into a gainful means of employment, or you may develop a new hobby that produces something of value to you. You may want to turn a romance into a relationship or kiss a frivolous romantic tie good-bye. Whatever you are drawn to, it is in your best interest to follow your dreams, because they will lead you to the right place at the right time. Your actions now set the stage for your rise over the next ten years and will play a large role in the level of success you achieve then, when you reach a thirty-year pinnacle. Key dates in Saturn's cycle are January 27, February 19, April 5 and 24, June 20, August 7, November 16, and December 5.

If you were born between March 27 and April 5, Uranus is creating greater inner activity in your life from its position in Pisces and your solar Twelfth House. You may find yourself doing and saying things that are unusual for you—things that you realize are true, but you didn't know about until they came out. You could make "Freudian slips" that reveal your true feelings to yourself and others. These actions could even lead you in a new life direction as you realize things about yourself that you never knew before. You may also find yourself drawn to spiritual pursuits; you will be more likely to feel like retreating from the world periodically, whether through a vacation, an actual spiritual retreat, or just closing the door to your private space more often. You could even experience an enforced solitude, as with an illness or a major project that forces you to cut back on social contact. Whatever the source, you are being led to find inner peace and healing. The more you go with the flow of the forces that draw you inward, the more graceful will be your experience. Events related to this cycle will occur near March 1, June 5 and 19, September 5, November 19, and December 2.

If you were born between April 5 and 10, Neptune will be contacting your Sun through a harmonious sextile aspect from its position in Aquarius and your Eleventh House of group activities. Neptune will change the amount and type of interaction and activity you experience in a group environment—everything from professional networking organizations and associations to extended family, your social milieu, and even your biological or ethnic affiliations. You are more likely to feel drawn to people on the basis of their inner qualities than their external similarities to you. It won't be enough to join a group because they like to go dancing; you will want them to share your political or spiritual views or other interests as well. You're looking for something deeper and healthier than before, and you're willing to make sacrifices to join in a group that means something more to you. Ideals are very important to you right now, and you don't want to be around people who are "downers." You want to share support and encouragement, to be with like-minded people who live in a world of possibility like you do right now. It is possible that, with your starry-eyed notions of what can be real, you could be taken advantage of. Look to those you trust for insight into whether your new-found friends and acquaintances are right for you. The thread of this theme in your life will surface around January 27, February 5, March 15, May 10 and 22, August 10, October 29, and November 9.

If you were born between April 13 and 18, Pluto in Sagittarius is giving you a power boost from your solar Ninth House. Pluto transforms, but it does so in the most harmonious and empowering way from this position in your chart. With its energy, you can accomplish great things this year, and your vision will be broadened to accommodate dreams larger than you've experienced in the past. Pay attention to those dreams, even if they seem to be larger than life, because you'll have about twenty years to realize them. Don't be afraid to set some long-term projects and goals before yourself, because you are reaching toward the pinnacle of a lifetime now, as Pluto moves across the top of your chart. Since it takes 250 years for it to move all the way around the Zodiac, not everyone gets this chance. This year, it will be easy for you to see the big picture and take actions to set yourself on your new path. You will be able to gather the resources you need with relative ease. You will find that others support you. This new path will lead you to greater appreciation, joy, and enthusiasm for life. You may feel inspired to help others as you experience the magnanimity of the universe. You may teach or simply share the love you feel for being alive. Key dates in this cycle are March 17 and 29, June 16, September 4 and 16, and December 18.

If you were born between March 19 and 23 or April 19 and 21, the major planets are giving you a rest, at least where your Sun is concerned. However, the chances are good that you'll have opportunities to grow and expand through contacts to other planets in your chart. Jupiter, the planet of enterprise and education, touches every degree each year, so you're assured of plenty of action to keep you busy. You can use this time to make changes and go places with little direction or opposition from external forces in your life. And it never hurts to take it easy or have fun—we seldom get enough of that in our busy modern lives.

Aries/January

Planetary Hotspots

Issues with career and authority figures that arose at the end of the year are with you through January as Venus remains retrograde all month. Now it's time to delay moving ahead with career plans and projects. Instead, look ahead, plan, and finish up what's still on your plate. You've got eighteen months to fulfill the goals you're setting now, so relax and let things emerge gradually. This can be the beginning of something really big if you take it seriously.

Wellness and Keeping Fit

You're in a very serious frame of mind now, but don't let the emphasis on progress keep you from taking part in a healthy lifestyle. Ignoring this could build to immune weakness in March.

Love and Life Connections

Relationships are a bit rocky this month, and not just for you. Previous challenges with children or romantic partners come to a head on January 27, but you have a chance to smooth things over before problems arise on January 17.

Finance and Success

As Jupiter squares Neptune on January 27, you're checking in on how well you're doing at fulfilling dreams you hatched nine years ago. After a rough autumn, you're looking at what is left to accomplish in the next four years. These four years include a pinnacle, so the best may be yet to come. The coming year will be seminal in what you are able to create this time, and you'll be given your first hints of the issues that will shape your success. In the short run, tensions continue related to finances as you stretch your resources toward your goals, but they are already releasing. You'll get clues about how to do so on January 15, 18, 23, and 27.

Rewarding Days

1, 2, 5, 6, 7, 10, 11, 15, 16, 25, 26, 29, 30

Challenging Days

12, 13, 14, 20, 21, 27, 28

Aries/February

Planetary Hotspots

Tensions at work release now as Venus returns to direct motion on February 3. Relationships will settle into their new pattern, and you can move on to other concerns. However, the excitements of the last half of January continue as the Sun and Mercury trigger new patterns. From February 1 to 5, Mercury brings new information that leads to solutions. With the Sun's contacts from February 5 to 19, you can launch into action to accomplish your objectives.

Wellness and Keeping Fit

You enter a two-month period of vulnerability where health is concerned on February 8, as Mercury enters Pisces and your Twelfth House. Take care of yourself by following your regular fitness routine and eating well. Taking time to relax and enjoy a movie or a night out is also revitalizing.

Love and Life Connections

Once Venus starts moving forward again on February 3, the window on rejuvenating your relationships closes and your bonds with others settle into a new type of stability for the next eighteen months. While the emphasis has been on relationships with bosses and fellow professionals, parental ties could also be involved. You'll be involved in more social activity now, whether it's for business or leisure. Your contacts will bring new awareness that leads you to a deeper understanding of what you want in life and how to accomplish it, especially on February 1.

Finance and Success

You'll be busier than ever for the first week of the month, with new situations arising and throwing you off schedule. However, the next two weeks give you the breathing room you need to get caught up. February 19 is a watershed date, after which pressures reduce.

Rewarding Days

2, 3, 6, 7, 11, 12, 21, 22, 25, 26

Challenging Days

8, 9, 10, 16, 17, 23, 24

Aries/March

Planetary Hotspots

Planetary pauses punctuate the month as Mercury, Jupiter, and Pluto change direction. Around March 2, obstructions come out of nowhere as Mercury slows down in your Twelfth House. On March 4, Jupiter's four-month retrograde signals a time when spending cuts will be a benefit. Pluto's five-month backward trek starts on March 29 at the same time as the last solar eclipse in your sign. They will empower you to make changes you've wanted for many years.

Wellness and Keeping Fit

Activities could stack up on you through March 25, resulting in a dip in your resistance to disease, especially on March 2. The prevailing Mercury retrograde virus could get you if you ignore your need for sleep and good nutrition.

Love and Life Connections

The solar eclipse on March 29 in your sign underscores the impact you have on others. As you become more aware of this, you are inclined to act with greater sensitivity to their needs, but you'll move ahead nonetheless because you know it will all work out in the long run.

Finance and Success

This is the time to set your intention for the mission you want to accomplish this year, as Uranus starts its new cycle on March 1. The more you emphasize service to others, the more successful and satisfying your initiative will be. It will make sense to think of it as part of a major process you began in 2003. On March 11, new information will invigorate your sense of direction and desire to act when Mars triggers Uranus. The lunar eclipse on March 14 also spurs you to action.

Rewarding Days

1, 2, 5, 6, 7, 10, 11, 12, 20, 21, 25, 26, 29, 30

Challenging Days

8, 9, 15, 16, 17, 22, 23, 24

Aries/April

Planetary Hotspots

You've had to be very productive since last November, when Saturn began to travel backward through your Fifth House. Release from this extra burden arrives on April 5—or at least you've gotten used to the higher level of activity. This ties in with events occurring around last November 22 and January 27 of this year. A number of incomplete projects demand your immediate attention through April 17. Although you're good at putting out fires, even you may get a little overwhelmed this time.

Wellness and Keeping Fit

You may be stuck at home doing videotaped exercise routines this month, what with all the busy work you have now. Don't let those niggling details suck up all your time and attention—stay with your usual fitness routine, or pump it up a little if you've strayed from the path. You're more accident-prone after April 13th.

Love and Life Connections

Love connections become more challenging after April 18 as Venus contacts Uranus on April 18 and Pluto on April 30. Events on the first date will tie in with those at the end of the month, so don't think it's over if you make it through mid-month without a hitch. There's an issue that seems innocent enough now, but needs closer attention and deeper study to resolve. This is likely to involve anger and emotional responses.

Finance and Success

Financial matters get put on the back burner as work and home life assume greater prominence. Don't forget to "tend your financial garden" as needed, or problems will arise later. You're moving on a steady trajectory toward success in two years' time, and you don't want problems created now to hold you back. Patience is key.

Rewarding Days

2, 3, 6, 7, 8, 16, 17, 18, 21, 22, 25, 26, 29, 30

Challenging Days

4, 5, 11, 12, 13, 19, 20

Aries/May

Planetary Hotspots

As Mars, Jupiter, and Uranus form a grand trine in the heavens in early May, an opportunity for financial and emotional fulfillment comes your way. Although it may seem to come out of the blue, it ties in with events around November 27 of last year. This opportunity will not come without effort, but you will be rewarded starting at the end of summer and through the fall. This adds impetus to the trajectory you're traveling as part of a twenty-year success cycle that began in May 2000. If you think in these terms, you'll see a common thread that runs through the events that play out this month, and you will be able to respond with purpose and intent. Key dates are May 4 to 15, and 22.

Wellness and Keeping Fit

You will not feel in control of events and circumstances in your life this month as the planets interact at a fever pitch. While this may pull you out of your routines, do your best to fit good habits into what you have to do: take the stairs instead of the elevator, practice deep breathing while waiting in line, and go for the healthy fast-food restaurant.

Love and Life Connections

Your personal relationships flow smoothly this month, building toward something special around May 26. Take the initiative to make that a special date.

Finance and Success

There's so much going on this month, it's hard to keep a business head as you spend most of your time responding to situations as they arise. While you're good at that, don't let the tide of events keep you from taking care of logistics, like paying bills and keeping accounts. You'll pay more than the usual price for a lapse.

Rewarding Days

4, 5, 14, 15, 18, 19, 22, 23, 27, 28, 31

Challenging Days

1, 2, 3, 9, 10, 16, 17, 29, 30

Aries/June

Planetary Hotspots

Your finances—and your resources in a more general sense—have been in a squeeze off and on this year, but when the fixed-cross pattern recurs this month it has a positive twist. You get the chance to cash in around June 7 as Venus in peak contact with Jupiter magnetizes money into your pocket. This may come with strings or with pre-arranged demands placed on you by those in your social realm, from family to romantic partners to groups. This is all part of the progress you've been making in reaching for your big-picture goals—the ones formed from 1997 to 2000.

Wellness and Keeping Fit

Your physical vitality is high this month, especially around June 16 when the Sun opposes Jupiter. Don't overshoot your capabilities, especially on June 17.

Love and Life Connections

You are gifted when it comes to quick and appropriate responses to rapidly developing situations, and those kinds of events are happening to the people around you. They come to you for support, knowing where your expertise lies. It helps that you are not as affected by this month's planetary patterns, but they are dealing with difficult circumstances that can't be easily overcome. Do what you can, but don't make yourself responsible. Avoid risky behaviors in romantic encounters.

Finance and Success

This is not a good time for high-risk endeavors due to the Mars contact to Saturn, Chiron, and Jupiter on June 17, 18, and 19. You could be out some serious cash with investments you choose on these days unless there's a way you can greatly reduce the risk through superior knowledge.

Rewarding Days

1, 2, 10, 11, 14, 15, 19, 20, 23, 24, 27, 28, 29

Challenging Days

5, 6, 7, 12, 13, 25, 26

Aries/July

Planetary Hotspots

Starting July 4, Mercury's latest retrograde brings out the need for repairs at home, including relationships. However, situations will not be complicated by compound problems, and misunderstandings will be overcome with few after-effects. It's full steam ahead after July 28, as Mercury returns to forward motion.

Wellness and Keeping Fit

You feel like playing this month, and so you should, as Mars dashes through your Fifth House of fun and games. Sports, dates—even a vacation—revitalize you, and you have the time to do these things now. After July 22, you'll be working harder, so enjoy it while it lasts.

Love and Life Connections

Communication snafus come out of nowhere and revive unresolved issues in relationships, especially on July 5 and 14. It's a good time to get in touch with submerged factors in your own character, because they are affecting the way others feel about you. Listening attentively to your loved ones now will help you grow as you improve your bond with them. You also have the opportunity to help others get beyond a conflict in a group setting around July 30. You may be called upon to mediate, or perhaps just to be a good sounding board.

Finance and Success

Beware of taking financial risks around July 5, as Mars moves into a challenging contact with Neptune. Gambling, including speculation in the markets, is not likely to go well because your judgment will be impaired by hidden factors. After July 6, Jupiter's retrograde period ends and your income production settles into a new normal. With a regular cash flow re-established, your life becomes calmer and more predictable.

Rewarding Days
7, 8, 9, 12, 13, 16, 17, 20, 21, 25, 26

Challenging Days
2, 3, 4, 10, 11, 22, 23, 24, 30, 31

Aries/August

Planetary Hotspots

The Neptune cycle reaches its culmination point on August 10, bringing the full manifestation of challenges from groups and organizations. This is an area where you've been making consistent sacrifices, probably by performing volunteer work. The pressure is on to be more than usually productive as this date passes. Take note of what happens on August 7, and take charge of what you do, because you're setting the tone for a new yearly Saturn cycle. Saturn supports your creative productivity and draws your focus to ways in which you can make your life happier and more meaningful. Think in terms of what you want to do over the next year to build a better life and make a plan. Your actions now will bear their finest results in twelve years.

Wellness and Keeping Fit

Inflammations, injuries, cuts, and bumps are more possible than usual as Mars makes its way through your Sixth House. The most critical dates are August 12 and 29, when it makes contact with Uranus and Pluto. If surgery is indicated, it is best to avoid having it on these dates.

Love and Life Connections

Problems in groups and organizations could land on your lap around August 10, and just what's going on could be difficult to pin down. If you wait a few days, new facts will emerge that will end the confusion.

Finance and Success

Lots of social activities—perhaps a vacation or special event—put pressure on your finances all month. This is not a bad thing, just something to plan for. These are part of a long-term development process in response to your desire for a more interesting and meaningful life. Events related to this occur all month, from August 2 to 27.

Rewarding Days

4, 5, 8, 9, 12, 13, 16, 17, 18, 21, 22, 23, 31

Challenging Days

6, 7, 19, 20, 26, 27, 28

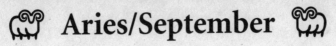 Aries/September

Planetary Hotspots

Work and health assume great importance as the planets pile up in your Sixth House. This reaches a peak around September 7 as Pluto turns direct, Uranus's cycle culminates, and the lunar eclipse occurs in rapid succession. Mercury and Venus provide triggers throughout the month to help you make sense of what's happening and respond fruitfully to what occurs.

Wellness and Keeping Fit

There never was a better time to focus on your wellness, as the planets cluster in your health houses. In fact, if you've ignored the odd symptom or persistent pain, you're likely to find out what's really going on. Now it's time to apply your ever-ready willingness to try new things to this area and get back in balance. Key events occur all month, but especially from September 3 to 9.

Love and Life Connections

You'll notice that others appear more aggressive than usual after September 6, as Mars enters your Seventh House. This could be in response to past behavior on your part, or it could be from subtle cues of frustration that you're sending out. A cool, non-reactive response will produce the best results; however, the issues raised may be valid and worth considering.

Finance and Success

The tension between your ideals and what you do to earn money comes up on September 24 as Jupiter contacts Neptune for the third and final time. When this first arose in January, you were inspired to pursue new goals, and now you get the chance to see how well you've done. Even though this is the last contact, it is only one more step in the process of fulfilling your ideals—one that produced some results but not the whole enchilada.

Rewarding Days

1, 5, 6, 9, 10, 13, 14, 17, 18, 19, 27, 28, 29

Challenging Days

2, 3, 4, 15, 16, 22, 23, 24, 30

Aries/October

Planetary Hotspots

The tensions that have built up in various situations over the year get a major release this month as the planets align in harmonious positions through October 15. Watch closely what occurs on October 5, 15, and 22. A seemingly harmless event could mushroom into a larger difficulty near the end of the month that will leave a contrail in your life through December 9.

Wellness and Keeping Fit

The emphasis on your Eighth House makes this a great time to enhance the transformative processes in your life. If there are any things in your wellness profile that you want to change, from liver congestion to personality patterns, now is a great time to do it. Once Mercury enters Scorpio on October 1 you can start the process.

Love and Life Connections

The harmonizing planets are principally felt in your social life, where difficulties in groups are healed with the help of a few friends. This involves the mediation of several people to open the channels to negotiation and accord. Key dates are October 3, 10, 13, 18, and 19.

Finance and Success

Finance and indebtedness come to the forefront as the fast-moving planets congregate in your Eighth House toward the end of the month. Events on October 5, 15, and 22 feed a long-term process that affects your flow of income. This is the result of past outreach efforts and is likely to involve a project that brings income but is not a perfect match to your skills and ways of working. The challenges with this will max out around October 28, when Mercury begins its three-week retrograde period.

Rewarding Days
1, 2, 3, 6, 7, 10, 11, 15, 16, 25, 26, 29, 30

Challenging Days
12, 13, 14, 20, 21, 27, 28

♈ Aries/November ♈

Planetary Hotspots

With Mercury retrograde until November 17 in your Eighth House, you're open to the world's transformative processes. The emphasis is on the challenges you have faced all year, sort of a last hurrah if you deal with them effectively. Starting November 23, the universe feels kinder. Jupiter enters Sagittarius and your Ninth House. This is completely harmonious with your Aries energy and fills you with inspiration to fulfill your life quest.

Wellness and Keeping Fit

This is a good month to work on healing old wounds, injuries, and scar tissue. Your energy field is particularly open to the benefits of energetic healing, as Mars trines Uranus on November 8.

Love and Life Connections

Changes in your understanding of the universe have a positive ripple effect in your relationships as well. This does not come without some soul-baring, however. You may need to fess up to your own mistakes and frailties, but if you are willing to do so, friction that you experienced in groups or organizations dissipates dramatically. The most harmonious dates for such interactions are November 1, 8, 11, 14, and 22.

Finance and Success

You can already feel it coming—the time when you can start reaching for the newest peak in your cycle of personal success. The coming year, starting officially November 23, will be a combination of final preparation for and manifestation of the goal you've been reaching toward for the past eight years, since Jupiter was last in your sign. This will be a year to circulate, travel, get the word out, and expand your horizons. Sounds like fun, doesn't it?

Rewarding Days

2, 3, 6, 7, 8, 21, 22, 25, 26, 30

Challenging Days

12, 13, 14, 20, 27, 28

♈ Aries/December ♈

Planetary Hotspots

Teaching, travel, publishing, higher learning, spiritual growth, and aspirations—these are in the spotlight now and for the next year. Six planets throw their weight here for added emphasis now, giving your related affairs a big boost. This is a good time to take a vacation to rural, foreign, or faraway places. Or you can use this time to boost your career and educational plans.

Wellness and Keeping Fit

Although you are not usually the dreamy-eyed type, this month may be the exception. In fact, you'll be more accident- and injury-prone because of it. You do need some time to get away and recenter yourself. If you prefer not to get away, at least retreat from the world by closing the door as you go into your sacred space.

Love and Life Connections

There's not much to complain about, but you recognize that you could be happier, and you could contribute to the happiness of others more as well, as Saturn starts its retrograde on December 5. This is a good time to renew your commitment to connect with children and other loved ones—not just in the abstract, but by agreeing to an activity that affords you regular time together. Taking your son to his basketball practice, your daughter to her dance lessons, or meeting a romantic partner for dinner on Wednesdays—these are investments in relationships that lead to fulfillment.

Finance and Success

Even if you are enjoying some time away, take the time on December 18 to think of what you want to accomplish over the coming year. This is when Pluto's new annual cycle begins, and with Jupiter joining it this year in Sagittarius, you will be greatly empowered to achieve your goals.

Rewarding Days

1, 4, 5, 8, 9, 10, 18, 19, 23, 24, 27, 28, 31

Challenging Days

6, 7, 13, 14, 15, 20, 21, 22

Aries Action Table

These dates reflect the best—but not the only—times for success and ease in these activities, according to your Sun sign.

	JAN	FEB	MAR	APR	MAY	JUN	JUL	AUG	SEPT	OCT	NOV	DEC
Move						3-28	29-31	1-10				
Start a class					20-31	1, 2						
Join a club	23-31	1-8										
Ask for a raise	29, 30		5-31	1-5	3-29							
Look for work	4-22							28-31	1-30	2		
Get pro advice	20, 21, 25	16, 17, 21	15-17, 20	11-13, 16	9, 19, 14	5-7, 10	2-4, 7-9	5, 26-28	1, 22-24	20, 21, 25	16, 17, 21	13-15, 18
Get a loan	22-24	18-20	18, 19	14, 15	11-13	8, 9	5, 6	1-3, 29	25, 26	22-24	18-20	16, 17
See a doctor		9-28	26-31	1-30	1-4		27-31	1-30	1			
Start a diet			13, 14				27-31	1-12				
End relationship				12, 13								
Buy clothes								11-31	1-5			
Get a makeover			29, 30	16-30	1-28							
New romance							25-27	13-31	1-5, 30	1-23		
Vacation	25, 26	21, 22	20, 21	16-18	14, 15	10, 11	7-9	4, 5, 31	1, 27-29	25, 26	17-30	8-27

TAURUS

The Bull
April 20 to May 22

♉

Element:	Earth
Quality:	Fixed
Polarity:	Yin/Feminine
Planetary Ruler:	Venus
Meditation:	I trust myself and others
Gemstone:	Emerald
Power Stones:	Diamond, blue lace agate, rose quartz
Key Phrase:	I have
Glyph:	Bull's head
Anatomy:	Throat, neck
Color:	Green
Animal:	Cattle
Myths/Legends:	Isis and Osiris, Cerridwen, Bull of Minos
House:	Second
Opposite Sign:	Scorpio
Flower:	Violet
Key Word:	Conservation

Your Ego's Strengths and Weaknesses

You're so strong, consistent, and solid, Taurus, that sometimes you feel like a rock, both to yourself and others. This comes from your fixed earth nature. As a fixed sign, you respond to the forces of the world around you by trying to preserve the status quo. You prefer things to be the same. When you build something, you try to make it as long-lasting as possible. This is why you are known as the architect or builder. You stabilize, calm, construct, and solidify. You resist change because change destabilizes things. However, you must also remember that everything eventually breaks down. Change creates a temporary disruption, but it can bring about a new, better stability if it is wisely directed. By becoming a master of change, you master your own ability to create lasting structures.

As an earth sign, you look at the immediate and the practical. Your physical, tangible surroundings are what you think of first, and physical security—having enough money, a sturdy house, well-made clothes, and nutritious food—is very important to you. You have a knack for crafts and mechanical skills and you are gifted at working with three-dimensional objects. Whether you are inclined to work on cars or do fine needlecraft, you are driven to produce and exemplify beauty in whatever you do. A car that purrs smoothly is as beautiful to a mechanic as a finely woven rug is to a weaver. But a down side to your nature can be a tendency to forget about the inner needs and qualities that make the material world more enjoyable. If you get mired in worry about finances, you can't enjoy the security you have. In the worst case, you could feel that there's never enough for you to feel comfortable. By cultivating your awareness of what's really important, such as love and health, you'll naturally place your need for material comforts in perspective.

Shining Your Love Light

You like to build things that last, and love relationships are no exception. It may take you time to warm to a partner, to learn to trust, but you are in it for the long haul. You do not make commitments lightly, and you break them even less lightly. For you, financial stability is essential in a relationship, and you will hesitate to commit unless you are sure you can create a relationship with a firm material foundation.

Aries signs may seem a little too impulsive for you, but they certainly get you motivated and fill you with inspiring ideas. A fellow Taurus will understand your need for a deliberate approach to life, but you can get stuck in a rut together. Geminis will lead you to experiences you never dreamed possible, and you'll be the better for them, but this sign's chatter may annoy you at times. Cancer shares your appreciation of security and brings emotional energy to your bond, but you will not be known for your adventurousness as a couple. Leo's attention-seeking can rub you the wrong way, but the joy and generosity this sign brings reassures you. Virgo is a true and loyal helpmate, a companion who shares your values and sees the world as you do. Your mutual supportiveness and productivity can be used to build a strong relationship. Libra brings out your eye for elegance and harmony. You share a love of aesthetics, and together you can explore the many expressions of beauty, both practical and cultural. Scorpios may seem your nemesis, but they are really teaching you the flipside of your own character—the need to recognize transformation as an element of true stability. Sagittarians, with their wild ways and wide-ranging focus, may seem to have little in common with you, until you recognize that they are as interested as you are in the principles that give life its value. Capricorn adds broad perspective and worldly savvy to your pragmatic skills to make the business side of your relationship a success, but don't ignore the emotional needs that lie beneath. You may feel irritated by Aquarius's fascination with the social and political world, but you share a rational approach that allows you to work through any problem. Pisces's tenderness makes it easy for you to trust, but your occasional stubbornness may be difficult for this sign.

Making Your Place in the World

You are so comfortable manipulating the physical world that your skills are in demand in any business. Your high mechanical aptitude makes you a natural for any career requiring highly developed motor skills, from sports to carpentry to dressmaking. You also have a refined sense of beauty that can be expressed in more symbolic ways, such as through the design side of any of field, from fashion or architecture to landscaping and urban planning. Your interest in finances will lead you to develop skills in managing money, whether you apply them to bookkeeping or go into the more conceptual worlds of accounting and markets. Financial planning, loan or mortgage lending, insurance services, or banking may also provide satisfaction to you. Because of your desire for financial predictability, you will feel better in a job where a regular paycheck and good benefits are featured rather than in a situation with more sporadic payment.

Putting Your Best Foot Forward

Before you can be at your best, Taurus, you need to make sure you've overcome your fear of change. Your stability makes you a rock to stand on when all else is shifting—a port in a storm. When you establish something, everyone knows it will last. However, change is a part of life, and if you experience all change as too risky, you are resisting the flow of the universe and making the changes harder when they do come. It is true that not everything needs to change just because somebody thinks it does, and it's your job to determine which changes are good and which should not be enacted. However, you have to be friends with change, or you can't make wise decisions about it. You have to know that your security does not come from the nature of your external surroundings or how much money you have in the bank, but in how well you deal with what life throws at you. You have a gift for building firm structures and lasting foundations. If you can add the flexibility to move and bend to your rock-like steadiness, you'll have the best of both worlds and feel more comfortable in the bargain. We must let go in order to have.

Tools for Change

Your earthy pragmatism and ability to make things grow and multiply, from gardens to bank accounts, have their charms, but to prevent yourself from becoming overly materialistic or stuck in a rut, you should lift your consciousness to other levels to create balance. At the core of this process is the need to introduce mind, heart, and spirit into the mix without neglecting the physical body. One of the best ways to cultivate and maintain this balance is to immerse yourself in a liberal education. A liberal education focuses on teaching dialogic technique and places a high value on critical enquiry. These in themselves could be said to broaden the mind, but this education goes further to encompass philosophy, history, language, culture, and theory—all stepping stones to creating a broad mind and powerful analytical process. To hone your natural emphasis on values, philosophy is especially helpful, because our values are based on what we believe. The study of history adds depth to your awareness by allowing you to see the rhythms of human evolution and how they play into current events and individual behavior. You can also benefit from "lightening up." You can put your good sense of humor to work by taking a class in stand-up comedy, or just by immersing yourself in a comedic world on a regular basis. Plays, movies, and sitcoms on TV can teach you to laugh at yourself and to recognize that the obstacles that fall in your path do not signal the end of the world. Meditation can also remove you from the cares of daily life. You will benefit from meditating in a garden or engaging in "open-eye meditation," which can be done while gardening (or in another tranquil activity) if you maintain the proper focus.

All earth signs need to counteract their natural tendency toward immobility by engaging consciously in a program of physical activity. If you do not engage in physical work as a part of your work life, it's important to compensate for that by working out before or after. Although you may tend toward strength training, aerobic exercise and flexibility training are more important for you. Yoga offers a blend of all three, or you can engage in them as separate practices through other means. Hiking appeals to your love of the outdoors, and it will also soothe the soul. Pilates works with the core muscles and encourages proper alignment. Dance may be especially enjoyable to your creative spirit. No matter what you choose, it should mean something to you and be something you can build into a healthy habit.

Affirmation for the Year

I can listen to others and make adjustments.

The Year Ahead for Taurus

Relationships have a high profile in your life this year, Taurus, as Jupiter makes its way through your solar Seventh House. If you work in a field where more "people contact" is good, this will be a year of increased prosperity for you. You may even find that new partnership opportunities open up to you. This could also be true in your personal life. One or more new personal relationships may come your way—you may even have to choose from a short list of viable candidates! Your existing partner may bring more prosperity to you or teach you something new. Things you started six years ago, if you've pursued them consistently, will bear the fruit of inner satisfaction and happiness.

Saturn is in Leo and your solar Fourth House, drawing attention to your home and private life. There may be deferred maintenance projects or repairs that you must handle this year—usually ones that provide basic services but are invisible and so offer little gratification, like re-roofing or rewiring. You could find that the place you are living is too limiting in terms of your future plans, so you may decide that it's time to move. You may also be required to fulfill greater responsibilities to family.

Chiron spends its second year in Aquarius, teaching us all how to be better team players. In your solar Tenth House, it challenges you to overcome obstacles of bias that lie in your viewpoint of the world, to see how all people are equally worthy of the chance to experience life's finer delights. This doesn't detract from the fact that each of us has something unique to offer or that we all have to work for those experiences. When you view life as a level playing field, you will open doorways in your career and life calling because of your more open attitude.

Uranus is at the midpoint of its transit of Pisces and your solar Eleventh House. Uniqueness is the key word: you want to do something exceptional. This is not empty action lightly taken, especially for you. You have a deeper vision of what can be. You see a new and different world that is just around the corner if we enact it, based on the ideals that everyone spouts but cannot seem to realize. You are a voice of altruistic change for which you will gladly sacrifice if you can but imbue others with your vision.

Neptune is once more in Aquarius and your solar Tenth House. Since 1998, you have followed a trajectory toward a deeper, more meaningful calling which will eventually replace the job or career you fulfilled before this time. As long as you don't get caught up in some fly-by-night operation or get-rich-quick scheme, you'll benefit by this transit.

Pluto in Sagittarius and your solar Eighth House is bringing adjustments to the way you handle finances, especially where you are using the resources of others. Transformative financial events could also occur, from gaining a large inheritance or winning the lottery to losing it all on the stock market. A balanced approach with an unswerving sense of responsibility is key to whatever changes come your way.

This year the eclipses darken the skies in Virgo and Pisces, and your Fifth and Eleventh Houses receive the focus. Your social life will be under the magnifying glass, and you may change directions there in some way, perhaps beginning a new romance, joining a new organization, or trying a new sport. Fun will be in the picture, and life will be more meaningful by the time the eclipses leave these areas in 2007.

If you were born between April 24 and May 16, Saturn is directly contacting your Sun from your solar Fourth House. Since July of last year, your home and private life have required more of your attention. You may be in a quiet phase of your work life (even unemployed), or have greater responsibilities to family that pull you home more often. This is a period of relative anonymity, but it is nonetheless full of activity for you, for you are working hard to develop a new foundation that will withstand the challenges of the next thirty years. Your literal foundation—your home—may need dramatic structural changes, or you could decide to voluntarily improve its value. An elder in your family may require more care as they age, or your immediate family may require more attention in some way. You may also spend more time looking inward, discovering the keys to your own deep-seated behavior patterns so that you can mend them. Facing these matters squarely is always the best where Saturn in concerned, and by the end of the year you'll have the situation sorted out, if not completely resolved. Related events will occur around January 27, February 19, April 5 and 24, June 20, August 7, November 16, and December 5.

If you were born between April 22 and May 1, Uranus in Pisces will bring the opportunity for harmonious change from your solar Eleventh House. People make the world go 'round, and your contacts with people are essential this year. If you make a consistent effort to engage with others socially, you will find a gold mine of new options and opportunities there. Even if your work does not directly rely on making connections, new acquaintances bring new ideas, perspectives, and techniques. Innovation is the key word, and you will have the chance to change your life and the way you work. You could be up for an award, recognition, or career advancement for past efforts. You could stand out as a voice for progress, because you see flaws in the tried-and-true systems around you. Humanitarian causes may grab at your heartstrings, and you could become involved in volunteer work to make the world a better place. If you emphasize novel experiences and watch for the unexpected, you'll be able to gain maximum benefit from this planetary event. March 1, June 5 and 19, September 5, November 19, and December 2 are important dates in Uranus's cycle.

If you were born between May 5 and 10, Neptune in Aquarius will stir yearnings for deeper meaning in life and career. You may feel trapped by your current work situation and want to inject more creativity into what you do. You may find that it isn't necessary to change your job title—rather that your sense of purpose and meaning will deepen within the job you already carry out. Even if you throw over the work you've done in the past for an entirely new path, the meaning is at least as important as the money to you. You won't gain the full benefit of Neptune's contact unless you make sure that your work meets your deeper need for meaning and purpose. It is also possible to find purpose outside the workplace, through hobbies, part-time small business ventures, or leisure activities. Adding more variety to your life may be all it takes. Spirituality and your notion of a higher power may be under development as well, as you see more reasons to make these a part of your life. Turning points in your Neptune experience occur around January 27,

February 5, March 15, May 10 and 22, August 10, October 29, and November 9.

If you were born between May 13 and 18, you'll feel pressure to make dramatic changes as Pluto contacts your Sun from your solar Eighth House. Your finances and the way you handle them need to be transformed. Perhaps your income has dramatically increased; this means you need to develop new financial managements skills to use those new resources wisely. If your income has been reduced or your debt increased, you will need to tighten your belt and develop a new budget to pull yourself through a tough time. All Pluto transits are about self-empowerment, and taking responsibility is the first step to gaining personal power and control over your own life. You may find that studies of the inner workings of human behavior help you cope with your new world, whether through psychology, the occult mysteries, astrology, or the I Ching. Transformative processes may fascinate you now as you grapple with your ability to change under pressure. Pluto's energy will be felt most around March 17 and 29, June 16, September 4 and 16, and December 18.

If you were born between April 20 and 23 or May 19 and 22, the planets are giving you a break this year, at least as far as your Sun is concerned. This means that your efforts to accomplish your next great goal(s) will not be hampered, but neither will they be guided. Sometimes an obstacle turns us away from loss or harm. Therefore, it pays to extra vigilant in listening to your inner voice, because the other planets in your chart will speak to you there. It never hurts to use this time to introduce a little more leisure into a busy life or to tackle a big project when it's easier to accomplish.

Taurus/January

Planetary Hotspots

Jupiter squares Neptune on January 27, with related triggers on January 15, 18, 23, and 27 by other planets. This signals a new phase in the career or profession you began in 1997. New people come into your life now who may be able to join you in an enterprise. However, you will have to sort through which ones they are. Since Venus is retrograde through the month, people encountered now may be less appropriate no matter how good they look. You'll have plenty to choose from and four more years to go before you reach the top.

Wellness and Keeping Fit

You need an unhurried perspective after January 14 to keep your life on track, when someone may try to pull you off center. Even a long weekend will do if that's all you can manage, but don't stay home— go someplace that will allow you to get some perspective on the current events in your life.

Love and Life Connections

You've been pondering how to be in contact with more people in new groups and venues, to brighten your prospects and increase your social interaction. Investigate and experiment with some new contacts throughout this month. By the end of the month, you'll have some ideas of who to link up with. Relationship matters clear up after January 17.

Finance and Success

Don't let others push you into something before you're ready. It's a sure sign that their offers won't stand up to deeper scrutiny. If you ignore your internal radar, problems will crop up in May, August, and November as well, and may last long after that. This ties in with obstacles you encountered last fall.

Rewarding Days
3, 4, 8, 9, 12, 13, 14, 17, 18, 19, 27, 28

Challenging Days
1, 2, 15, 16, 22, 23, 24, 29, 30

Taurus/February

Planetary Hotspots

The first week of February is hot as Mercury and the Sun provide the final triggers to the situation you've been dealing with since last fall. Mercury brings a new understanding of all the changes you've been dealing with. Although they became highlighted last summer, they really tie in to a slow shift you're making in your career and family life. Now you can begin to move more steadily toward those goals. After the new information provided from February 1 to 5, you'll have two relatively calm weeks to get caught up. The emphasis is on your personal life—partnership and home—but the situation at work is really behind what's happening there.

Wellness and Keeping Fit

It's not too late to take that vacation you put off. This is a great time to get away from it all, if only for a few days. Activities in nature will soothe your soul and give you an energy pick-up.

Love and Life Connections

As Venus returns to direct motion in your Ninth House, this is a good time to write letters to people far away with whom communication has fallen off. Social activity picks up for you on February 8, especially in group and public settings.

Finance and Success

After February 17 when Mars enters your Second House, expenditures go up, but probably because you're going shopping. There are items that you've wanted to get that suddenly seem more important, but it may be just because you feel bold enough to finally spend the money. Whatever the motivation, a modicum of discipline will make this a harmless adventure. On February 5 a new year-long cycle begins which brings about spiritual growth and the fulfillment of wishes.

Rewarding Days

1, 4, 5, 8, 9, 10, 13, 14, 15, 23, 24, 27, 28

Challenging Days

11, 12, 18, 19, 20, 25, 26

Taurus/March

Planetary Hotspots

Planetary standstills mean transitions in perspective and direction, and this will be the theme for March. After the intensity of events starting last fall, you had a chance to redirect forces on the desired path last month. Now it's time to let go and let the planets do the work for you as you respond to what you previously set in motion. Uranus's new cycle starting on March 1 feeds positively into the social changes you want to bring about in your life. Think of what you want and make a plan.

Wellness and Keeping Fit

Experiences and events will inspire you to take a healthier approach to life around March 29. Your new methods could include a different type of fitness, diet, or inner growth program.

Love and Life Connections

The area of greatest enterprise for you this month is in social relationships, but don't expect results right away. Mercury trines Jupiter all month long, but since it is retrograde, results will be delayed. When they do come through, they'll be more powerful. If you're getting the brush-off when you approach people with your ideas, don't take it as a final "no." Come back after March 25 with a subtle reminder of your intent, and you'll receive a warmer reception.

Finance and Success

March 4 and 15 bring hints of what's to come with the dreams you began pursuing on January 27. This is a good time to be aware of the opportunities and insights that come your way from others, because they will portend the concrete results that will manifest later. Pluto's change in direction on March 29 motivates you all the more to keep moving toward a career or business idea with more income potential. The time to begin the transition is now.

Rewarding Days

3, 4, 8, 9, 13, 14, 22, 23, 24, 27, 28, 31

Challenging Days

10, 11, 12, 18, 19, 25, 26

Taurus/April

Planetary Hotspots

It's as if a great burden is being lifted from your shoulders when Saturn returns to direct motion on April 5. You've been working extra hard with no apparent progress or recognition since November 22 of last year, but that behind-the-scenes effort has kept others from interrupting you or throwing obstacles in your path. Now you can advance, but still in your own quiet way. Year One of this two-year process will be over on August 7.

Wellness and Keeping Fit

After April 16, you'll want to retreat more than ever as Mercury follows the Sun into your Twelfth House, and it's a good idea to succumb to the urge. It's one of those rare times when you can recharge your batteries. That doesn't mean to laze about, however, or to work harder behind the scenes. It means to return to your center and renew your focus, reasserting discipline, if necessary, to follow your regular fitness and health routines.

Love and Life Connections

If someone in your life has gone into a cave, let it be. He or she won't be there forever, although it will still be three months before this person returns to you unreservedly. If you interfere in the process, it will take longer.

Finance and Success

On April 8, you're alerted to the fact that your finances need more attention than usual, as situations come to light that you overlooked due to the recent intensity of events. Take the time to update and audit your accounts and portfolios. You'll find errors and will have to take the time to fix them, but they're nothing irreversible. Key dates are April 13, 18, and 30.

Rewarding Days

1, 4, 5, 9, 10, 19, 20, 23, 24, 27, 28

Challenging Days

6, 7, 8, 14, 15, 21, 22

Taurus/May

Planetary Hotspots

A grand trine with Mars, Jupiter, and Uranus supports your plans, and you experience unexpected breakthroughs, especially at the beginning of the month. This accelerates the speed of life to a fast pace that continues through May 14. You may feel like you've run off the edge of a cliff after that, but the processes have just begun to work in a submerged way as the retrogrades of Chiron and Neptune activate on May 15 and 22. There is a common theme in all these events that ties in with a nibble you got November 27 of last year and the twenty-year cycle that started in May 2000.

Wellness and Keeping Fit

Your lifestyle routines don't have to be disrupted if you incorporate healthy patterns into the flow of events. Step into your garden, pull a few weeds, or listen to relaxing music as you work to keep those alpha waves flowing in your brain.

Love and Life Connections

You could use the support of those close to you now, but they may be busy in their own whirlwinds of activity, especially from May 4 to 14. If so, just take the time to be emotionally supportive of each other as you pass in the doorway.

Finance and Success

It seems as if you'll never fulfill all the obligations that have suddenly landed in your lap as you experience the effects of too much success in the moment. The first half of the month will be hectic, with your "to do" list getting longer rather than shorter. The second half will give you more breathing room, however. Don't let the enormity of the task make you less effective—just look at what's directly in front of you in the moment and get that done before looking at the next item on the list.

Rewarding Days

1, 2, 3, 6, 7, 8, 16, 17, 20, 21, 24, 25, 26, 29, 30

Challenging Days

4, 5, 11, 12, 13, 18, 19, 31

Taurus/June

Planetary Hotspots

In spite of your cheerful attitude, a difficult dilemma arises this month with regard to home and career obligations. You have been making sacrifices in order to fulfill the desires of your employer or to further your career. However, now the needs of your loved ones call you home quite urgently, and you can't ignore them. Which are you going to fulfill? Clearly, some adjustments need to be made to the balance of your public and your personal life, and the private side is getting more of your time now. Making the transition is tricky, but you can find help and support. This pattern is strongest from June 17 to 22.

Wellness and Keeping Fit

Your energy levels are not at their peak this month, so "low and slow" is the key. Respond to what your body is telling you, because it is listening to the Mars-Saturn conjunction in your Fourth House. Walking is an excellent routine now, since it gets you out of the house—the most important thing of all.

Love and Life Connections

Although others need support at home, it doesn't always have to be you providing it. If someone requires health care, you can hire people to assist you, giving you a needed rest as well as some time away from your public life.

Finance and Success

In the context of the long-term process of financial self-empowerment you've been engaged in since 1995, you're able to "draw down the power" around June 16, as the Sun contacts Pluto in your money houses. There is likely to be an influx of cash, either from your own efforts or as a loan or bequest. This is timely after the changes you experienced on June 5.

Rewarding Days

3, 4, 12, 13, 17, 18, 21, 22, 25, 26, 30

Challenging Days

1, 2, 8, 9, 14, 15, 27, 28, 29

Taurus/July

Planetary Hotspots

The high level of activity you experienced last month is history by July 5, but there are still some leftover loose ends to tie up as Mercury retrogrades in your Third House from July 5 to 28. You may also be inconvenienced by activity in your neighborhood or events involving siblings. However, as this retrograde is not complicated by other planetary contacts, solutions to the dilemmas that arise should be straightforward. This is a golden opportunity to get your house in order, both metaphorically and literally.

Wellness and Keeping Fit

You'll feel more energized after July 21 when Mars enters your Fifth House. It's a good time to take a vacation—and to make room for more sports activities in your schedule. Even if what you like to do is low-key, such as working in the garden or hiking in the hills, taking a friend or two will increase your pleasure exponentially, which is as important to health as a good diet.

Love and Life Connections

After July 6, when Jupiter returns to direct motion, unusual circumstances in your partnership dissipate, and you return to a new normal. There is a flurry of activity around this date and then a feeling of moving forward. This has to do with a process of positive development that started four months ago.

Finance and Success

Around July 30, it's okay to let activities at home take you away from work. You are needed, and you'll just have to rely on the goodwill of your colleagues and employers to see you through. Minimize potential problems by being clear about what you're doing and why.

Rewarding Days

1, 10, 11, 14, 15, 18, 19, 22, 23, 24, 27, 28

Challenging Days

5, 6, 12, 13, 25, 26

Taurus/August

Planetary Hotspots

You'll have plenty on your plate this month as situations at home and work come to a head around August 10, but there are plenty of contributing activities and events from August 2 to 27. This is a complex situation that requires consistent effort to see it through. However, it benefits you in the long run financially. Set your intention carefully for what you plan and do on August 7, the start of the yearly Saturn cycle. This opens Stage Two of the two-year process of restructuring your home and family life. This involves extra effort on your part, but it will result in a more secure and comfortable foundation from which to launch your newest climb to success, which will peak in thirteen years.

Wellness and Keeping Fit

Sporting activities could result in clashes and injury as Mars makes its way through your Fifth House. This is most likely on August 12 and 29.

Love and Life Connections

Your home and family life is a beehive of activity. You're on the cusp of new possibilities, and your private life is abuzz as your plans are being laid and fulfilled. You're at the halfway point in the overall project, and now you have the urge to put focused effort into it to make more visible progress. This will not be without its obstacles, but you'd expect that with work of this nature.

Finance and Success

It seems like activities at work and home are equally demanding now—and both want too much from you in August. It may be the right time to adjust your career reality now by delegating more or providing constructive input in a workload-adjustment process.

Rewarding Days

6, 7, 10, 11, 14, 15, 19, 20, 24, 25

Challenging Days

1, 2, 3, 8, 9, 21, 22, 23, 29, 30

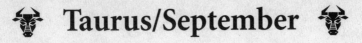

Taurus/September

Planetary Hotspots

The efforts you undertook in January to create the ideal career path are moving into a new phase, as the cycle that prompted them winds down. Jupiter and Neptune make their final of three dynamic contacts on September 24 and leave you with two more months before you feel ready for a new challenge and approach to success. You have paid the most attention to your relationships and how they support your path. This may have resulted in a business partnership or the support of those close to you as you continue toward success.

Wellness and Keeping Fit

You're more prone to stress after September 6 once Mars enters your Sixth House. You're under more pressure at work, and life has gotten more complicated outside your job as well. However, Mars also invigorates you, and as long as you don't overdo it, regular exercise now will go far to keep you in balance.

Love and Life Connections

Children or romance are in the spotlight now as the planets congregate in your Fifth House. Exciting, perhaps challenging, events occur from September 3 to 9, but you're more than equal to the contest. Your heart and mind are drawn toward projects in your home and personal life more than usual for the next two months, culminating at the end of October. You can head off some of the crush of activity that will occur then by taking care of preliminaries now.

Finance and Success

Financial barriers give way around September 4 as Pluto returns to forward motion. You've been working on creating greater stability since the end of March, and now the results are more apparent. Tests of your new reality arise on September 16 and 22, making you aware that there's more room for growth.

Rewarding Days

2, 3, 4, 7, 8, 11, 12, 15, 16, 20, 21, 30

Challenging Days

5, 6, 17, 18, 19, 25, 26

Taurus/October

Planetary Hotspots

You've worked hard this year to satisfy others' expectations so you can get what you want. This month you start to see some results, with more enjoyable and fulfilling work and some recognition for your steady efforts. Although the obstacles you've been whittling away at all year still exist in a lesser form, the planetary doors open this month to bring you more visible progress gained much more easily.

Wellness and Keeping Fit

Your energy level is high and your health good, especially through October 15. This is a good time to get advice from those who can give you new ideas to make it even better. You can benefit from restructuring your health goals now for the coming year.

Love and Life Connections

If it seems as though you have another full-time job taking care of your home and family duties, that's Saturn speaking. You've been carrying more responsibility there, and that pulls you away from what you've been working toward in your career since 1998. Although you have another year of this push-pull process, it gets tremendously easier now. It helps to remember that personal and family happiness and security are the goal of career growth, not the other way around. Listen to what those closest to you have to say early in the month. Although spoken mildly, it's important to them, and they will become more insistent after October 28. Key listening dates are October 5, 15, 22 and 24.

Finance and Success

The opportunity for more satisfying work comes your way this month, becoming part of your long-term drive to create a more fulfilling career path. You've been making sacrifices in order to build this new reality, and now you see some results.

Rewarding Days

1, 4, 5, 8, 9, 12, 13, 14, 17, 18, 19, 27, 28, 31

Challenging Days

2, 3, 15, 16, 22, 23, 24, 29, 30

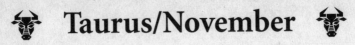 Taurus/November

Planetary Hotspots

Relationships are in the spotlight as the planets cluster in your Seventh House. If you are in a helping profession, you'll have more client contacts than usual. Other contacts will be numerous also, and possibly contentious, as Mars is involved. Mercury retrograde increases the possibility of misunderstanding, but also of clarification of communications. Jupiter's new cycle starts on November 23, starting a year of greater prosperity for you. You could also leave behind some sources of income in order to follow others that promise better returns on investments or your efforts. This is the first of four years when you will be at the top of your game.

Wellness and Keeping Fit

Working out with a friend is the way to go all month long, as you're feeling more companionable now. It's also a good time to seek health and medical advice, especially on November 14, 21, 22, and 27.

Love and Life Connections

This is an excellent time for working out issues in personal relationships, as Mercury retrogrades through your house of partnerships. Undermining influences, such as unconscious factors or career and family pressures, can be brought to full awareness and resolution. November 15 is a special date for love.

Finance and Success

You've been working hard toward your long-term goals all year, and this month the pressure heats up again, with the emphasis on your interactions with others. This could mean more foot traffic in a business, a major business deal, even a new business partnership. Confusion, misunderstanding, and disorganization are possible as you adjust to the higher level of activity. Wait until after November 17 to sign contracts. The best dates are November 21 and 22.

Rewarding Days
1, 4, 5, 9, 10, 13, 14, 15, 23, 24, 28, 29

Challenging Days
11, 12, 18, 19, 20, 25, 26, 27

Taurus/December

Planetary Hotspots

Even though it's the end of the year, it's the beginning of a year of increased prosperity and expanding prospects for you, Taurus. The fast-moving planets join Jupiter and Pluto in your Eighth House, bringing an explosion of resources flowing toward you. You've been working since 1995 to get where you are, and now you begin the four-year pay-off period as Jupiter arcs across the top of your chart. You can maximize the potential of the coming year by setting your intention to create the things you want the most on December 18, when Pluto starts its new yearly cycle. This can be a bold plan that substantially advances the deeper plan you have for your life.

Wellness and Keeping Fit

You're ready for some time off to recharge your batteries, and getting away from your home environment looks good after December 18. Key dates are December 3, 9 to 11, and 15.

Love and Life Connections

Projects and people at home take more of your time around December 5 as Saturn begins its retrograde period. This is the beginning of five months of focused effort that should be aimed at increasing your stability and rejuvenating your inner being. Much of what happens for you now is invisible to those not close to you, yet this part of your life is full of growth.

Finance and Success

The limitations you are dealing with at home are supported by, and support, the wealth cycle you are entering now. There is a boost or bonus coming sometime between December 9 and 11 that will set the tone for the year, but you should not rely on results being that good consistently. There will be peaks and dips over the year, with a big boost next fall, so keep that in mind when making plans.

Rewarding Days

2, 3, 6, 7, 11, 12, 20, 21, 22, 25, 26, 29, 30

Challenging Days

8, 9, 10, 16, 17, 23, 24

Taurus Action Table

These dates reflect the best—but not the only—times for success and ease in these activities, according to your Sun sign.

	JAN	FEB	MAR	APR	MAY	JUN	JUL	AUG	SEPT	OCT	NOV	DEC
Move						28-30	1-3, 25	11-27				
Start a class			26-31			3-27	29-31	1-10				
Join a club		9-28		1-15								
Ask for a raise		27, 28		6-30	1-3, 29-31	1-23						
Look for work	23-31	1-8							13-30	1-26	19-30	
Get pro advice	22-24, 27	18-20, 23	18, 19, 22	14, 15, 19	11-13, 16	8, 9, 12	5, 6, 10	1-3, 6, 7	2-4, 25	1, 22-24	18-20, 23	16, 17, 20
Get a loan	25, 26	21, 22	20, 21	16-18	14, 15	10, 11	7-9	4, 5, 31	1, 27-29	25, 26	21, 22	18, 19
See a doctor				16-30	1-19				12-30	1-26	19-30	1-7
Start a diet									12-30	1		
End relationship				12, 13								
Buy clothes								27-31	1-30			
Get a makeover				27, 28	5-19, 29			23-25	6-30	24-31	1-16, 18	
New romance						1-23						
Vacation	3-22, 27	3-28	1-5, 22	19, 20	16, 17	12, 13	10, 11	6, 7	2-4, 30	1, 27, 28	23, 24	11-31

GEMINI

The Twins
May 22 to June 21

Ⅱ

Element:	Air
Quality:	Mutable
Polarity:	Yang/Masculine
Planetary Ruler:	Mercury
Meditation:	I explore my inner worlds
Gemstone:	Tourmaline
Power Stones:	Ametrine, citrine, emerald, spectrolite, agate
Key Phrase:	I think
Glyph:	Pillars of duality, the Twins
Anatomy:	Hands, arms, shoulders, lungs, nervous system
Color:	Bright colors, orange, yellow, magenta
Animal:	Monkeys, talking birds, flying insects
Myths/Legends:	Peter Pan, Castor and Pollux
House:	Third
Opposite Sign:	Sagittarius
Flower:	Lily of the valley
Key Word:	Versatility

Your Ego's Strengths and Weaknesses

You flow with the breezes of life, exploring every nook and cranny of experience. It's your mutable air nature that you're expressing, Gemini—your desire to connect. Your mutable side gives you flexibility. You move around obstacles rather than through or over them. You prefer to avoid confrontation, and you will rely on your considerable social skills to put others at ease. You can be a master negotiator, finding the right words to assuage ruffled feelings, so adept are you at using your mind. You are better at follow-through than you are at starting something new because you go with others' impulses, connecting the dots or integrating the bits of data that others present to you. You complete processes and make them whole. With your desire to avoid friction, you may find yourself revising the data to fit the situation, but this is not from any mean-spiritedness or scheming on your part. You may also become scattered and nervous when your circumstances overwhelm you. When this happens, you may tend to chatter mindlessly to distract yourself.

As an air sign, you are an assimilator and a communicator. You move rapidly from thought to thought or place to place, absorbing new data and impressions and then sharing them as you travel to your future stops. You talk, spreading the word of your latest discoveries, using dialogue as a source of discovery. However, communication is not the only way to connect, and you also link people to objects, as in commerce; people to each other, as in negotiation or facilitation; ideas to students, as in education; or words to form, as in writing. Because of your curiosity, you know a little bit about many things, and you pick up skills quickly. This adds to your versatility, which is a gift in today's world. Just like a breath of fresh air, you bring objectivity into a room. Where passionate emotions may prevent agreement, you bring logic and intellect to bear on disputes and difficulties. Whether you are encouraging a friend to think better of themselves or teaching students how a chemical reaction occurs, your insights are a valued contribution.

Shining Your Love Light

You're the ideal companion, Gemini, because you love to connect with those around you. You always feel that your experience is better if there's someone there beside you. What is most meaningful is the ability to communicate, and you are uneasy with a partner who doesn't want to talk about everything. However, your desire to enjoy everything you encounter may make your relationships brief, causing you to miss out on the depth that can develop in something longer term.

Aries has the spark to light the fires of your curiosity, and the two of you will be off on many adventures together. Taurus calms your flightiness and gives you a common-sense perspective. Another Gemini will be a true companion, sharing your gift of gab and love of experimentation. You'll learn more about your feelings with Cancer, who can also benefit by your more rational approach to life. Leo enjoys the social whirl as much as you do, inspires your actions with ideas, and brings a playful spirit to your life. You appreciate Virgo's cool logic because it is so much a part of your own nature, but you both must learn to overcome the tendency to avoid life's challenges. Fellow air sign Libra supports your world view and appreciates how vital social connections are. You will enrich each other's lives with your abilities to communicate. Scorpio has a deep well of emotion that, once appreciated, can take you to new heights of passion, while you can help this sign to lighten up. Sagittarius holds the mirror, showing you how valuable sticking to one thing is. Without it, you may not stay long enough in one place to build a lasting success. Capricorn brings gentle wisdom that may seem confining but calms the nerves. Aquarius is right beside you during social events and can work a room as well as you can. You each understand the value of loose connections, but may miss out on intimacy if you don't share your feelings. Your Pisces partners will wear their feelings on their sleeves and give you a faithful reflection of the emotional side of your relationship, just as you can provide an objective viewpoint to them.

Making Your Place in the World

Communication is probably the most important skill we have as humans. Since this is your strength, you will always be able to make your way with little difficulty, no matter what career path you choose. Writing is one of the best ways to use your skills, possibly through journalism, technical writing, or fiction, to name a few possibilities. You can learn languages so quickly that you may find translation an effortless pursuit, and a valuable skill in business and education. Teaching will satisfy your curiosity, and your desire to share your understanding with others. Marketing and public relations are also good areas to express yourself, since you have a natural insight into how people think and what they want. Your adeptness at using your hands suggests you will do well in fields such as hairstyling, computer repair, music (playing an instrument), or detail-oriented work such as word-processing or needlework.

Putting Your Best Foot Forward

To put your best foot forward, Gemini, you must make sure that your penchant for exploration and experimentation does not make you scattered and ineffective. You have a marvelous talent for discovery. You're always looking for something you didn't know or haven't done before, and there are plenty of things that fall into those categories. For that reason, it is possible for you to be so busy trying your hand at something new that you don't take the time to express what you have learned or apply those lessons to your daily life. If all you are doing is taking in information, it becomes garbled rather than integrated, and such inner disorganization leads to external chaos. It can also lead to stress, which causes illness. To avoid this, you need only slow down your pace of activity—to give your curiosity a rest once in a while. This will give you time to absorb what you take in and put it in the context of the knowledge you already have. It gives you time to share with others—a process which in itself induces integration of the data you've collected. Ultimately, it permits you to achieve mastery.

Tools for Change

Unlike Taurus, who needs to lift energy up, you need to ground yourself, Gemini. You have a tendency to become scattered and lose effectiveness when you over-express your Gemini nature. The most important thing for you, then, is to develop your ability to develop and maintain focus. You can start by developing goals. Goals give you a long-term focus that can operate beneath your daily decision-making processes and provide guidelines and support. They will make individual decisions easier, and you'll find it takes less effort to stay on track. Develop your goals in rhythm with the planetary cycles. Set monthly goals at the New Moon, yearly goals at your birthday and the winter solstice, and use the longer term cycles to plan long-range trajectories of action. Jupiter's cycle is twelve years; since you are in the sixth year of this cycle, think back to what you wanted to do five years ago and write those goals down. By now you can see how those ideas are developing, or you can initiate their development if you dropped them prematurely.

It sounds odd for a Gemini, but you can also benefit from taking communications training. Typically, your airy way of conversing conveys information, not self-expression. Communication training can teach you to engage in interaction that is more personally satisfying, and emphasize the expression of feelings, which you may need to get in touch with. Chatter does not connect with people, and you can become aware of the difference and choose to truly bond with others through your refined communication skills.

Another thing you can do to calm your inner being is to engage in non-verbal artistic and creative pursuits. No one disputes your skill, but you will benefit from learning to channel your creativity into something more visually or actively oriented. Drama, painting, gemstone cutting, stained glass, pottery, and sculpture, to name a few, can help calm and reinvigorate your spirit. Getting your hands in the earth or getting in touch with real products, as through sewing or crafts, are excellent sources of balance as well. Finally, physical exercise will also assist in grounding you. Exercise draws energy down into the lower part of the body when you focus on your feet, as with dance, step aerobics, and running or walking. Focusing and grounding meditation can also help.

Affirmation for the Year

Improving my habits brings long-term benefits.

The Year Ahead for Gemini

The emphasis this year is on completing activities and projects you've been working on for up to seven years, as the planets stimulate each other from your Third, Sixth, and Ninth Houses. Jupiter travels through Scorpio until November 23, lighting up your solar Sixth House. This is a good time to spruce up your lifestyle to improve your health and well-being. You may also encounter an opportunity to expand your career potential if you are willing to do the below-the-radar work required to accomplish an important task. You will generally feel good this year—energetic and vigorous. Don't let those feelings lull you into a sense of false security about past unresolved difficulties. Weight gain is a possibility if you don't maintain a disciplined approach when the going is easy. When Jupiter moves into Sagittarius on November 23, your relationship life will light up. Look for more partnership activity—perhaps a romantic commitment or business agreement to enrich your life for years to come.

Saturn spends another year in Leo and your Third House. You're discovering limitations in the ways you think, and perhaps in your education and communication style as well. You can increase your charisma by enhancing any and all of these through further training in areas of weakness. If you are a writer, teacher, or merchant, you may find your efforts in these areas suppressed or more difficult than normal, but confronting the issues will make you stronger.

Chiron is in Aquarius and your solar Ninth House. This ties in with Saturn's sojourn through your Third House and brings you a new awareness of your weaknesses. Both houses have to do with educating—giving it and getting it. You may feel drawn to the great task of getting a new degree or diploma. You can choose to broaden your horizons through more than higher education—travel, self-study, and spiritual explorations accomplish the same goal.

Uranus in Pisces sparks new life for another year in your solar Tenth House. Freedom has never been more important to you—the freedom to think for yourself, to direct your own activities, and to live by your own values. You may be in the process of bringing this about. Your direction may seem random to others, but to you it is perfectly justified by deep inner urging and a new sense of purpose that has emerged since 2002.

Neptune continues making its fourteen-year transit through Aquarius, your solar Ninth House. You've been turning ideals into goals, reaching beyond the confines of the life you would have found acceptable ten years ago. Since 1998, you've been charting a new path for yourself which will fulfill your egalitarian and humanitarian ideals. This may involve higher education, travel, or the exploration of other languages and cultures. You may choose to remove yourself from the fray of civilization to study it from afar.

Pluto is in Sagittarius and your Seventh House. Since Pluto entered Sagittarius in 1995, you've been going through a complete transformation in the way you see yourself as you realize more about what others are really like. In particular, you've become sensitive to power plays and subtle manipulations. You'll continue learning more about the balance of power between yourself and others, and gain more insights into human nature, as this year unfolds.

The eclipses move into Virgo and Pisces this year, falling in March and September. They open new chapters in your life and your comfort zone through your Fourth and Tenth Houses. You may find that this is the time to make that long-anticipated career change, or move house to a better location.

If you were born between May 25 and June 17, Saturn is contacting your Sun from your solar Third House. This is a time to broaden your mental horizons, but first you must recognize the limitations that you impose on yourself from within your own mind. You may find that you go through clever mental gymnastics to avoid thinking about something you feel is threatening. Or you may decide that you want to improve your options by getting more education in a critical area. You could take on an important mental project. You may even be inspired to take active listening training, since listening is an often-missing but key ingredient in good communication. Anything that opens your mind to new ways of seeing things will fulfill the promise of this year's encounter with Saturn. Since the Third House rules siblings and extended family, you may be challenged in some way by the people who fill those roles in your life. They may ask you to take on more responsibility—perhaps more than your fair share. Important dates in Saturn's cycle are January 27, February 19, April 5 and 24, June 20, August 7, November 16, and December 5.

If you were born between May 28 and June 6, Uranus in your Tenth House challenges your career choices. You have felt discontented with some aspects of your career for some time now, perhaps as long as ten years. However, your feelings have become more urgent since 2003. Now the time of change is upon you. If you want to be the master of your change, you must face it squarely and take steps to mitigate negative effects coming to you from others. For instance, perhaps you see the potential to be "downsized" out of a job. Updating your resume and checking the in-house job postings are ways to put the ball in your court. If you are discontented with your line of work, some honest soul-searching now may prevent you from unconsciously sabotaging your current position, giving you the breathing room you need to create something new. If you "stuff" your feelings out of fear of change or a sense of complacency, Uranus may wreak its worst in your life in the form of the actions others take. This is the universe's way of bringing you back into balance with your natural path, which is sometimes a blessing when we can't figure out what to do. Events related to Uranus's cycle will occur near March 1, June 5 and 19, September 5, November 19, and December 2.

If you were born between June 6 and 11, Neptune in Aquarius brings you new adventures from its position in your solar Ninth House. Your head is filled with visions of the future and ways to recreate your life. You may aspire to travel to exotic places or enroll yourself in a course of study at the university of your dreams. Most important will be the need to inject more creativity into your life, even if that means creating your own business so that you can carve out your own niche in the world. Spiritual studies may assume more importance now as you succumb to the allure of the mysteries of life. You want to expand your consciousness, and this can be done in many ways, from meditation practice to sky-diving. You can also be taken advantage of under Neptune contacts. Make sure when you travel that you secure all your belongings with care. When you become confused or disoriented, you are most vulnerable, so plan well. It is also possible that some vague obstacle appears to block your path. To clear it, check your intention: Do you really want what you have set out to accomplish, at least in the way you are pursuing it? Chances are that the answer is "no." Make the answer into a yes, and the blockage will clear. Key dates in Neptune's cycle are January 27, February 5, March 15, May 10 and 22, August 10, October 29, and November 9.

If you were born between June 14 and 19, Pluto in Sagittarius gives you new awareness of your relationships. You have probably felt changes coming in your close ties for a while, since Plutonian experiences, powerful as they are, rarely take us by surprise. Those around you are removing their masks, revealing parts of themselves that have been dormant or suppressed. And as they change, you must accept the changes—and change yourself. Although such advances can be unsettling, in the long run they are relieving, because you and your intimates are brought back into balance through these changes. Where tension and turmoil were created to maintain equilibrium, now that equilibrium is naturally maintained. You can breathe a sigh of relief, even though your world may be dramatically different from what it was before. Such changes may occur in business partnerships and close friendships as well—anyone to whom you have a commitment, spoken or not. Issues around levels of commitment and the balance of power will arise. You may be asked to make a deeper commitment in a long-term relationship, or a long-standing relationship may break up. Responding with flexibility and responsibility to the transformation at hand will permit you to make the most of it. Dates related to this cycle are March 17 and 29, June 16, September 4 and 16, and December 18.

If you were born between May 22 and 24 or June 20 and 21, there are no outer planetary contacts to your Sun this year. This does not mean, however, that you get a year off. First, other planets or points in your chart are undoubtedly being contacted. While this may not be as momentous as a contact to your Sun, these connections are nonetheless significant—but they may be easier to deal with since they are not as all-encompassing as contacts to your Sun.

Second, a "year off" is a time when you may be able to accomplish your goals with relatively few obstacles. However, you have to be self-motivated, as the planets will not be there to goad you on into ground-breaking new experiences.

Gemini/January

Planetary Hotspots

With a grand cross in fixed signs in the heavens right now, health and stress management are key issues in this busy month in the aftermath of last fall's challenges. Then it was just putting out fires, but now it's time to look at the root of the problem and make some hard choices. Although it's difficult to face what's real, you'll be able to truly change your life for the better if you do not shrink from the situation and agree with yourself to take it on. Give yourself time and space to get there.

Wellness and Keeping Fit

You've got so much on your plate right now, you're not even sure you'll remember to breathe. Since last October, you've been on overdrive—perhaps due to a little too much success. The best way to guard your health is to renegotiate your deadlines. This will allow you to relax and carry on with the routines that keep you healthy, from exercise to meditation to having fun.

Love and Life Connections

Negotiations are important this month, and there won't be much room for you to change your position, because life has you "on call" with Venus retrograde in your Eighth House. You'll just have to rely on your foundation of trust as you inconvenience others a little. They can cope, and you'll be able to meet your own needs.

Finance and Success

Success this month is a matter of finishing what you started. With the grand cross falling in your houses of completion, you're inundated with paperwork and all the consequences of your past initiatives. Asking for help, hiring a temporary worker, and delegating are all options for empowering yourself to get through this time. Tensions are highest on January 15, 18, 23, and 27.

Rewarding Days

1, 2, 5, 6, 7, 10, 11, 15, 16, 20, 21, 29, 30

Challenging Days

3, 4, 17, 18, 19, 25, 26, 31

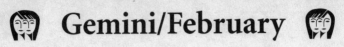 Gemini/February

Planetary Hotspots

The first week of February is full of activity to keep you distracted, but if you pay attention, the universe is in receptive mode on February 5 at the start of Neptune's new yearly cycle. This is your "make a wish" time, as well as the moment to set new spiritual goals. Other planetary contacts on February 1, 5, 6, and 19 will boost you toward those goals.

Wellness and Keeping Fit

This is a good month to get away, with the Sun in your Ninth House of travels. A vacation trip can lift you out of the cares of daily life and rebuild the strength that overstimulation takes away. A getaway to a foreign, or at least unfamiliar, metropolis is just the ticket. Visit museums, go to a play, or take a tour of a historic part of town. Build in some exercise for a totally rejuvenating experience.

Love and Life Connections

Your partner's finances take a turn for the better, or at least show signs of recovery. It's okay to help out a little, but not to rescue. A little guidance, if asked for, is better than a hand-out. Although communications are difficult through February 5, much good comes of what is revealed if you take the long view.

Finance and Success

Financial pressures release as Venus turns direct on February 3. You've taken care of those extra expenditures, or at least have a plan for doing so. You've got eighteen months to develop whatever strategy you have in mind now, whether it's to strengthen your investment portfolio or to get out of debt. Don't blow off an incident that occurs after February 7. It could go underground and flare up in March to take more energy than it deserves.

Rewarding Days

2, 3, 6, 7, 11, 12, 16, 17, 25, 26

Challenging Days

1, 13, 14, 15, 21, 22, 27, 28

Gemini/March

Planetary Hotspots

If career changes catch you by surprise this month, you'll be able to make a smooth transition into the next and better situation, as Mercury, Jupiter, and Uranus interact harmoniously. They tie in with actions you initiate around March 11, which don't turn out quite as intended—but that's all for the good.

Wellness and Keeping Fit

Unexpected turns of events could throw you off course in your efforts to live a healthier life. However, you'll be able to get back in the saddle after only minor disruptions. You could be more accident- and injury-prone around March 11 as Mars contacts Uranus from your sign, so be sure to stay more focused and grounded around that time.

Love and Life Connections

It feels like a make-or-break time, and you're ready to break for it as the lunar eclipse triggers your home vs. career choices. This event could spark you to move either house or job, or both. However, you don't have to take draconian measures. This change has been in the works for a long time, and unless it's overdue, you can go about it more gradually than you think.

Finance and Success

Avoid careless talk related to your career or profession, or you could alienate an ally or friend. Don't make promises you're not sure you can fulfill about deadlines or your skills and experience. However, if you can respond quickly to another's sudden and dire need, you will benefit greatly, and for years to come. Pay attention to the new Uranus cycle, which begins on March 1. It will enable you to break free of old restrictions in business and get what you really want if you dare to go for it.

Rewarding Days

1, 2, 5, 6, 7, 10, 11, 12, 15, 16, 17, 25, 26, 29, 30

Challenging Days

13, 14, 20, 21, 27, 28

Gemini/April

Planetary Hotspots

You get a wake-up call on April 8 related to events that occurred on March 11, as others, probably in the workplace, give you significant and perhaps unpleasant feedback. You can mitigate this if you own up to your part in the situation, especially if you do so before April 8. Follow-up events occur on or near April 13, 18, and 30. A charm offensive won't work, but taking appropriate responsibility will.

Wellness and Keeping Fit

Getting organized is the key to being at peace with yourself, as feng shui teaches us. With Saturn going direct in your Third House and Jupiter still moving backward through your Sixth House, this is your quickest path to more leisure time for play, sport, and health. While you're having a good clear out, invite friends over to make it fun, but don't interrupt your regular healthy habits and routines.

Love and Life Connections

Even if you get some constructive criticism from others this month, you can make it into a win-win if you use their comments to improve the way you interact with the world. Those who offer their advice are not trying to hurt you, only to help. You can smooth things over with actions you take on April 19 and 20.

Finance and Success

After five months of intensive activity and study, it's time to get organized so you can find those important papers you lost. Better yet, why not work out a system for staying organized? Saturn returns to direct motion on April 5, so now you can get caught up. It also invites you to create preventive structures so you don't have to spend so much time periodically dealing with chaos.

Rewarding Days

2, 3, 6, 7, 8, 11, 12, 13, 21, 22, 25, 26, 29, 30

Challenging Days

9, 10, 16, 17, 18, 23, 24

Gemini/May

Planetary Hotspots

You'd like to retreat and get your work done, but events keep calling you out of your cave and disrupting your peace of mind. The fixed-grand-cross pattern of January is repeated in May and carries a reverberation of that time. However, there are golden opportunities this month that make it more rewarding as a Mars-Jupiter-Uranus grand trine forms in houses of money and work. It will help if you can see this as part of a thread started in May 2000, where you began a new economic initiative. Innovation is the key word now that Uranus is in the mix.

Wellness and Keeping Fit

This is not the best time to plan a vacation, especially one that involves unfamiliar places or long-distance travel, as Chiron and Neptune begin their retrograde periods in your Ninth House. Instead, take mini-breaks, since your desire to withdraw for a yearly refueling is strong right now.

Love and Life Connections

This is a great time to connect with other people—especially new contacts. If you are at loose ends in your love life, this is a great month to meet potential new partners, so get out and circulate.

Finance and Success

You gain by seeing sudden changes in your work world as opportunities. Others may come to you with startling news that you see as a call to action. This is not the time to retreat, although short bouts of uninterrupted time can be hugely beneficial to the creative side of your effort and help to ground you. Events are spaced farther apart after May 14.

Rewarding Days

4, 5, 9, 10, 18, 19, 22, 23, 27, 28, 31

Challenging Days

6, 7, 8, 14, 15, 20, 21

Gemini/June

Planetary Hotspots

Uranus and Pluto are activated this month, on June 1, 5, 16, and 19. Since the planets affect you directly, these will be key dates for you, invoking changes in career, relationship, and the way you see and present yourself. On June 19, Uranus turns retrograde, initiating its five-month test of the new ideas you began to enact around March 1. While your plans may seem overly ambitious, even overwhelming, as you try to follow through on them, they are also exciting, and you will carry them to completion and success if you stay focused. The testing process is over November 19.

Wellness and Keeping Fit

Although activities in other arenas tantalize you, don't slack off on the new health and fitness routines you've been trying out. A consistent rhythm, such as thirty minutes in the morning before you pick the day's duties, will serve you well now.

Love and Life Connections

The culmination of Pluto's yearly cycle occurs on June 16, bringing to the surface whatever change has been brewing in your close relationships. This does not have to be conflict, although it could be. However it expresses itself, transformation is the familiar result—a part of the process Pluto has represented in your life since 1995. Events now will tie in with those of March 29 and April 16.

Finance and Success

Your activity level rises to a fever pitch as the grand cross that formed in January and May reassembles. Although somewhat milder, it is also more sustained, lasting from June 4 to 22. It requires you to think on your feet to find priorities, responsibilities, and opportunities. Delegate what you can and stay as organized as possible so that nothing falls through the cracks.

Rewarding Days

1, 2, 5, 6, 7, 14, 15, 19, 20, 23, 24, 27, 28, 29

Challenging Days

3, 4, 10, 11, 16, 17, 18, 30

Gemini/July

Planetary Hotspots

You come up with new solutions to the ongoing changes and challenges you face in your career and relationships, as Venus travels your sign and triggers Uranus and Pluto on July 5 and 14. Your friendly way of presenting yourself helps to ease the process along.

Wellness and Keeping Fit

Health matters you've been working on for the past four months finally do a turn-around as Jupiter returns to forward motion on July 6. You've had the chance to develop a new routine and a fresher, more optimistic outlook on your well-being, and now it's showing visible results. Keep it up!

Love and Life Connections

You may not be able to make everything okay, but your charm quotient is high through July 17, while Venus is in your sign. If there's a sensitive topic you need to broach with someone near and dear, this is a good month, so long as you avoid July 5 and 14.

Finance and Success

Around July 30, you become painfully aware of how much further you have to go to reach your goals—and you may even question whether these are the right goals to pursue. While it is good to be alert for the need to change, it doesn't automatically follow that encountering an obstacle means you need to alter course. You can turn it into a test of your resolve, look for ways to overcome the difficulty, and work it through. This strengthens your character while sending the universe a message about your intentions. If you realize that you really do need to change, this is a good time to do so.

Rewarding Days

2, 3, 4, 12, 13, 16, 17, 20, 21, 25, 26, 30, 31

Challenging Days

1, 7, 8, 9, 14, 15, 27, 28, 29

Gemini/August

Planetary Hotspots

It seems as if you're dealing with stress in every important area of your life—career, home, relationships—and you're feeling self-doubt. This has to do with the volatile planets of Mars, Uranus, and Pluto contacting each other in the signs that affect you the most. If you can wait before you respond to events, you'll find that your perception of how significant they are will shift. You'll be less likely to overdramatize the situation to yourself. Key dates are August 13 and 29.

Wellness and Keeping Fit

It will reduce your stress and make you more efficient if you only attempt to do one thing at a time. It will keep your head clear, and you'll stay healthier and more energetic.

Love and Life Connections

Be careful not to take out your frustration with your career situation on those at home, or you could lose the support you find so important now. Instead, try to be completely aware of how you feel about what's happening at work and be clear about your priorities. You've been feeling confined and rebellious, and at no time will that be more on your mind than on August 12 and 13. If someone at home challenges your authority, take the position of a team member rather than a parent or boss, and the problem will disappear.

Finance and Success

You've set your sights on a goal that will take your career in a new direction or help you lay a new foundation for your next rise to the top. The target date for this is August 7, when Saturn's new year-long cycle begins. Set your intention and write down your preliminary plans for how you will accomplish your goals. You've been at least thinking about this for a year, if not working on it—now it's time to get busy.

Rewarding Days

8, 9, 12, 13, 16, 17, 18, 21, 22, 23, 26, 27, 28

Challenging Days

4, 5, 10, 11, 24, 25, 31

Gemini/September

Planetary Hotspots

You've had some dicey situations arise as you move toward a more satisfying career path, especially in March, April, and June. The influences from home and family on your direction come to the surface now as either supporting or undermining your efforts, and they propel you forward with new vigor and insight. The key dates for this are September 3 to 9, 15, 16, 22, and 25.

Wellness and Keeping Fit

The approach you've been taking to improve your health over the past eight to ten months is providing visible results. The positive results also produce less tangible benefits, such as optimism based on the sense of accomplishment you feel. This can spur you on to successes in other areas of your life as well.

Love and Life Connections

Any issues that have lain dormant in your family and personal relationships come to the surface now, especially through September 9, as the planets form an intense pattern in your Fourth, Seventh, and Tenth Houses. You feel an urgency about declaring your freedom from the past—especially from the messages you received in childhood. You don't want any authority holding you down. Events now confirm your resolve to take dramatic steps, but later you may regret actions taken in haste.

Finance and Success

You'll multiply your success if you focus on social activities and events after September 7. That may not seem like the best way to network, but it will be this month. In addition to having fun, you'll run into just the right people. Hard work on the job now will produce results in November and lay the foundation for successes in the next two years.

Rewarding Days

5, 6, 9, 10, 13, 14, 17, 18, 21, 22, 23, 26, 27, 28

Challenging Days

4, 5, 10, 11, 24, 25

Gemini/October

Planetary Hotspots

Your educational efforts of the past year are beginning to pay off in the form of broader horizons and new opportunities. Something from your past which has held you back will continue to nip at your heels for the next year, but the situation will be much more manageable than this past year.

Wellness and Keeping Fit

You benefit from paying close attention to your body's signals all month, but especially on October 5, 15, 22 and 24. On October 28, when Mercury begins its three weeks of reverse travel, your body will begin to speak more loudly. By listening to it in the early part of the month and responding to what it's saying, you can avoid more dramatic symptoms and the problems that underlie them in November and December. It may be advantageous to seek the perspective and support of medical and healing practitioners to sort out what's going on.

Love and Life Connections

You have more time this month for doing what you love most—socializing. From parties to dinner with a few friends to a romantic evening with your partner, you will revel in the joy of what has been a rare experience for you this year—relaxation and appreciation of life with those you love.

Finance and Success

Your new level of training opens doorways, and you can launch creative plans you've had in the can for many years. This is an excellent time to drag those plans out of the closet and surprise your bosses and colleagues with your new ideas. The best dates for making a proposal or pitch are around October 10.

Rewarding Days
2, 3, 6, 7, 10, 11, 15, 16, 21, 22, 29, 30

Challenging Days
4, 5, 17, 18, 19, 25, 26, 31

Gemini/November

Planetary Hotspots

Health and work routines are the focus all month, but especially before November 22, as the planets cluster in your Sixth House. The better organized you are, both personally and at work, the better you will fare now. When Jupiter enters Sagittarius on November 23, a new year of growth in relationships begins. It will be a good time to bring in new clients and partners.

Wellness and Keeping Fit

The key to resisting health imbalances is stress management. Organize your affairs to keep track of the big picture, then as you execute each detail, stay in the moment without thinking ahead or behind.

Love and Life Connections

As Pluto has traveled its path through your Seventh House, you've been working on the balance of self versus other in relationship since 1995. You've been identifying the ways you give away your self-sovereignty to others, and slowly taking charge of your life. This has meant taking responsibility for your own actions as well as having the strength to say no to others when warranted. When Jupiter enters Sagittarius on November 23, you'll begin to receive more tangible recognition and reward for what you've learned. This is the beginning of an upward arc toward greater success based on your developing sense of self-command.

Finance and Success

In your field of expertise, you've been developing new competencies and skills for four years. Beginning this month, others will acknowledge you as a peer in your chosen field. The extra work that you put in this month is easy for you, even a delight, because it will feed directly into the dream career you are building. Key connections occur on November 1, 8, 11, and 15.

Rewarding Days

2, 3, 6, 7, 8, 11, 12, 16, 17, 25, 26, 27, 30

Challenging Days

1, 13, 14, 15, 21, 22, 28, 29

Gemini/December

Planetary Hotspots

Contractors, bosses, romantic or business partners—these are all highlighted now as the planets gather in your Seventh House. The emphasis is on social interactions, sometimes adversarial ones, as events this month unfold. The early part of the month is the most eventful, but even when there are stresses, there are planetary harmonies that support a good outcome.

Wellness and Keeping Fit

If you worry too much about pleasing others, you'll weaken your body with stress and be less able to do so. By being consistent, even when people and events seem destined to push you off-center, you'll remain strong and peaceful.

Love and Life Connections

You're learning to deal with authority figures as a free spirit, without feeling like they can control you. Avoidance of the situation is not the way to go—honesty and self-responsibility will win the day. This is a time of very pleasant interactions, from intimate dinners to grand parties, which lighten the energy and make this an enjoyable time. December 18 starts a new yearly cycle in the ongoing transformation of the way you relate to others, as Pluto starts its new yearly cycle. This is a good time to be conscious of how you want your relationship life to be and set your intention to create it.

Finance and Success

You've been working for a year on getting better organized and communicating more thoughtfully and responsibly. You may also be in school or training to improve your career prospects. Your steady efforts are starting to have a positive effect. As Saturn starts its new retrograde on December 5 in your Third House, there is still much to learn and do, but it will be much easier this year.

Rewarding Days

1, 4, 5, 8, 9, 10, 13, 14, 15, 23, 24, 27, 28, 31

Challenging Days

11, 12, 18, 19, 25, 26

Gemini Action Table

These dates reflect the best—but not the only—times for success and ease in these activities, according to your Sun sign.

	JAN	FEB	MAR	APR	MAY	JUN	JUL	AUG	SEPT	OCT	NOV	DEC
Move								25, 27-31	2-22, 1			
Start a class						29, 30	1-3, 24-26	11-27				
Join a club			29, 30	16-30	1-4							
Ask for a raise			29, 30	1-15	3-28	24-30	1-18					
Look for work	1-3	9-28	26-31							2-26	18-30	1-26
Get pro advice	2, 3, 29, 30	21, 22, 26	20, 21, 25	16-18, 21	14, 15, 18	10, 11, 15	7-9, 12	4, 5, 8, 9	1, 5, 6, 27	2, 3, 25	21, 22, 26	19, 19, 23
Get a loan	27, 28	23, 24	22-24	19, 20	16, 17	12, 13	10, 11	6, 7	2-4, 30	1, 27, 28	23, 24	20-22
See a doctor	1-3				5-31	1, 2				2-26	18-30	1-26
Start a diet					11-13					2-26	18-30	1-7
End relationship						10, 11						
Buy clothes									13-30	1-23		
Get a makeover					20-31	1-3, 24-30	1-18					
New romance									30	1-23	17-30	1-10, 18-20
Vacation	3, 22-31	1-8, 26	5-31	1-5, 21	18, 19	15, 16	12, 13	8, 9	5, 6	2, 3, 29	26, 27	23, 24

CANCER

The Crab
June 20 to July 21

Element:	Water
Quality:	Cardinal
Polarity:	Yin/Feminine
Planetary Ruler:	The Moon
Meditation:	I have faith in the promptings of my heart
Gemstone:	Pearl
Power Stones:	Moonstone, chrysocolla
Key Phrase:	I feel
Glyph:	Crab's claws
Anatomy:	Stomach, breasts
Color:	Silver, pearl white
Animal:	Crustaceans, cows, chickens
Myths/Legends:	Hercules and the Crab, Asherah, Hecate
House:	Fourth
Opposite Sign:	Capricorn
Flower:	Larkspur
Key Word:	Receptivity

Your Ego's Strengths and Weaknesses

You've got plenty of warmth and nurturing to go around, Cancer, with your active nature. Yours is the cardinal water sign—active water, as in a waterfall or spring. Your energy is fresh and caring, providing the purest sustenance. The mothering instinct lies at the core of your nature, and this is an active role. Those you care for often cannot act on their own, so you must think, feel, and act for them. This is how your cardinal side works, but it can also be used in a more extended sense of nurturing, as when you care for a non-family group such as a tribe, organization, company, military unit, or country. As with any cardinal sign, you can overdo it. You may overextend yourself when taking care of others, giving them more nurturing than they want or need. You could become attached to the people you care for, living through them instead of cultivating your own life independent of them.

As a water sign, you live in a world of feelings and sensations. You are acutely aware of the unseen sensory impulses moving around you, and you can benefit from learning how emotion and energy exchange between people works through the study of psychism and energetic healing. Your instincts are strong, and you often take actions based on what your "gut" tells you. Sometimes your feelings may be so strong that it's hard to manage them. This is especially difficult in a world that places a premium on suppressing feelings. However, feelings are meant to be acknowledged, accepted, and channeled into positive action. You know that they are an accurate signal system to keep you happy and safe. You can also use your emotional depths in creative pursuits, such as art, music, or drama. These will also keep the emotional fountain of life flowing through you in a healthy way. One thing you may lack is the ability to step back from your feelings and observe yourself objectively. Developing this skill will do much to introduce balance to your self-expression and bring greater self-confidence.

Shining Your Love Light

The love you offer is tender and caring, Cancer. You are the original romantic, dreaming nostalgically of days gone by when love contained mystery. You can find your mystery in the here and now if you are willing to hold something back, to allow your love to grow slowly. This works better for you anyway, since emotional insecurity is your weak point. Although you may want to rush in eagerly, it is better to let trust build gradually.

Aries signs bring optimism and joy to your relationship, but their needs are less emotionally based than yours. Taurus steadies you and is as interested in living a low-risk life as you are. This sign brings grounding and practicality to your outlook. Gemini's inquisitiveness will open doors of experience to you, but you may have a hard time keeping up verbally. You'll have a partner as loyal and sensitive as you in another Cancer—someone to build a family with. Leo's desire for the limelight is fine as long as you don't have to join in: this sign will bring drama to your life. Virgos reassure you with their loyalty and an industrious commitment to your partnership. Their attention to detail relaxes you, but it does not free you from responsibility to share the workload of life together. Libra signs share your need for harmony. They'll bring objectivity to your bond, but don't expect them to take the lead. Passions will run high with Scorpio and emotions will flow freely. However, you'll have to develop objectivity to balance the high emotional pitch each of you tends to have. A Sagittarian's abstract approach may be hard for you to understand, but it will help you gain a removed perspective, while your emotional approach is something this sign can learn from. Capricorn reflects the need to develop filters and structures to help you manage your contacts with the outer world—and shield your tender feelings from the slings and arrows that fly there. Aquarius shares your interest in groups, although the bond will be more intellectual than emotional. Fellow water-sign Pisces has much in common with you, especially the immersion in the ocean of feelings that surrounds us. You need not fear sharing your sensitivities here.

Making Your Place in the World

With your watery nature, you do well in any environment where caring for others is key. One way to fulfill this gift is to take up a career in the medical profession. Nursing involves you in direct general care for those in need, while other fields such as radiology or physical therapy allow you to specialize. You may also enjoy the work of a medical doctor, or, less traditionally, offer care as a naturopathic doctor or chiropractor. Outside the medical field, you can give healing to others as a healer or psychic counselor, or even as a hairdresser or personal style consultant. You can extend your empathic ability to animals and go into veterinary science. Since emotion feeds creative expression, you may find deep satisfaction in writing (especially fiction or poetry), music, or the visual arts. Finally, having and raising a family can be the most rewarding of all pursuits. Even if you do this through animal husbandry rather than with your own children, you will feel fulfilled.

Putting Your Best Foot Forward

You're at your best when you can learn to distinguish between your needs and those of others, Cancer. You have a gift for anticipating what others require in order to thrive, especially with children, animals, or those who cannot take care of themselves. This is where you excel: your warmth comes out, and you become a selfless and generous nurturer. However, you can become so involved in fulfilling someone else's needs that you forget about your own. It is possible to project your needs onto someone else, truly thinking that it is that person's need instead. It is important to nurture yourself, just as it is important to stay attuned to the signals coming from the object of your care. With growing animals and children, their needs change daily and caring for them is a process of letting go. The best care you can give is to have a life of your own that will give you fulfillment when they stop needing you. This makes you the wisest of "mothers," and because your charges are free to leave, they will always be yours.

Tools for Change

Your watery cardinality gives you a strong focus and sensitivity to the world around you. Your gift is your ability to turn that focus single-mindedly toward those who need care—mostly your family and loved ones. This close focus, often extending no further than the walls of your home, is necessary to your admirable task, but it narrows your perspective. It prevents you from seeing the big picture—and it's necessary to see that picture so your responses to the world stay in balance. What's more, this focus keeps you from developing yourself. You can do many things to fill in this gap and empower your nurturing style. A major but simple step you can take is to get out of the house on a daily basis. You don't have to go far. You can take a walk, work in the garden, or just run a few errands. It helps, however, if you vary your activities and do something unusual once in a while, like visit a museum or take your walk on the beach. Another way to extend this step is to travel. This really gets you out of your local focus—and perhaps your comfort zone—but travel gives a "long-distance" perspective on your life that cannot occur while you are at home. Challenging your comfort zone isn't a bad idea either, because that builds emotional strength and teaches you about yourself, which is a need that can be overlooked in your drive to take care of others. Nurturing and healing yourself is also essential and will counterbalance this tendency. Treat yourself to a weekly massage or a beauty bath, or go to your favorite place for some time alone—or let a friend or lover take care of you for a change. It helps if you establish self-care habits into your daily and weekly routines. Exercise almost every day at the same time of day so you and others get used to a consistent pattern. This works especially well with children. Make sure that the exercise is something you enjoy, and not just an event to endure and get over with. Develop your own nature through a hobby or career that contrasts with the activities you engage in at home. If you are a caregiver at home, take up work that does not call on that skill so much. If you work as a caregiver, pick up a hobby that satisfies your other needs and brings out other capacities. Finally, closing the door to your own space and meditating will boost your energy reserves.

Affirmation for the Year

I can take time to delight in the joys of life.

The Year Ahead for Cancer

With Jupiter in Scorpio and your solar Fifth House, play and creativity are your keys to future success. Dream big, and in four years you'll reach your goals. For now, pursue your interests and let your mind take flights of fancy. There's something deeper that you need to bring forth—something that comes from deep within you. Build on that spark now, while your optimism and confidence are strong. You'll be inspired and rejuvenated. Children, romance, or sports may also play a featured role in your life this year and be a source of joy. When Jupiter enters Sagittarius on November 23, a year-long cycle of increased work starts. Overwork is a possibility, and health issues could arise as a result. Kept in balance, your efforts could launch a great enterprise that builds on the inspiration you have during the earlier part of the year.

Saturn continues its course through Leo and your Second House, suggesting the need for more discipline in your financial affairs. If your spending is out of control, you may be scrutinizing your spending patterns to see what you find unnecessary or of little value to you. Saturn may also require some belt-tightening: perhaps you will decide to save money for a new venture or future need, such as starting a business or taking early retirement. The need for security is the driving force.

Chiron remains in Aquarius and your solar Eighth House, reminding you that one of the keys to personal security is a solid relationship with your financial connections. Insurance policies kept up to date, loans and taxes paid on time, honesty in all financial dealings—these are critical to your stability. It's time to correct errors and shore up weaknesses here. Chiron could also take you on an exciting ride into the hidden world beneath the surface of what seems to be true. You may discover the truths buried in occult studies, depth psychology, or astrology.

In Pisces and your Ninth House, Uranus is awakening you to higher truths and a more global perspective on just about everything. Studies that universalize your awareness, from meditation to philosophy to foreign languages to alien life, will fascinate you now. You may delight in being unpredictable and rise to any challenge—

and you may even be drawn to take risks you would never have considered before. Allowing this awakening to take place will sharpen your mind and put a new spring in your step.

Neptune also makes its home in Aquarius and your solar Eighth House, leading you toward a deep spiritualizing process. You know that there is something beyond what can be perceived by the senses, and you feel compelled to pursue an understanding of what makes the world tick. Neptune here could also blind you to what is happening in your finances—or perhaps you don't want to look too closely. You may feel helpless about it, or think that you have to make sacrifices for others. Although you are the only one who can decide what's right for you, you may be sacrificing too much.

Pluto is in Sagittarius and your solar Sixth House, continuing to transform your health and daily habits, including work. You may see upheaval in your workplace, and your work environment and tasks are directly affected by these changes whenever Pluto contacts one of your own planets. This is the time to make sure your health is the best it can be by adjusting your daily habits and lifestyle.

The eclipses move into Virgo and Pisces in 2006, your Third and Ninth Houses. They highlight your intellectual pursuits, encouraging you to gain more knowledge for practical purposes, so that you can work smarter or get paid more.

If you were born between June 24 and July 17, Saturn will contact your Sun from your solar Second House of personal resources such as time, money, and skills. You're prompted by feelings of insecurity to examine your life—particularly how you spend what you earn. An important factor is what you want in life, and that is based on your goals. So, this is a good time to ask yourself the big questions: "What is my purpose?" "Who am I?" We do best with Saturn when we face what comes up with courage and take on the big tasks that are required to get us where we want to go. When we do, the greatest rewards come our way in the fullness of time. You are likely to discover that some reward can be gained by curtailing your spending. You may want to save for a home project, a new big-ticket item, or your retirement. You may want to use other resources that you place a high value on in a new way, such as your skills or your time. Finally, you may find that love, the most important of all resources, becomes more important to you. Critical junctures in Saturn's cycle occur on January 27, February 19, April 5 and 24, June 20, August 7, November 16, and December 5.

If you were born between June 27 and July 6, Uranus in Pisces boosts your desire for adventure from its position in your Ninth House. You'll want to expand your horizons this year to explore what is foreign to you. You could travel to far-flung lands, study another culture and language, or follow an unusual spiritual path. With Uranus involved, you'll stretch your concept of what is comfortable and take greater risks than you have in the past. Spiritually, you may experience an awakening that leads you to pursue a new understanding of the universe. On a more mundane level, exotic locales and obscure cultures will spark your interest as you seek what is outside the mainstream. Opportunities to expand your horizons may come up unexpectedly. This could include the chance to follow a new path of self-fulfillment, which could lead to a new career when Uranus enters your Tenth House. You may be inspired to take on humanitarian work, even going overseas to help those in need. By following your heart, you will open the door to new insights and achievements based on a new awareness of humanity. Uranian events will occur near March 1, June 5 and 19, September 5, November 19, and December 2.

If you were born between July 5 and 10, Neptune in Aquarius and your solar Eighth House is helping you discover the true world beneath the world of appearances. You are learning about hidden motives—your own and those of others. The occult studies—tarot, magic, numerology, palmistry, etc.—may spark your interest. All of these really teach you to read the undercurrents of human interaction, and understanding them gives you vital insights that will help you make better, more successful decisions in your personal and professional life. Neptune can also symbolize confusion or illusion, and this is dangerous when it comes to the life-and-death matters of the Eighth House, such as taxes and borrowing money. Don't be tempted to think you can get away with something under this contact, because it won't work. Rather, be extra careful to be accurate, to stay organized, and to make sure you are living within your means. Although it goes against your lofty desires at this time, when you emerge from Neptune's "fog" in a year or two, you'll be happy you maintained some discipline. Neptunian issues will pervade your life around January 27, February 5, March 15, May 10 and 22, August 10, October 29, and November 9.

If you were born between July 13 and 18, Pluto is offering you the opportunity to make big changes in your health and work life from its position in Sagittarius and your Sixth House. Pluto may herald a realization that requires long-term efforts to make sweeping alterations in your way of living. A thorough health examination—recommended at this time—may reveal a hidden issue that requires immediate attention if a serious illness is to be avoided. You are likely to find it useful to change your diet, reduce the amount of work you do, or find ways to reduce your stress. Living more simply, engaging in regular meditation, and taking the time to enjoy life more may all be part of your new health equation. No doubt your work world has been troubled, whether due to downsizing, a poisonous interpersonal environment, or outright job loss. A change that seems catastrophic can often release tension and create a firmer foundation in a new place. Although it's too late to prepare for the changes once you're in them, letting go gracefully can lessen the negative effects of a break in income. This may be the time to enhance your earning power by gaining additional training or education. You'll experience Pluto's energy most around March 17 and 29, June 16, September 4 and 16, and December 18.

If you were born June 20 to 23 or July 19 to 21, none of the slow-moving planets are in direct contact with your Sun this year. This is the time to put finishing touches on the changes you experienced last year or to prepare for the next round. You are likely to find that life is less challenging, even though you may feel less motivated to accomplish anything. If these planets are contacting other planets in your chart than your Sun, your year will still be colored with defining events that propel you in a direction that results from your own unique blend of you and your planets.

Cancer/January

Planetary Hotspots

It's time to add creative juice to the dreams you're building, as Jupiter contacts Neptune on January 27. You've been working toward lofty goals, often sacrificing what is safe for what is more fulfilling. Now it's time to put some energy into the new and wonderful ideas you have. You've got five more years to get to the pinnacle, so keep that in mind as you decide what to build. This is part of a major planetary configuration that began last September and continues throughout 2006, so the path will not be without its obstacles. With a firm resolve and steady pressure, you'll succeed. You'll catch glimpses of what's to come on January 15, 18, 23, and 27.

Wellness and Keeping Fit

Don't be tempted to give up your healthy routines when the pressure is on. Especially helpful now is contact with water—hot showers, beauty baths, or swimming.

Love and Life Connections

As Venus tracks retrograde through your Seventh House, your relationships will need more focus. The attention you give them now will lay out the issues you'll be dealing with for the next eighteen months, but you can head off future difficulties by being receptive now. Hearts are warmer on January 17, which makes it a good day for needed communication.

Finance and Success

You may be tapping your financial resources to fund your next enterprise as the year unfolds. This is a good month to plan how to use your resources most wisely, to stretch them the furthest. You could be duped into making unwise choices where these expenditures are concerned, especially around January 27.

Rewarding Days

3, 4, 8, 9, 12, 13, 14, 17, 18, 19, 22, 23, 24, 31

Challenging Days

5, 6, 7, 20, 21, 27, 28

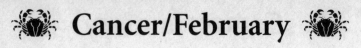 Cancer/February

Planetary Hotspots

If your creativity is limited only by your pocketbook, this is the right time to make a wish that will bring in the funds you need for your projects. The Sun conjoins Neptune on February 5, giving birth to a new cycle of imagination and spiritual growth. Tuning in now and setting your intention allows you to tap the powers of the unseen world to further your goals. Venus turns direct on February 3, and the challenges you've been facing in relationships and business partnerships abate. Your bonds with others have reached a new normal that will bear fruit over the next eighteen months.

Wellness and Keeping Fit

Although this is an exciting time for you and your energy levels are generally good, after February 17 you could be more vulnerable to viruses and inflammations. You'll benefit from more sleep then, and your imaginative processes will too, as your dreams are likely to be vivid, productive, and memorable.

Love and Life Connections

You've had six weeks to develop new agreements with those close to you, and now you can move forward again on the basis of those changes. Others contribute valuable ideas from February 1 to 5 that give wings to your dreams.

Finance and Success

Instead of letting fear run your portfolio, let optimism play a role. That doesn't mean you should take extraordinary risks, but instead let go of unnecessary limitations to your actions. Neptune is teaching you a long-term lesson in your Eighth House about relying on inner guidance to create your own security. Putting what you've learned into practice will help you accomplish your dreams.

Rewarding Days

1, 4, 5, 8, 9, 10, 13, 14, 15, 18, 19, 20, 27, 28

Challenging Days

2, 3, 16, 17, 23, 24

Cancer/March

Planetary Hotspots

You experience a rare flow of energies and events this month, Cancer, as Mercury, Jupiter, and Uranus entwine with your Sun to give you the opportunity to further your loftiest dreams and goals. However, it may not look that way on the surface, as hidden factors seem to impede your progress. Don't let that stop you, because facing down obstacles and adversaries will empower you to move forward when the time is right. Delays will last from March 2 to 25, with some forward motion after March 11. Tune in on March 1 to your deepest aspirations. A new Uranus cycle starts then, which supports fulfillment of your long-term goals.

Wellness and Keeping Fit

Stressing out over what you can't do right now could result in sickness or injury. Preemptively boosting your immune system will help you avoid downtime. Possible dates of difficulty are March 2, 11, and 29.

Love and Life Connections

Your love life receives extra attention as you experience a watershed event around March 4 that will determine whether your romance moves forward or dies away. Activities with children also assume greater importance on this date. Making specific plans to enrich your life in either area will produce positive results in two to four months.

Finance and Success

The dreams you have for creating a new life—the ones you had around January 27—get their first tests on March 4 and 15. Be aware of what you experience on those days, because events will give signals of how your plans are developing in both visible and invisible ways. The solar eclipse on March 29 highlights your Tenth House, spurring dramatic but harmonious change in work and career.

Rewarding Days

3, 4, 8, 9, 13, 14, 18, 19, 27, 28, 31

Challenging Days

1, 2, 15, 16, 17, 22, 23, 24, 29, 30

Cancer/April

Planetary Hotspots

Your financial picture improves considerably starting on April 5, as Saturn returns to forward motion in your Second House. You've had a greater number of restrictions than usual on your budget, as you've had to cope with reduced income or increased expenses. However, you can loosen your belt a little now and breathe more easily. There's still just a little more to come next year, but for now you're through the worst.

Wellness and Keeping Fit

Health concerns rise to the surface, perhaps unexpectedly, on April 8. If you've stayed on top of your health with a thorough examination prior to this time, you may be able to head this situation off or at least mitigate its significance. Related events will occur on April 13, 18, and 30.

Love and Life Connections

Events beyond your control take charge of your life now. If you need help from someone else for a change, don't be afraid to ask. With all that you give, you are not used to asking, but you're certainly entitled to. If it's hard for you, it's a good lesson, too.

Finance and Success

With Mars triggering Pluto in your service/health houses on April 8, chances are good that you'll have some time off from work this month, but not because you necessarily want to. It's a necessary hiatus, and although you'll be missed, others will be able to carry on. Make the most of it by turning it into a vacation.

Rewarding Days
1, 4, 5, 9, 10, 14, 15, 23, 24, 27, 28

Challenging Days
11, 12, 13, 19, 20, 25, 26

Cancer/May

Planetary Hotspots

As Mars, Jupiter, and Uranus make a grand triangle in the heavens early in May, the world is your oyster, and you feel energized and full of inspiration. Your emphasis on the creative process is bearing fruit, and what you've felt you could do is now in the works. This does not come without its struggles, however, as the fixed pattern that happened in January is mimicked through May 22. The challenges you face will be exacerbated by your current financial restrictions, but you'll find a way to make things work. Key opportunity dates are May 4 and 7.

Wellness and Keeping Fit

Your step is light and your vitality high, but you're also a little more accident-prone this month as well because you are more in a rush. Watch your feet and keep your focus to avoid this possibility.

Love and Life Connections

Just when you thought your financial woes were going to seriously curtail your current activities, someone comes through for you and gives you the support you need. The key date for this is May 7, and this is before much of the action in May occurs. If you think you may need assistance ask then, and the person will be more receptive. After all, it's for a good cause.

Finance and Success

An infusion of cash or other resources will come around May 7, and you can stretch it to take care of your backlog. That doesn't take care of all your obstacles, but it helps, especially if you use it as wisely as you usually do.

Rewarding Days

1, 2, 3, 6, 7, 8, 11, 12, 13, 20, 21, 24, 25, 26, 29, 30

Challenging Days

9, 10, 16, 17, 22, 23

Cancer/June

Planetary Hotspots

You've got more than enough to keep you occupied in June, as the grand cross of planets forms once again in the heavens—but in a slightly different form. Situations that arose in January, April, and May are carried forward as Act IV now. However, there is a beneficial energy coming in the form of support from others. You are not as strongly affected as many around you, but the circumstances will touch your life—if only through those whose lives you touch. This pattern falls into place on June 4 and does not dissipate until June 22.

Wellness and Keeping Fit

Find some time to retreat this month, as the Sun moves through your Twelfth House. You'll be able to reorganize both your inner and outer lives—a vital step in managing the circumstances you find yourself in now. As June 16 approaches, tensions could rise as we reach the culmination of Pluto's yearly cycle. Take care of this by emphasizing relaxation and stretching.

Love and Life Connections

Although you do not bear the brunt of events this month, others around you do. You can be an invaluable support—not just to those nearest and dearest, but to those who number you as an acquaintance or colleague. Although it won't bring a direct benefit to you, it is the right thing to do.

Finance and Success

There's a weakness in your finances that you've been trying to remedy. You feel an urge to keep a tight grip on your money now to stay on track with your goals as Mars and Saturn conjoin in your Second House. However, multiple events may require you to let go of the purse strings a little and have faith that it will all work out for the best. Key dates are June 17 to 22.

Rewarding Days
3, 4, 8, 9, 16, 17, 18, 21, 22, 25, 26, 30

Challenging Days
5, 6, 7, 12, 13, 19, 20

Cancer/July

Planetary Hotspots

With Mercury going backward from July 5 to 28, you have plenty on your plate. You are questioning the way you've been handling things, including your own time and energy. Your ability to communicate may be a bit off as well—a sign of your inner uncertainty. If your birthday falls during the retrograde, you have the added excitement of knowing that you'll be learning about some major area of your life through hands-on experience.

Wellness and Keeping Fit

Minor illness could strike this month as external events heighten your inner tension. If you can dole out some of the work to others and respond calmly to events, the prevailing bug doesn't have to get you. Focus on taking care of your body, and your body will support you through this busy time.

Love and Life Connections

Any time after July 6 is a great time to take a vacation with your loved ones, even with the Mercury retrograde. Chances are, you want to go to someplace completely new, and this is good. This is a relatively uncomplicated Mercury retrograde, so difficulties will be largely limited to the effects of dealing with the awkward and unfamiliar.

Finance and Success

Your finances are in a steady state now, and you're ready to move forward with new plans for a new year of your life. Jupiter assists you with innovative insights as its retrograde period ends on July 6, and you will want to incorporate creativity into your activities more than ever now. Input from others spark new ideas on July 5 and 14.

Rewarding Days

1, 5, 6, 14, 15, 18, 19, 22, 23, 24, 27, 28, 29

Challenging Days

2, 3, 4, 10, 11, 16, 17, 30, 31

Cancer/August

Planetary Hotspots

It's time to reformulate your financial goals as a new yearly cycle related to your use and conservation of resources starts on August 7, when Saturn in your Second House starts its new cycle. This is more than simply adjusting your budget and paying off debts; it is also examining your plans for future security. Are you saving all that you should? Is your retirement fund in a safe place? Do your insurance coverages correspond to your current needs? You'll have ample opportunity to work on this area as Saturn is triggered multiple times during the month, so give this area the attention it deserves.

Wellness and Keeping Fit

Long-standing health imbalances may flare up around August 13 and 29, especially in response to unusually high levels of stress. The best thing you can do for yourself is to plan some downtime into your schedule—time away from other people, which includes staying away from the phone or email. Sleep is also very important, as is safe and gentle exercise. Injuries are also possible on these dates.

Love and Life Connections

The last of the three harmonious and innovative contacts between Jupiter and Uranus occurs on August 29—a contact you can use all month long. The connection falls in your Fifth House of romance and children, but it will help you in any pursuit that gives you joy and fulfillment.

Finance and Success

The Jupiter-Uranus connection can also be used for business innovation or artistic expression. You are capable of coming up with truly unique innovations now, ones that will bring value to you and others, so don't minimize the quality of your ideas, even if they come easily.

Rewarding Days

1, 2, 3, 10, 11, 14, 15, 19, 20, 24, 25, 29, 30

Challenging Days

6, 7, 12, 13, 26, 27, 28

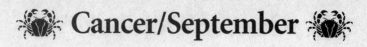 # Cancer/September

Planetary Hotspots

New information comes in which helps you better focus your plans for the future, as a cluster of planets forms in your Third House. You may receive training or arrive upon a new idea that spurs you in a slightly different direction, and that is going to fuel your progress. This could involve writing, outreach, or interaction with the community in some way. Key dates for this are from September 3 to 9 and September 15.

Wellness and Keeping Fit

Rising tensions at work could spill over to affect your health, especially around September 4, 16, and 22. This is part of a familiar pattern which you've learned to abate with many techniques, both by supporting your health and by dealing with your job environment. Consistency and responsiveness to your body's signals are most vital. Exercise is the great balancer.

Love and Life Connections

Your attentions are drawn to your home environment, and you are called upon to exert more than the average amount of effort there after September 7. This may tie in with a household repair that needs doing, or the preparations for and presence of visiting relatives. This will generally be a pleasant experience that distracts you from the more serious aspects of your life.

Finance and Success

Your workload may seem overwhelming, especially early in the month, but it's not as bad as you think. Prioritize your tasks, then take them one step at a time. Find a time slot when you will not accept interruptions and get your paperwork organized. It's when the stacks pile up in no particular order that everything seems unmanageable.

Rewarding Days
7, 8, 11, 12, 15, 16, 20, 21, 25, 26

Challenging Days
2, 3, 4, 9, 10, 22, 23, 24, 30

Cancer/October

Planetary Hotspots

Planetary harmonies permit you to indulge your nesting instinct this month. You can stay home with your family more, enjoying the rich connection you have with them. Financial needs are reduced now as the demands others have on your money have been satisfied. The financial challenges of the past year will be largely complete as of October 29.

Wellness and Keeping Fit

Health concerns can be de-emphasized now, but your routine cannot. Stick with the program you've been following. Consistency brings results.

Love and Life Connections

Life is rich with pleasure, especially through October 24, because you can focus your attention on your home once more. Children go through an adjustment period to new influences starting October 1, which becomes apparent as the month waxes. They need to know why about something before they'll accept it. Key dates are October 5, 15, and 22. If you prepare them well, follow-up events in November and December will flow more smoothly. Romantic ties go through an adjustment period as well, backtracking to a previous stage in the relationship to accommodate your partner's emotional needs.

Finance and Success

Although you're nearly through the times of tight budgetary discipline for this year, seemingly innocuous events on October 5, 15, and 24 may prolong the process through December. Alertness and a creative approach can minimize expenditures. Opportunities in the markets are not what they seem during this time, and if something seems high-risk despite advice to the contrary, it is high-risk right now. Trust your instincts.

Rewarding Days

4, 5, 8, 9, 12, 13, 14, 17, 18, 19, 22, 23, 24, 31

Challenging Days

1, 6, 7, 20, 21, 27, 28

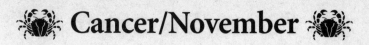 # Cancer/November

Planetary Hotspots

This may be the best month for you this year so far, as the planets form a grand trine with your sign. All the fast-moving planets conjoin in your Fifth House of fun, romance, and children, giving you the opportunity to focus on pleasure for a change. You'll have more leisure time, and you'll want to spend it in total enjoyment, but there is a catch. Mercury will also be retrograde in this area through November 17, suggesting that you'll be busy doing things for others as you plug back into their lives. You'll pack the kids off for their favorite playground or theme park, and you'll finally get the chance to engage in your favorite hobby—but there may be a pile of paper on top of it. By November 17, you're settled back into your groove.

Wellness and Keeping Fit

Injury, primarily through sports activities or horsing around with the kids, is possible, especially on November 1, 8, 11, and 17. This will be due to impulsive actions or distraction, which can be prevented by staying centered in your body and not overdoing it.

Love and Life Connections

The fun part of relationships is emphasized now, whether it is with children, friends, or romantic partners. This is an ideal month to take a vacation involving travel, especially between November 11 and 22.

Finance and Success

Your creative energies are running strong, and you feel inspired to express yourself in some artistic way. Giving free rein to this part of your nature will enrich your path as you pursue the new life options that have intrigued you since 2003. Glitches with equipment and technique are overcome by November 17, when you can proceed full steam ahead!

Rewarding Days

1, 4, 5, 9, 10, 13, 14, 15, 18, 19, 20, 28, 29

Challenging Days

2, 3, 16, 17, 23, 24, 30

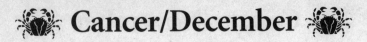 **Cancer/December**

Planetary Hotspots

Six planets populate your Sixth House, putting the focus on health and work. A lot of energy is required to fulfill the goals you've set for yourself, and by the end of the month you'll have the satisfaction of accomplishing a great deal. Saturn's retrograde period begins on December 5, initiating a five-month period when you will be observing greater financial restrictions, much as you did last year. These restrictions continue to support your long-term goals.

Wellness and Keeping Fit

Health is a major focus this month—a part of the long-term transformation you've been enacting in your lifestyle, habits, and well-being. You've taken a no-holds-barred approach to getting your being to its peak, not just physically, but in spiritual, mental, and emotional ways as well. Your drive right now is to focus on the physical, but there's a spiritual component to what's going on. A holistic assessment, or several from different types of practitioners, will give you the information you need to make your own decisions about what to do.

Love and Life Connections

Others are supportive of your intensified efforts to improve your life and fulfill your work obligations. As you provide services to others, you have to take care of yourself. The extreme efforts required now, especially at the beginning of the month, are of a short duration.

Finance and Success

Due to the trials of the past year, you've realized that the plan you had before wouldn't work in its original form. Now you've hit upon a better way to achieve what you want, and you can hardly wait to make up for lost time. Enthusiasm is great, but don't overdo it. You'll end up overspending and depleting your energy stores.

Rewarding Days

2, 3, 6, 7, 11, 12, 16, 17, 25, 26, 29, 30

Challenging Days

1, 13, 14, 15, 18, 19, 22, 23, 24, 27, 28

Cancer Action Table

These dates reflect the best—but not the only—times for success and ease in these activities, according to your Sun sign.

	JAN	FEB	MAR	APR	MAY	JUN	JUL	AUG	SEPT	OCT	NOV	DEC
Move									12-30	1, 19-21		
Start a class								25, 27-31	1-12, 20			
Join a club				27, 28	5-19							
Ask for a raise				27, 28	29-31	1-23, 26	19-31	1-11				
Look for work	1-22			16-30	1-4							8-27
Get pro advice	3, 4, 27	1, 23, 24	22-24, 27	19, 20, 23	16, 17, 29	12, 13, 16	10, 11, 14	6, 7, 10	2-4, 7	1, 4, 5, 31	1, 23, 24	20-22, 25
Get a loan	27, 28	23, 24	22-24	19, 20	16, 17	12, 13	10, 11	6, 7	2-4, 30	1, 27, 28	23, 24	20-22
See a doctor	1-22				19-31	1-28	29-31	1-10				8-31
Start a diet	1-3					10, 11						8-27
End relationship							10, 11					
Buy clothes										2-27	18-30	1-7
Get a makeover					3-28	10-21	1-12					
New romance		3-28	1-4		1, 2, 20	16-18				24-31	1-20	
Vacation	3, 4, 31	1, 9-28	25-31	1-30	1, 2, 20	16-18	14, 15	10, 11	7, 8	4, 5, 31	1, 28, 29	25, 26

LEO

The Lion
July 22 to August 23

♌

Element:	Fire
Quality:	Fixed
Polarity:	Yang/Masculine
Planetary Ruler:	The Sun
Meditation:	I trust in the strength of my soul
Gemstone:	Ruby
Power Stones:	Topaz, sardonyx
Key Phrase:	I will
Glyph:	Lion's tail
Anatomy:	Heart, upper back
Color:	Gold, scarlet
Animal:	Lions, large cats
Myths/Legends:	Apollo, Isis, Helios
House:	Fifth
Opposite Sign:	Aquarius
Flower:	Marigold, sunflower
Key Word:	Magnetic

Your Ego's Strengths and Weaknesses

Your flair for the dramatic and passion for life is both inspiring and invigorating, Leo! It's your fixed fire nature that steadies your flame and gives you such remarkable energy. One of your most dominant traits is courage, or heart. You have the heart to commit yourself to a path based on the ideals you wish to fulfill, leading others with your enthusiasm alone. Because of your fixed nature, you respond to life's experiences by trying to maintain the forms that already exist. For you, this means constancy of belief and effort. You want to create something because you believe in it. You won't be the first to have thought of it, but you're the right person to carry forth the initiative, because you know how to muster forces and get them moving. You enjoy being with people. You love their attentions, for this is where the exchange of love occurs, and love is the constant you try to preserve. You resist forces that threaten the things you wish to hold true to, which are mostly inner principles, like love and joy, rather than external conditions or circumstances. You may have difficulty recognizing when it's time to stop resisting, especially when it doesn't benefit you personally. It's not that you're selfish, only that your fiery energy makes it hard to see beyond your own viewpoint.

As a fire sign, you provide the spark that ignites others' motivation and lifts them to a better reality. Fire's movement is upward, and that's where your gaze is directed, toward bigger and better things. You are ambitious as well as optimistic, which is an unbeatable combination for success. With your passion for life, drama is one of your strengths if you pour it into the arts or theater. However, if you expel it into your work environment or personal relationships, you may generate unnecessary turmoil.

Shining Your Love Light

Since love is your forte, relationships are important to you. Your passionate nature and persistent optimism, as well as your loyalty, make you a good partner. However, you love the support, even the adoration, of more than one person. You need to know how far to go in satisfying this urge outside your primary relationship, or disagreements will arise. You may find yourself in a series of short-term relationships rather than one long-term one, since they require less commitment on your part.

Fellow fire-sign Aries shares your optimism and joy in life, but may compete for the spotlight with you. Taurus wants consistency just as much as you do, but may pull in a different direction, seeking financial and physical security. You'll get along fine with companion-sign Gemini. This sign's talkative style blends well with your need for a rich social life. Cancers may seem too fussy at times, but their warm and caring love is hard to beat. Another Leo is able to keep up with you in style, substance, and inspiration. You'll have to share the stage, though. You can feel comfortable with Virgo's dedication to your relationship, and this sign will take care of the details you would prefer to overlook. Libra is as compatible as they come, with a love of social interaction to rival your own and the objectivity to tone down your dramatic approach. Scorpios may seem too deep and intense, while you're trying to have fun and spread the warmth and joy you feel. However, you'll find they care just as much as you about making the world a better place. Sagittarius extends and expands upon your ideals, creating a goal and a path upon which to reach it. You'll explore the universe together along the way. Capricorns have a different style from yours, but their hearts are in the right place. Aquarius supplies exactly the quality you need the most: the detachment to think things through and see the value for all beings. Pisces's attunement to the inner realms is something you can relate to, especially when you see how this sign's holistic perspective empowers you and your objectives.

Making Your Place in the World

You like to create your life as you go along, so a career with too much predictability or drudgery will leave you tired and uninspired. You want every activity to be unique, chosen by you, and something you care about. You could be drawn to fields such as sales (especially where you work on your own to develop relationships with clientele), or public relations (where you let others know about the value of a product or person's abilities). Other professions allow you to express your creativity more directly, such as drama or comedy, the visual arts, or musical performance. You are a gifted leader, especially if you are willing to take your role as more than titular and make sure all the responsibilities of office are fulfilled. You could enjoy spearheading the development of creative endeavors, perhaps by producing plays or movies. Because of your entrepreneurial spirit, anything you care about passionately can be turned into business gold.

Putting Your Best Foot Forward

When you participate in a true give-and-take with those around you, Leo, you're at your best. The danger is in getting carried away by the energy others give you. You love it when you generate joy and enthusiasm (other words for love) when you walk into a room. You have a unique talent for creating this by drawing others' attentions your way with a performance or display. This is an exchange of energy—if you give back the energy they give you. However, if you forget that step in the process in the excitement of the moment, you stop the flow and lose your rapport with your audience. The easiest way to maintain the flow is to move into a state of gratitude. When you engage in this magical process with others, you trigger a healing experience. During the healing, you reach peaks of emotional energy, and your audience is carried along with you. Trigger, release, integration, gratitude—these are the steps of healing. They correspond to the stages in a story or drama. You complete the process when you express thanks, which your audience does in turn as well.

Tools for Change

Leo, you'll be much more able to fulfill your heart's desires if you can place internal limits on your energetic outpouring of vitality. You have so much vigor and enthusiasm that you can bowl people over. This potential downside can be avoided if you temper the expression of your ebullience. First, you can downplay your own role in any group initiative or project: get involved in groups that operate as a team, where everyone is an equal player; do your work without seeking credit; let others take the lead or be the hub of group operations. Make an effort to pull your fair share of the load. For you, the hesitation may be that you won't seem to be at your best, in terms of appearance and skill. However, people will appreciate your efforts and see you as one of them. Another thing you can do is to play in team sports. Even if you are a star player, you still have to play as part of a team, and this will balance your Leo side, giving you a chance to express the competitive and dramatic fire side and cultivate counterbalancing team-oriented skills.

You are such a warm, creative type that you bounce joyfully along through life, sometimes overlooking the practical structures that keep you going—things like paying your bills, washing clothes, making sure you have food in the cupboard, and fixing the pipes. You will find that life's flow breaks down pretty quickly when these constructs are not maintained. If you do manage them well, however, you are freer to be yourself. While it's nice if you can hire a maid, accountant, and personal manager to do these things for you, you may need to assert the discipline to handle them yourself. As a fire sign, you are likely to find it more natural to be in expressive rather than receptive mode. A lack of receptivity cuts you off from others; they are less open to you. Communications training will help you develop listening skills and teach you to express your feelings in a variety of ways to enhance your bond with those around you. This will also teach you to step back from a situation and look at it more objectively, so you can decide whether your passion is a helpful component. Meditation focusing on moving energy into the heart, as is done with Sufi dzikr or chakra-clearing practices, is also supportive of your Leonine spirit.

Affirmation for the Year

I enjoy taking time to nurture my inner self.

The Year Ahead for Leo

In 2006, your opportunities will emanate from within yourself. This is the time to look inside to see what sparks of creativity and purpose move you, because you're beginning a six-year climb to the top. This is part of the cycle of Jupiter, which is traveling through Scorpio and your solar Fourth House. You are inclined to spend more time at home now, perhaps because you're doing some renovations. There is a possibility that you'll move, although anything to rejuvenate your home environment will satisfy that urge to brighten up your surroundings. If you sell your home, you stand to make a tidy profit; if you're buying, take care not to pay too much for it. When Jupiter enters Sagittarius and your solar Fifth House on November 23, you'll feel more energetic and focused in the way you express your creative initiative. This placement will bring you more joy, more fun—even more romance if you want it. This will be the time to set your sights on a new dream.

Saturn continues its course through Leo and your First House. You have found the value—perhaps the necessity—of greater-than-normal discipline in managing your personal energies and circumstances. If you are not happy with yourself, you will bear the full brunt of that awareness now. You will continue to scrutinize your relationships, letting go of those that do not match the person you are now becoming. This is a good time to reform your overall health and appearance.

Chiron remains on course in Aquarius and your solar Seventh House, driving home any relationship issues you are dealing with. Chances are that you're dissatisfied with your experiences with your partner. However, the problem may lie within you. At least, look very hard at what you have contributed and own up to your role. This will make the healing process go much more quickly—and you will find out if healing is possible within the current structure.

Uranus is in Pisces, your Eighth House, again this year, bringing unexpected events. You may feel as though fate has a hand in your finances, or unusual experiences may characterize your contacts with others. Uranus disrupts our patterns so that new, healthier patterns can be formed. Your finances may go through a sudden change, either for the better or worse. If you are prepared for the occasional hiatus which occurs in anyone's cash flow, you will benefit from what you experience.

Neptune continues its slow path through Aquarius and your solar Seventh House, dissolving old patterns in relationships so that you can form new ones. Old commitments fall away as you shed old unhealthy parts of yourself. You may simply forget old pains and approach intimacy with a new sense of innocence.

Pluto is lifting and empowering you from its position in Sagittarius and your Ninth House. You've been transforming your goals, your ways of seeing the world, since 1995. You've come a long way since then, but there are still a few more miles to go in your quest for something greater than yourself. Whether you encounter that greatness through travel, education, or spiritual expansion, you are aware of being on an inner journey.

The eclipses begin their sojourn through Virgo and Pisces in March. They will enliven and enlighten your resources and financial contacts with others. This is a good time to review your financial plans, correct erroneous ways of handling your resources, and make plans for a secure future.

If you were born from July 26 to August 18, Saturn in Leo will touch your life in the most basic ways. It is in your own sign—your First House—an event that occurs once in thirty years. You are likely to feel obligated to others in new ways, to carry a larger burden of responsibility than before. You may feel as though you must curtail your old behavior to achieve a new rapport with others or to advance your goals in some way. This is a great time for a makeover. A new hair style and new fashions are ways you can make a difference in the way you come across to others. Of course, beauty is more than skin deep, so corrections to health through diet and exercise are also helpful. Whatever changes you decide to make will stem from a rigorous self-examination process. You have the opportunity to reassess who you are, where you're going, what you want to accomplish in your life, and how you are going to get there. It's never too late to start anew, and it's never too late to forgive yourself your mistakes; in fact, both are essential if you are to make the most of this powerful transit. Saturn events will occur on or near

January 27, February 19, April 5 and 24, June 20, August 7, November 16, and December 5.

If you were born from July 29 to August 7, Uranus in Pisces will be in your solar Eighth House. If your financial affairs were at all tenuous in the past, they will become even more so this year, requiring you to make changes in the way you manage them. Unexpected events are sure to occur no matter what, and you may have to draw on your cash reserves or borrow money to manage them. You could lose or gain large sums of money through inheritance, investments, or insurance claims. On a deeper level, you will go through an awakening process. You will begin to recognize what really matters to you and begin to pursue those things. They are likely to be intangibles like love, trust, and mutual support, and they are likely to involve other people. You could even dig into your past to discover the unconscious patterns that move you to act and behave as you do. In this opening process, you can gain assistance and support by taking up studies in the occult tools, which have been specifically designed to enhance a spiritualization experience such as yours. The tarot, numerology, and magic can help you understand the mysterious world you are entering now. Events related to Uranus will occur on or near March 1, June 5 and 19, September 5, November 19, and December 2.

If you were born between August 7 and 12, Neptune is making direct contact with your Sun from its position in Aquarius and your Seventh House. Since 1998, you've been experiencing a slow, subtle shift in your perceptions of and interactions with others. This is especially true in your committed relationships—marriage, business partnerships, and close friendships. Much of what you have been discovering is intimately tied up with your own nature. It is as much who you are attracted to as who you attract. You are half the equation in making relationship choices, and this is the key part that you can change. When Neptune is involved, you may find that old bonds are fading away, or that there was nothing there to begin with. You may have been carrying the relationship, thinking there was more support for you than there really was. You may discover that someone close to you is unreliable, untrustworthy, or unable to make a commitment. If so, you may be attracted to this type of person because you secretly fear commitment yourself. On the brighter side, you may find that a spiritual bond forms between you and another person. While this is no assurance that a more earthly connection will take place, it is a powerful experience nonetheless. Neptunian events will occur around January 27, February 5, March 15, May 10 and 22, August 10, October 29, and November 9.

If you were born between August 15 and 20, Pluto is transforming your path through a direct connection to your Sun from your solar Ninth House. You've been feeling this coming since 1995, and now it's time for some big changes. You could decide to completely revolutionize your career, going back to school for a degree or changing the focus of your career path to line up with your newly discovered sense of purpose. Purpose and life direction play an especially big role right now, because you want more than anything else to feel that your life has meaning. If it doesn't, you will change it so that it does. It will help if you broaden your horizons. This can come through higher education or through travel or other contact with unfamiliar cultures. You may want to take a hiatus from your usual forms of employment to do something with a more humanitarian slant, such as a foreign relief program or social support effort closer to home. There's also the sense of a quest: you want to grow, to challenge yourself, and to make progress toward being a better, perhaps more spiritual, person. Getting in touch with your ideals and then daring to pursue them is critical to the success of your journey. You will experience events related to this process around March 17 and 29, June 16, September 4 and 16, and December 18.

If you were born between July 22 and 25 or August 21 and 23, there are no major planetary contacts to your Sun this year. This means that you have the opportunity to choose your own path without "planetary interference." However, this also means that you will not have planetary guidance. Without guidance, you could lose momentum and fail to further your goals this year. Of course, taking time off to relax and enjoy life is essential to a healthy existence, and it's what all the hard work is about. This may be a good time to take a vacation or plan a long-awaited pleasure cruise. If other planets in your chart are contacted by the major planets, you will feel the forces of change operating in your life, but perhaps not as powerfully as if your Sun were involved.

Leo/January

Planetary Hotspots

You've been more focused and disciplined since last July, and now you feel it's time to put the pedal to the metal as the fixed grand cross contacts your Sun. However, there are complicating factors. Venus, retrograde since last year's end, confounds your efficiency— you have too many loose ends to tie up to be moving forward yet. Roadblocks may occur around January 15, 18, 23, and 27. If so, they are just another stage in the process, and they ensure you'll be able to iron the wrinkles out of the system.

Wellness and Keeping Fit

Although normally robust, you may suffer from more than the usual virus with Venus retrograde in your Sixth House, so take care of yourself. This is a good time to forego the parties and "cocoon" at home.

Love and Life Connections

Relationships at work may not be going so well with that Venus retrograde highlighting your Sixth House. The problems are not just something that arose this month but issues that have been building over time. It's time to face what's happening and adjust your methods and mannerisms. However, it's not all up to you. It takes two to make it work. If you're the only one receiving criticism, point out the common motivations you share with the other players in the situation to draw them into the peace-making efforts.

Finance and Success

A Jupiter-Neptune contact gives you a chance to check in on how well you're taking care of your private life. This is the time to look down that long tunnel of the future and see what potentials you can develop for the next six years. You'll also be looking back at the past nine years to see how far you've come, taking stock and tying up loose ends. The focal date is January 27.

Rewarding Days
5, 6, 7, 10, 11, 15, 16, 20, 21, 25, 26

Challenging Days
1, 2, 8, 9, 22, 23, 24, 29, 30

Leo/February

Planetary Hotspots

Through February 5, you'll continue following the journey on your new life path that you started in mid-January, as January's major configuration is triggered by Mercury and the Sun. Take the time to tune in to your inner reality on February 5, when Neptune's new yearly cycle begins. Insights may be reflected to you by others, who may be unaware of the messages they're bringing.

Wellness and Keeping Fit

Venus returns to forward motion on February 3. Now you can get back to managing your own schedule as you see fit, which should include a reinvigorated exercise routine and nutritious meals. You'll be back to normal by the end of the month.

Love and Life Connections

Work relationships have needed adjustments. If you manage a team, you could have had to hire or fire someone, or give someone additional guidance. Conflicts could have arisen within the group that need to be resolved. If they have not been resolved, they will go underground and become entrenched in the system, so it is best to clear the air now before that happens. The earlier in the month you handle it, the better it will be, since Venus, the key planet, changes course on February 3. It's time to look deeply into what you want from your closest relationships. If there are unresolved issues, you can't make them go away by ignoring them. A constructive approach is required to overcome serious problems, and the help of others may be necessary.

Finance and Success

You've been running behind schedule for at least six weeks, but you'll be able to catch up quickly now. Distractions ebb as everyone begins to pull together again.

Rewarding Days

2, 3, 6, 7, 11, 12, 16, 17, 21, 22

Challenging Days

4, 5, 18, 19, 20, 25, 26

Leo/March

Planetary Hotspots

Your home and family require more attention this month, whether it is because of repairs and renovations or family needs, as Jupiter turns retrograde on March 4 and makes its second of three contacts with Neptune on March 15. Finances are weak most of the month as Mercury treks retrograde through your Eighth House from March 2 to 25. An unexpected infusion of cash comes from family when it is most needed.

Wellness and Keeping Fit

You're working on creating happiness and fulfillment, and that's the most important factor in being healthy. Keeping this in mind will make it easier to maintain a buoyant mood and high level of vitality.

Love and Life Connections

Your social world has been through powerful alterations since 1995, and more occur this year as the lunar eclipse focuses Pluto's transformative forces. Children, if you have them, continue to go through dramatic change. Romantic ties invoke powerful feelings but may be troubling at the same time. Events related to this energy field in your life occur on March 14 and 29.

Finance and Success

The pressure has eased in career or business just in time for activities to intensify at home. With the current unpredictability of your finances, family provides much-needed sustenance this year, even if it is only emotional or mental. Starting March 4, this sustenance may be interrupted or become more regular as a reflection of your situation. If times are tough, it helps to realize that it's only temporary and that current restrictions will achieve a worthy goal, because you're headed in the right direction. Other key dates this month are March 1, 14, and 29.

Rewarding Days

1, 2, 5, 6, 7, 10, 11, 12, 15, 16, 17, 20, 21, 29, 30

Challenging Days

3, 4, 18, 19, 25, 26, 31

Leo/April

Planetary Hotspots

A load lifts from your shoulders on April 5 when Saturn returns to forward motion. Last July, when it entered your sign, you found it useful to take on additional responsibility and self-discipline in order to accomplish new goals. Your choices were tested in the fall, and you had to commit to a plan of action starting November 22. Your enterprise reached a crescendo on January 27, and now you can begin to see how things will shape up. There are still four months to go with this phase of your plan, then another year before the pressure shifts to a new area.

Wellness and Keeping Fit

Part of your self-improvement program involves presenting yourself in a new way. You're seeing yourself differently and changing your appearance to reflect your new identity. As Saturn changes direction, you're clearer on what the new you looks like and what you need to do to accomplish your goals most effectively, and you can move ahead with a greater sense of clarity and optimism.

Love and Life Connections

Although you can see changes coming down the road, it's not time for them yet. In the meantime, facing what's happening will permit you to prepare. For now, you can empower your life in many ways by branching out socially. Charismatic types that you meet around April 8 may be more challenging than you bargained for.

Finance and Success

Networking now will bring success in the future, even if it doesn't seem like the potential is there. There are planetary harmonies on April 16, 19, and 20 to give your public life an extra boost. This is a good time to make those phone calls that spark new business.

Rewarding Days

2, 3, 6, 7, 8, 11, 12, 13, 16, 17, 18, 25, 26, 29, 30

Challenging Days

1, 14, 15, 21, 22, 27, 28

Leo/May

Planetary Hotspots

This month could feel like January in all but temperature as the fixed grand cross is repeated through May 14. However, there are patches of blue amongst the clouds as a Mars-Jupiter-Uranus grand trine forms simultaneously, giving you the chance to capitalize on the events that occur.

Wellness and Keeping Fit

You're feeling more withdrawn this month as Mars highlights your Twelfth House, and you want to step out of the spotlight for a time. Even though you're busy, you get the support you need to take this time out and get revitalized. You can get support for the tasks that require your constant vigilance while you get out from under the pressure.

Love and Life Connections

Emotional and creative support comes from family and business ties alike; the most valuable thing to you now is to know that others have faith in you and your goals. Challenge points occur May 4 to 15 and 22.

Finance and Success

It may feel like you're starting over, but there's more to it than that. You need to broaden your perspective to see other parts of the picture. In fact, what you're stuck in right now started in May 2000. Just as you know what goes up must come down (and it has), you also know that you will return to the top in a new and better way. As Jupiter reaches the halfway point in its cycle on May 4, you can feel a bit of relief, but the best part is knowing that real freedom is only two more months away. It will be a coast downhill to complete this year's enterprises, which will be fully integrated into your life by the end of the year.

Rewarding Days

4, 5, 9, 10, 14, 15, 22, 23, 27, 28, 31

Challenging Days

11, 12, 13, 18, 19, 24, 25, 26

Leo/June

Planetary Hotspots

Pressure intensifies now as Mars reaches Saturn in your sign on June 17. This is only another stage in the situation that emerged last July and became better defined in the fall. Since then, you've had major turning points occur in January, April, and May. From June 4 to 22, you'll be engaged in activities that further resolve the associated issues, with peak events from June 17 to 22.

Wellness and Keeping Fit

You need time to yourself now to gain clarity on the issues confronting you, so it's a good time to plan that into your schedule. You can economize on time by doing things by yourself that you normally engage in with others present, such as office work (close the door), exercise, and spiritual practice.

Love and Life Connections

There's a weakness in your relationship life that you've been trying to mend since last summer. It will take a long process of self-examination and healing, as well as a willingness to engage honestly with your partner if you have one. Now there's a chance to bring new insight more gently into the equation, especially around June 7. Although it's not a panacea, it is a step in the right direction.

Finance and Success

Disruption of your normal stream of income may occur around June 19 when Uranus's retrograde period begins. It's part of a bigger change in the way you gain sustenance. You've been seeking to free yourself of financial limitations, but it also opens you to greater financial risk. The next five months give you a chance to strengthen your base, so that when your income fluctuates downward you have a reserve to rely on.

Rewarding Days

1, 2, 5, 6, 7, 10, 11, 19, 20, 23, 24, 27, 28, 29

Challenging Days

8, 9, 14, 15, 21, 22

Leo/July

Planetary Hotspots

The pressure is off and now you can make steady progress toward your personal goals. Jupiter assists you in the form of support from home and family once it returns to forward motion on July 6. Projects and people at home require less intense effort, and you have more free time.

Wellness and Keeping Fit

Mercury's retrograde starts off in your sign on July 4 but quickly regresses into Cancer and your Twelfth House. This is a good retreat time for you, when you can replenish your energy supplies after a tiring few months. An important component of the retreat is having time to do what you need to in order to locate the place of peace in yourself. This may be reorganizing your home office, finishing up a project, or taking a spiritual retreat. The less you are exposed to others' energies, the better it will be for you. Illness could be a factor if you ignore the need to restore yourself and find the way back to your center.

Love and Life Connections

Your home is a better place to be now, whether it is because relationship dynamics are better or because you finally finished that remodeling job. It's a good time to celebrate life: throw a party or just raise a glass with those you love. If you've been waiting to move, you'll be able to go ahead with your plans as of July 6.

Finance and Success

You experience a financial blip around July 5, but it won't amount to much in the long run, so don't waste emotional energy on it.

Rewarding Days

2, 3, 4, 7, 8, 9, 16, 17, 25, 26, 30, 31

Challenging Days

5, 6, 12, 13, 18, 19

Leo/August

Planetary Hotspots

This will be the most active month of the year for you, as the Sun and Saturn connect to start Saturn's new yearly cycle on August 7. You have a clear view of how to create the new you, and you're completely devoted to accomplishing your goals. Over the next year, you'll have to decide how to balance fulfilling your plans against meeting your obligations and commitments to others. Events related to this issue come to the surface on August 10.

Wellness and Keeping Fit

You have a tendency to be a little too serious these days, but you can temper this by taking time to laugh and enjoy life. Schedule some free time if you find it hard to break away, and make a commitment to yourself in your life to do something fun during that time.

Love and Life Connections

Events on August 10 bring a new awareness of the obstacles you face in your relationship life. If you have a partner, there is a way in which he or she is not there for you—in fact, your partner may drain your energy due to illness or personal weakness. It is necessary to set boundaries on the situation in some way so that you can pursue your goals. If he or she needs consistent extra support, perhaps it is time to get someone else to help out when you can't, no matter how your loved one feels about it.

Finance and Success

You could feel like soothing your frustrations by shopping this month, which is likely to inconvenience you in terms of fulfilling your plans for the future. Don't let your need to do what your friends are doing goad you into spending what you really can't afford. The danger of this is greatest on August 13 and 29.

Rewarding Days

4, 5, 12, 13, 16, 17, 18, 21, 22, 23, 26, 27, 28, 31

Challenging Days

1, 2, 3, 8, 9, 14, 15, 29, 30

Leo/September

Planetary Hotspots

You have the satisfaction of seeing visible progress for your past year's efforts, and now you get some relatively uninterrupted time to work toward your goals. Financial matters require extra attention, however, especially from September 3 to 9, and you could feel as though the risk level you have in your income is unacceptable. Although you'll feel calmer later, greater stability is a worthy goal that can be accomplished by maintaining a bigger reserve.

Wellness and Keeping Fit

You'll bring more energy to your fitness routine after September 6, once Mars begins a supportive contact to your Sun. For the sake of variety, try staying closer to home when you exercise, whether exploring your neighborhood as you run or walk, or taking advantage of facilities nearby.

Love and Life Connections

Although those with whom you are only acquainted see little of you these days, those who are close to you see how busy you are. Your life is full of events and activities both with them and for them. You have big goals in mind, especially when it comes to the comforts you want to afford yourself and your family. Your efforts now peak at the end of October and lead to other successes in the next two years.

Finance and Success

The third of three contacts between Jupiter and Neptune occurs on September 24, stimulating you to revisit the goals you set for yourself in January. You have surmounted many obstacles to get where you are now. The next two months will see you finish with those plans as you formulate the ideas that will get you up the next rung on the ladder. Continued consistent efforts will empower you next year to create even greater things.

Rewarding Days

1, 9, 10, 13, 14, 17, 18, 19, 22, 23, 24, 27, 28

Challenging Days

1, 2, 3, 8, 9, 14, 15, 29, 30

Leo/October

Planetary Hotspots

Your drive to improve your home and relationship life is producing results, and this is more evident in October. If it has seemed at times as if your best efforts and good intentions have fallen on deaf ears, you'll find out by the end of the month that this is not so. Although there are still two months to go before the final results are in, some subtle indications, especially before October 15, will reveal that you've done good.

Wellness and Keeping Fit

You feel more energized as Saturn in your sign is not so heavily triggered by other bodies. You'll enjoy physical activities more if they are outdoors and involve friends.

Love and Life Connections

Mercury's latest retrograde, which starts on October 28, will bring issues out at home, enabling you to clear the air about suppressed issues. Communications early in the month will reveal the form the relevant situations will take, even though the underlying issues will be the ones you've been dealing with all year. Observe what you experience on October 15, 22, and 24, for events then will give you clues to what's up, and you may even be able to head off misunderstandings at these times. You can smooth over emotional issues by spending time together outside your home—go to a movie or community event to bring your relationship back to neutral ground.

Finance and Success

Rely on your instincts on October 9 and 10 to tell you what to do with a financial opportunity that arises then. This seemingly random opportunity is really based on your past kindnesses, and someone is trying to return the favor. Don't take it up, however, if it doesn't feel right.

Rewarding Days

6, 7, 10, 11, 15, 16, 20, 21, 25, 26

Challenging Days

2, 3, 8, 9, 22, 23, 24, 29, 30

Leo/November

Planetary Hotspots

Activities at home increase as the planets cluster in your Fourth House, and your family life is your main focus. This could involve renovations or repairs, preparations for and entertainment of guests, and lively interactions with other family members. It's a good time to do a fall cleaning, get the carpets steamed, and put a new coat of paint on the walls. You can have fun while you increase your enjoyment of your home.

Wellness and Keeping Fit

If you are working on repairs or redecorating around the house, it's important to do some exercise that uses muscle groups differently from the ways they are being fatigued as you work. Take a walk or run sometime during the day. You may be more sensitive than you think to fumes from cleaning and construction products, so keep your workspace well-ventilated. Be extra careful on November 1, 8, 11, and 17.

Love and Life Connections

In spite of the minor challenges you face with all the activity at home, life with your family is good. However, in a time of tiredness or stress, it is possible to say the wrong thing, especially on November 11. An immediate and simple apology will go far toward recreating harmony.

Finance and Success

If you feel inspired and optimistic as the month wears on, it's because Jupiter is about to enter Sagittarius and your Fifth House of fun and creativity. You've worked hard over the past year to build something new, and now it will go much more smoothly, feeding into your big plans for success. Now is the time to let your creative side run free, because it is through what you do now that you'll discover and later fulfill your greatest potential.

Rewarding Days

2, 3, 6, 7, 8, 11, 12, 16, 17, 21, 22, 30

Challenging Days

4, 5, 18, 19, 20, 25, 26, 27

Leo/December

Planetary Hotspots

This is Year Two of your self-improvement scheme, and now it's time for you to buckle down and get serious about the tasks you set for yourself around August 7. On December 5, Saturn's retrograde demarcates a five-month period of focused action to fulfill your personal goals. This will require self-discipline and perhaps discomfort as you restructure your life, but you know that it will be better once you adjust.

Wellness and Keeping Fit

Some of the discipline you are exerting in your life extends into taking care of yourself in new ways. A new diet, lifestyle, and fitness program will go down well now. Saturn's strong energy makes it easier to set limits on yourself now, so if you want to change habits for the better, this is an ideal time to do it.

Love and Life Connections

It's easier to manage your self-development process when you've got pleasant distractions. This is certainly the case now, with a gaggle of planets in your Fifth House of fun and romance. Love ties are in the front of your mind, whether they involve romantic partners, children, or friends. Sports activities, cultural events, parties, and dancing at your favorite club could be part of the plan. There are powerful energies at work, so don't be too eager to trust people you don't know. This promises to be a unique holiday season that will stand out among others.

Finance and Success

Around December 19, your work is recognized in a way that will result in more income, even if it does not come right away. Keep up your consistent good efforts, and you'll solidify this outcome in the months to come.

Rewarding Days

1, 4, 5, 8, 9, 10, 13, 14, 15, 18, 19, 27, 28, 31

Challenging Days

2, 3, 16, 17, 23, 24, 29, 30

Leo Action Table

These dates reflect the best—but not the only—times for success and ease in these activities, according to your Sun sign.

	JAN	FEB	MAR	APR	MAY	JUN	JUL	AUG	SEPT	OCT	NOV	DEC
Move										2-26	18-30	1-7
Start a class									12-30	1		
Join a club					20-31	1, 2						
Ask for a raise					27, 28	24-30	1-18, 25	12-31	1-5			27-31
Look for work	3-31	1-8			5-19							
Get pro advice	2, 3, 6	2, 3, 26	1, 2, 25	21, 22, 25	18, 19, 22	15, 16, 19	12, 13, 16	8, 9, 12	5, 6, 9	2, 3, 6, 7	2, 3, 26	1, 23, 24
Get a loan	3, 4, 31	1, 27, 28	27, 28	23, 24	20, 21	16-18	14, 15	10, 11	7, 8	4, 5, 31	1, 28, 29	25, 26
See a doctor	3-31	1-8				3-30	1, 2, 29-31	1-27				
Start a diet							10, 11					
End relationship								8, 9				
Buy clothes											18-30	1-27
Get a makeover							1, 2, 25, 26	11-31	1-5			
New romance			5-31	1-5							17-30	1-10, 18
Vacation	6, 7	2, 3	1, 2, 29	16-20	1-28	19, 20	16, 17	12, 13	9, 10	6, 7	2, 3, 30	1, 27, 28

VIRGO

The Virgin
August 22 to September 22

♍

Element:	Earth
Quality:	Mutable
Polarity:	Yin/Feminine
Planetary Ruler:	Mercury
Meditation:	I can allow time for myself
Gemstone:	Sapphire
Power Stones:	Peridot, amazonite, rhodochrosite
Key Phrase:	I analyze
Glyph:	Greek symbol for containment
Anatomy:	Abdomen, intestines, gall bladder
Color:	Taupe, gray, navy blue
Animal:	Domesticated animals
Myths/Legends:	Demeter, Astraea, Hygeia
House:	Sixth
Opposite Sign:	Pisces
Flower:	Pansy
Key Word:	Discriminating

Your Ego's Strengths and Weaknesses

Your industriousness and selfless commitment to the community good endear you to others, Virgo. From your perspective, you are doing nothing unusual or exemplary—in fact, you see much to improve—but you provide a rare dedication to others, quietly working in the background for the greater good. Yours is the mutable earth sign. Your mutability contributes two characteristics: flexibility and problem-solving capabilities. You are able to flow around obstacles, avoiding impediments to your objectives rather than confronting them. You can easily adapt to circumstances and identify obstacles and difficulties, and this gives you a unique ability to solve problems. You think on your feet, dispassionately assessing a situation without self-interest, and this frees you to make decisions that would not occur to others. This also gives you the ability to heal, but because Virgo is an earth sign, you are as likely to "heal" a bank account as you are a person's ills. However, your non-confrontational style can lead others to take advantage of you, especially if they detect that you are insecure about your competence. You may also tend to over-commit yourself and then become overwhelmed by events. Stress is one of your greatest difficulties.

Your earthiness makes you pragmatic. You use logic to discover the ways a procedure can be made more efficient, how to manage the details. Your mind is quick, and you're good with numbers. But there's more to you than that. You really care about others, although you are more likely to show it by cleaning the house than by saying "I love you." You are grounded and logical, and although earth signs can feel stuck in their circumstances or have difficulty changing, your mutability balances that. Your nature is a fluid, fertile environment for growth, both personal and on behalf of others.

Shining Your Love Light

With your modest demeanor and matter-of-fact style, you don't attract a lot of attention when it comes to love. However, that doesn't mean that you don't know how to give when the right person comes along. You're looking for specific qualities, and they are not the easiest ones to find: faithfulness and the ability to see the real person under the mask give you a thrill. Once in a relationship, you work tirelessly to support your beloved, but this may not fully communicate your feelings. It's important to remember more conventional means of showing your love as well.

Aries gives you energy and keeps you guessing, but you may tire of the competitive spirit. You recognize a common focus on practical matters in Taurus, with whom you can build structures of lasting value for yourself and others. You find your mental connection with Gemini quite stimulating, but you may have difficulty with this sign's frivolous side. Cancer adds tenderness and sensitivity to your world, reminding you of the importance of expressing your feelings. Leos teach you to be proud of yourself and more confident about your skills, while you help them apply their skills more effectively to gain greater success. A fellow Virgo will share the workload as well as the worry, but you'll have to learn to relax together, too. Libra's eye for the finer things in life will lift your spirits, but this sign's not one to get its hands dirty. Scorpio's understanding of human nature fascinates you, and softens the edges of your style by turning on your sensual side. Sagittarius signs inspire you to strive for new goals and possibilities, while you teach them the value of staying in one place long enough to achieve success. Fellow earth sign Capricorn has the breadth of vision and leadership skills to make your plans work in a big way. You'll build great things together as partners. Aquarius can teach you how to work a room and introduce you into many new social environments, while your logic bonds you through lively conversation. Opposite-sign Pisces reminds you of the missing link in your character and helps you fill the gap, letting you see the whole picture with compassionate understanding.

Making Your Place in the World

Your intelligence, practicality, and logic are highly valued business skills, especially in administrative or managerial roles. As such, you can apply them successfully in any field. Efficiency and organization make you an effective employee, and if you want to work on your own as an independent contractor or entrepreneur, you have the right foundation to be successful. You are probably happier working for someone else—not because you fear the risk of owning your own business, but because promotion, especially self-promotion, does not come naturally to you. However, if you can overcome your concerns over your imperfections, others will find you quite well qualified by the time you feel ready to put yourself forward. Other areas that suit you include civil service, nursing and medicine, healing, accounting, and financial services. You also have considerable mechanical aptitude, which permits you to work with three-dimensional objects with ease, from cars to computers to houses.

Putting Your Best Foot Forward

While Leo may get swept away in the fervor of the moment and forget to give back, you, Virgo, tend to get so busy giving that you forget to receive. You create a whirlwind of activity as you move efficiently through tasks and accomplish amazing things in a short period of time. However, you can undermine your productivity if you do not take care of yourself. The missing link is your ability to receive from others. You may feel like you don't deserve it. If you stop the flow here, you undermine your own energy stores, and illness results. You lose your resilience, get stressed out, and stop being able to produce. More important than this is that you deserve to take care of yourself, and to be taken care of in exchange for all you give. Once you establish a balance of influx and outflow, you will be a true fountain of life. Your mind will work with speed and logic, and your analytical abilities will be in top form, increasing your efficiency and giving you more time to enjoy yourself as well.

Tools for Change

You need to get out more, Virgo, and blow your own horn. You focus on making yourself useful, because you see the work that needs to be done to improve conditions around you. You are not afraid to get your hands dirty and do the lowliest job if that's required. However, you tend to sell yourself short. You work so hard at developing competency that you're usually over-prepared for any task. You may end up taking a "safe" job that presents no challenge to you because you're afraid you'll fail to do a more difficult job perfectly. This sells you and your abilities short. The first thing to do to overcome this tendency is to challenge yourself. Go a little beyond your usual realm of comfort to tasks that you know you are prepared for but require you to use more skill and take on greater responsibility. By stretching yourself a little at a time, you'll begin to see yourself in a new way and find it more natural to step into the role you deserve.

Since you tend to stress out easily, use calming techniques to balance the reaction you get to these new challenges. Meditation that focuses on deep breathing and letting go of thoughts will reduce anxiety and tension. Yoga is the ideal practice for Virgos: the stretching aspect relaxes the muscles and allows the spine to align properly; the strengthening part helps you resist being buffeted by others' emotions; the conditioning component gives you the endurance to see you through each day with optimism and confidence.

It doesn't hurt for you to increase your social contacts, particularly ones where you are not involved in a working role. Networking is an important skill, but one you may be reluctant to engage in if you feel uncertain about your abilities, social and otherwise. It's hard to feel you're worthy of receiving rewards when you don't allow yourself the opportunity to get them. This is where turning your natural tendencies upside down comes in handy: let other people do things for you. Rather than leaping in to do for others, as you normally do, wait. Let someone else fill in the gap of action. Delegate. It's not that you're better than anyone else, it's that you don't always have to be the one to respond to need.

Affirmation for the Year

I enjoy communicating my new ideas and
their mutual benefits to others.

The Year Ahead for Virgo

You're in your third year of a twelve year cycle, as Jupiter makes its way through Scorpio, your solar Third House. Two years ago, you got the inspiration for something new and exciting. If you've believed in yourself enough since then, you've been working to develop and profit by this seed concept. This year you begin to see that your project is taking on a life of its own—but a life that will be snuffed out if you neglect it during this tender stage. Your efforts will go relatively smoothly this year, but then you aren't putting your idea to the test yet; that will begin next year. In the meantime, talk it up, gather information, test your market, and develop a network to support your endeavor. After November 23, Jupiter will be in Sagittarius, beginning a year when you'll be challenged to let go of some of your old ways to make room for the new. You'll have to make a commitment to the new enterprise. This is the bumpiest phase as your jet leaves the ground for the first time.

With Saturn in Leo again this year, some of your attention is focused on issues that appear hidden and are hard to explain or justify to others. However, they are visible, and you will benefit from getting others' perspectives on your situation. Ailments, whether yours or someone else's, may arise that are difficult to diagnose, and you may feel confined in a situation or location this year. Whatever happens, you'll feel a spiritual obligation to stick with it. You've been dealing with these issues since Saturn moved into Leo in June 2005. As this year unfolds, you'll discover more definitive solutions to the dilemmas you've faced.

Chiron is in Aquarius and your Sixth House. Although you're always working on improving your health and lifestyle, this is the most opportune time to deal with those issues you've been putting off. Your motto could be, "Patient, heal thyself," as you take more responsibility for preventing health problems from recurring. This is also the time to deal with difficult situations in the workplace. If there are any circumstances that aren't healthy for you, you must change them, whether they are the physical dynamics of your desk and chair or the psychological and emotional undercurrents between people.

Uranus travels the middle degrees of Pisces and your solar Seventh House. This is one more year of learning how to relate to others in a new way. You're beginning to see yourself more objectively, as others see you, and you're discovering that you're not so bad. In fact, you deserve to have all the joys of success and intimacy that anyone with your skills and sincerity has. This is a freeing experience, and you feel lighter and more adventurous, especially when it comes to connecting with others.

Neptune remains in Aquarius and your Sixth House, continuing the process of sensitizing you to the subtle energies that influence all of us on a moment-by-moment basis. Particularly when you are working in close proximity to others, you become acutely aware of the ebb and flow of hidden messages. You've been developing a coherent awareness of them for several years, and you're finally able to put what you know into words, thanks to your tireless studies.

Pluto is in Sagittarius and your solar Fourth House for yet another year, maintaining the pressure on you to grow and change. You've looked deeply into yourself and your past, discovering the threads of influence that come from family and ancestors. This year you'll embellish on this knowledge and begin to reach out as you turn this knowledge into a new persona.

The eclipses are entering Virgo and Pisces—your First and Seventh House axis—starting March 14. This is a crossroads time, as you'll find that your desires are matched with opportunities. Look for others to help smooth the way once you know what you want to get out of the coming nine-year cycle.

If you were born between August 26 and September 18, Saturn in Leo is presenting subtle challenges from your solar Twelfth House. This placement is often accompanied by feelings of entrapment. You could feel caught in responsibilities or activities that are not of your choosing. Whether it is a personal illness, a sick family member, a job, a marriage or business partnership, or an educational path, you can see a better way for yourself. However, you have to wait, because the time isn't right. In the meantime, you can prepare. Visualize yourself in this new situation, and don't give up or think you are not worthy just have to wait for the right moment. No matter what your circumstances, your Saturn job is to "keep the faith" in your goals, to be patient, and to enjoy life as much as you can in the meantime. Saturn's energies will be evident in events on or near January 27, February 19, April 5 and 24, June 20, August 7, November 16, and December 5.

If you were born between August 29 and September 7, Uranus in Pisces is opening new doorways in relationships for you. Uranus will jar you awake through interactions with other people, from your intimate friends to those you meet in casual encounters. You will simply see how you deserve more, and you'll set a higher standard for your relationships. You will feel the urge to break away from difficult people, to clear the air in tense situations. You want to take the bars off your cage and clear the path to a new future. As you break with the old, you are clearing the path for new people and situations to enter your life, including new romantic or business partnerships. Your sense of self is the source of all these changes. It will dawn on you that you are really a very good, capable person. You've been preparing yourself for long enough, and now it's time to take action. Others will give you helpful feedback—even if it doesn't feel helpful at the time. Everything will point toward this call to action, especially events occurring on or near March 1, June 5 and 19, September 5, November 19, and December 2.

If you were born between September 7 and 12, Neptune in Aquarius is in your solar Sixth House. Since 1998, you've been discovering how important subtle influences are on your health and ability to conduct your everyday activities. You want more than anything to reduce stress and simplify your complex daily routines. Though you've been working on this in a general way, it now takes on a feeling of urgency. Perhaps you notice negative effects in your life that can no longer be ignored, from health imbalances to work situations with inexplicable problems. The challenges you encounter are likely to be difficult to pin down, and, in the case of health matters, hard to diagnose in mainstream medical terms. In reality, you are spiritualizing your Sixth House matters: work, health, lifestyle, and the rhythms of daily life. By examining this area in terms of what's really going on, you can get to the core of what's causing the difficulties, and truly solve them. Therefore, gentle approaches will work best, like meditation or alternative healing therapies. You'll experience Neptunian events around January 27, February 5, March 15, May 10 and 22, August 10, October 29, and November 9.

If you were born between September 15 and 20, Pluto is in your Fourth House and in Sagittarius. Pluto brings dynamic change to your world this year, uprooting old situations and circumstances so that you can enter a new world. You've been working yourself up to these changes for some time, knowing they were coming but not quite knowing how to accomplish them. This year, you'll take the plunge, ready or not! Because of your mutable nature, you'll flow through them, letting go of the past gracefully, even without knowing exactly what you're heading toward. From Pluto's position in your Fourth House, everything in your life will be profoundly affected, but most of all your foundation and sense of self will go through a powerful transformation. You may find yourself moving house, taking a daring new position in your career, or taking up a cause you hold dear to your heart. You may remodel your home, completely change your relationships with your family, or research your genealogy and find a wonderful story in your past. The thread of these changes will develop around March 17 and 29, June 16, September 4 and 16, and December 18.

If you were born between August 22 and 25 or September 21 and 22, none of the major planets is contacting your Sun this year. This suggests that you will encounter fewer obstacles in achieving your goals. However, you will also feel less stimulation toward those goals, because your areas of discontent probably won't bother you as much—although you will still have them. Crises that affect others' lives will still affect you, but it won't be the same as if it were a "direct hit." You can take this time to do what you want rather than what you feel you have to. This could be a project dear to your heart or some special experience like an extended vacation. It's a good time to relax and enjoy life—something you do too seldom—and to appreciate what's right in your world. If other planets in your chart are being contacted by the astrological movers and shakers, you will still feel guided toward specific goals by events and circumstances.

Virgo/January

Planetary Hotspots

The fixed grand cross puts the emphasis on following through with things that you've started. This is a time to be persistent in pursuing your dreams. The featured event this month is outreach, as Jupiter contacts Uranus from your Third House. Communicating your ideas to others is important all year, and doing so consistently will bring the best results of all your efforts. This will bring the plans you've been developing since 1997 into sharper focus.

Wellness and Keeping Fit

The challenges you've faced since September have created internal stress, and the first two weeks of this month are a good time to put more focus on your own needs. Withdraw a little, get plenty of sleep, and have some fun.

Love and Life Connections

There's a slowdown in your social life now, but that may be a blessing in disguise, since you've got enough on your plate already. Venus is heading backward, bringing focus to your Fifth House. Romance could be proceeding in reverse, and your relationships with your children may be going through a testing and adjustment period. This is a wonderful opportunity to renegotiate your agreements with your loved ones and accommodate each other's changing needs. That's all that's going on: people are growing, and by responding positively you'll ensure continuing good will.

Finance and Success

Jupiter highlighted in your Third House gives you the opportunity to communicate through new venues starting now. Only you can decide which of the opportunities you encounter are the right ones, keeping in mind your overall goal to serve others. Significant dates are January 15, 18, 23, and 27, March 15, and September 24.

Rewarding Days

8, 9, 12, 13, 14, 17, 18, 19, 22, 23, 24, 27, 28

Challenging Days

3, 4, 10, 11, 25, 26, 31

Virgo/February

Planetary Hotspots

With Neptune's new yearly cycle starting in your health house on February 5, it's time to reassess your well-being and adjust your routines to move your health in the desired direction. Although it's part of an ongoing process, this is the right time to make a new beginning. The high level of activity of January is relieved after February 6.

Wellness and Keeping Fit

It's a good time to take a vacation before February 17, as Mars finishes its sojourn through your Ninth House of travel. You deserve a respite any time you can take one, and this may just be the time. You'll be a little more sensitive than usual to toxins and viruses over the month—but especially at the beginning. Keep your stress levels down with yoga and other exercise, and get plenty of sleep.

Love and Life Connections

Romantic ties become more harmonious after February 3, as Venus returns to direct motion. If you found that this Venus retrograde was the right time to let go of a bond that was not what you really want, you can now put the old tie behind you and prepare for a new one. Testy relationships with children are also easing, as they accept the new rules and expectations placed upon them.

Finance and Success

After February 17, you will assume a higher profile with regard to your profession as Mars enters Gemini and your Tenth House. You'll benefit greatly if you continue your steady efforts to complete recent projects. In another month the clouds will clear and you'll have more leisure time, plus the rewards of your accomplishments.

Rewarding Days

4, 5, 8, 9, 10, 13, 14, 15, 18, 19, 20, 23, 24

Challenging Days

1, 6, 7, 21, 22, 27, 28

Virgo/March

Planetary Hotspots

Mercury, Mars, Uranus, Pluto, and the lunar eclipse highlight the role of other people in your life all month. Mercury is retrograde from March 2 to 25, bringing communications from others that affect you deeply. Issues in business or career and at home coincide from March 11 to 14 with unexpected results.

Wellness and Keeping Fit

After March 5, you'll get more out of your fitness activities if you do them with a friend. This is also a good time to seek support services such as massage, acupuncture, and other treatments provided by health practitioners. Stresses could knock you out around March 4.

Love and Life Connections

Independence needs are inducing changes in your relationship life—part of a process that has been playing out since 2003, when Uranus entered Pisces. Although it may seem like your partner wants more freedom, it is actually you. A new yearly cycle in this process starts on March 1, which is a good time to set your intention for how you want to develop your individuality. Others may balk at the transformation you're going through, especially if you announce it. But by quietly pursuing your goals, they will come to accept it in time. The lunar eclipse on March 14 in your sign underscores this process.

Finance and Success

Don't get so lost in your desire to help other people that you forget to help yourself. Your overall career goal is to contribute, but you need to be compensated fairly as well, even if your project is less than complete. Attune yourself to what is happening on March 15, as Jupiter makes its second of three contacts with Neptune. Events now will clue you in to what you are creating during their nine-month interaction, which started on January 27.

Rewarding Days
3, 4, 8, 9, 13, 14, 18, 19, 22, 23, 24, 31

Challenging Days
5, 6, 7, 20, 21, 27, 28

Virgo/April

Planetary Hotspots

When Saturn turns direct on April 5, you'll feel like you've been sprung from a trap. Spring is truly here, and your optimism rises with the growing grass. You've spent the last five months working extra hard in a no-glory position with little to show, but now progress begins to be visible, and you can shift gradually to the next step in the plan. Disruptive events occur with Mars, Mercury, and Venus triggering the volatile planets Uranus and Pluto. Key dates are April 8, 13, 18, and 30. This thread of your life ties in with what happened on March 1, 11, 14, and 29.

Wellness and Keeping Fit

You've got more energy this month, but if you overexert yourself either at work or during physical activity, you could end up with a slow-healing injury. If you focus on remembering to breathe and to take breaks periodically, you'll do much to avoid such mishaps. You can also reduce your stress level by choosing when to accept interruptions and input from others—don't answer the phone or check email for a portion of the day.

Love and Life Connections

Although you've been going it alone lately, you get more support from others starting April 5 as Saturn begins to move in direct motion again and Venus enters your Seventh House. This is a good time to ask for what you need and to generate enthusiasm for your plans, especially on April 20.

Finance and Success

The more you steady yourself this month, the more you'll be able to accomplish all the tasks you've laid out in your ambitious plans. When you're centered, you're more efficient. You get some positive financial support on April 19.

Rewarding Days
1, 4, 5, 9, 10, 14, 15, 19, 20, 27, 28

Challenging Days
2, 3, 16, 17, 18, 23, 24, 29, 30

Virgo/May

Planetary Hotspots

The challenges that affect others dramatically do not touch you directly, but you can take advantage of all the energy flowing. On May 4, you reach the halfway point in a communications or education effort you're involved in. At this time, you will experience a breakthrough in perspective or an opportunity to get your message out to a larger audience. This will lead to more open doors in the next two months, which you will be able to use beyond that time.

Wellness and Keeping Fit

Chiron and Neptune turn retrograde in your Sixth House on May 15 and 22, signaling an opportunity to examine your health and lifestyle patterns and tweak them in whatever way you feel necessary. This could involve a change in habits that you reluctantly adopt. However, if you stick with it, you'll see positive results in early August and dramatic change by mid-November.

Love and Life Connections

You feel more support from others this month as a Mars-Jupiter-Uranus grand trine forms in your social houses. Their ideas for how to deal with your circumstances are ingenious, and they're willing to take action to help you out as well.

Finance and Success

Your life gets more dynamic after May 19, as Mercury starts to stimulate your career life. Around May 26, you get startling feedback from someone in that arena—something you'll be able to use to your advantage once you figure out what it means for you. It will put money in the bank, either now or in the future.

Rewarding Days

1, 2, 3, 6, 7, 8, 11, 12, 13, 16, 17, 24, 25, 26, 29, 30

Challenging Days

14, 15, 20, 21, 27, 28

Virgo/June

Planetary Hotspots

Relationships are highlighted as Uranus changes direction on June 19. As its five-month retrograde period begins, you can see what improvements can be made to create greater balance and individuality in your relationship life, and you're ready to move toward those goals now. This ties in with issues at home (especially on June 16), where a major transformative process is taking place. This process will have to be factored into the relationship's equilibrium, and it needs to be discussed, even if no one wants to talk about it.

Wellness and Keeping Fit

This is a great time to take a vacation, in spite of all the demands pulling at you. With careful planning, you can get all your ducks in a row so that taking time off won't set your efforts back.

Love and Life Connections

You are sensitive to others' energies more than usual around June 17, and there may be a not-so-subtle pressure on you to do extra work, or even to take on someone else's responsibilities. This is difficult to resist, especially as it may be coming from a person with authority over you. It's important to take care of yourself in whatever negotiation you agree upon.

Finance and Success

Business goes well now as you reach the peak in your yearly business cycle. You still feel the pull toward home and family duties, especially around June 16, but you'll be able to keep them in balance during a generally fruitful time. Busywork and detail-oriented tasks may seem designed to overwhelm you from June 4 to 22. Just keep chipping away at them—these are the tasks required to maintain your life and ensure your future success.

Rewarding Days

3, 4, 8, 9, 12, 13, 21, 22, 25, 26, 30

Challenging Days

10, 11, 16, 17, 23, 24

Virgo/July

Planetary Hotspots

Writing and outreach projects are completed around July 6 as Jupiter begins to move forward through your Third House. Now it's time to clean up the paperwork and other little projects you've set aside in order to focus on your main objective. It feels good to turn the page and start a new chapter of your life, while the results of your efforts start to come in.

Wellness and Keeping Fit

With Mars in your Twelfth House through July 21, you are drawn to solitary ways of managing your health and fitness. Yoga, an exercise routine you can do at home, meditation, or a solo walk through your neighborhood are great ways to meet your needs now. You are a little more sensitive now, so make sure to get enough sleep. Your dreams will be very vivid.

Love and Life Connections

You are more assertive than usual starting July 22, and you're more aware of what bothers you, but don't let it get out of hand. Because you're usually reluctant to express your disagreement with others, you may have a lot that you want to say—more than is helpful. You'll be more direct, and it can be a refreshing feeling to approach your needs in a straightforward manner. Others will be surprised by your atypical daring.

Finance and Success

You want to stay in the background through July 21 to get caught up on your work, but after that you'll want to be out front and ready to go with your next set of plans. While you're in your cave, you'll be refining your next set of steps and writing them down. This is much-needed integration time, and it will help revitalize your enthusiasm as well.

Rewarding Days

1, 5, 6, 10, 11, 18, 19, 22, 23, 24, 27, 28, 29

Challenging Days

7, 8, 9, 14, 15, 20, 21

Virgo/August

Planetary Hotspots

Mars in your sign gives you energy to burn, but there's a volatility factor to consider when it contacts Uranus on August 13 and Pluto on August 29. You'll get strong reactions from others then, especially partners and family members, that have to do with issues of freedom and responsibility. Your ability to think clearly and communicate well will assuage feelings, especially on August 29. You may come up with an innovative idea that will resolve the issue once and for all.

Wellness and Keeping Fit

The feelings of tension related to the Mars-Uranus-Pluto activity will extend all month, and it's important that you not carry them in your body. Take extra measures to stretch and relax your body using yoga, exercise, and emotional treatments such as Bach flower remedies.

Love and Life Connections

Your responsibilities are lighter this month, and you have more time to enjoy life. You'll especially benefit from cultural events and other social outings with your friends. They will inspire you—especially around the end of the month—and spur you to new forms of creative expression.

Finance and Success

Publishing and outreach efforts are especially fruitful now as Jupiter harmonizes with Uranus for the third time from your house of communications. This is a good time to complete a writing project or to launch plans you've been formulating over the past few months. Work becomes more difficult now as the planets line up in your service houses. You want to do more than you can, but it's important to learn to take care of yourself, too. You can become ill if you ignore your body's natural limits.

Rewarding Days

1, 2, 3, 6, 7, 14, 15, 19, 20, 24, 25, 29, 30

Challenging Days

4, 5, 10, 11, 16, 17, 18, 31

Virgo/September

Planetary Hotspots
From September 3 to 9, you reach a turning point in your life that becomes the springboard for your next year's accomplishments, as the planets line up in your sign. Pluto returns to direct motion on September 4, signaling your release from a situation you've been dealing with in your personal life. Now you can move ahead once again with the larger scheme.

Wellness and Keeping Fit
There's lots of energy coming your way from others, especially early in the month. However, the planetary deck is stacked in your favor. It's likely you'll be able to distance yourself from the emotions there and identify the real issues without getting stressed out.

Love and Life Connections
On September 5, Uranus reaches the halfway point in the cycle it began on March 1 and is further highlighted by the lunar eclipse on September 7. These events draw your attention to relationships—especially the balance of freedom vs. needs and responsibilities. Differences of opinion about the course of your relationship and how much freedom each person should have are likely. You have plenty of persuasive power, especially after September 4. However, others may try to convince you otherwise, especially on September 15 and 25, to win the argument.

Finance and Success
Quiet work in the background is the basis of your next successful initiative. You need the downtime now to bring out the best of your many ideas. Writing, reading, thought, and communication are key through November. The drive inward is part of a two-year period of creative fermentation that will result in new exciting projects when it is over.

Rewarding Days
2, 3, 4, 11, 12, 15, 16, 20, 21, 25, 26, 30

Challenging Days
1, 7, 8, 13, 14, 27, 28, 29

Virgo/October

Planetary Hotspots

The demands on your time are dramatically reduced as October opens, yet your income goes up. While the planets release their contact with your sign, it's a good time to set aside all the leftover tasks from previous months' busy-ness. A vacation would go down well now. A few small matters arise after October 14 that, if taken care of now, will prevent problems after October 28, when Mercury starts its latest retrograde period.

Wellness and Keeping Fit

Play is the key word for you now. You need time off, and you need to spend it enjoying yourself, with an emphasis on being active. Leave the leftover filing and mending, and treat yourself to a massage or healing session. Go to the latest special museum exhibit and take in your favorite sporting event.

Love and Life Connections

If your partner is more conciliatory now, it is because you are more relaxed. You can use this time to refocus your relationships in a positive direction, especially in the first half of the month. Listen closely to what others are saying, but don't ignore your own insights. As the month waxes, an issue will emerge that raises the old dilemma of who's right and who's wrong, and you'll find that it's somewhere in between.

Finance and Success

You've been working hard with little to show for it, including recognition, since May 22. When Neptune returns to forward motion on October 29, this changes. You reach a tipping point, where now your efforts are more effective and bring better results, both because of what you've learned and what you've built.

Rewarding Days

1, 8, 9, 12, 13, 14, 17, 18, 19, 22, 23, 24, 27, 28

Challenging Days

4, 5, 10, 11, 25, 26, 31

Virgo/November

Planetary Hotspots

The emphasis is on organizing, and you're ready to clear out those filing cabinets and rev up the shredder as the planets collect in your Third House. You have a plan, and it feels good to finally get to this part of it. There are projects to finish up and details to manage as you interface with bureaucracy. Completing this work now will empower you to move forward with a clean slate when the new planetary cycles begin over the next few months.

Wellness and Keeping Fit

You're wanting to put more energy into your health and fitness routine, but beware of overdoing it. There's a leftover health situation that you've been making adjustments for, and you still need to do this until November 22.

Love and Life Connections

Social contact is highlighted now, especially with siblings, neighbors, and extended family. There may be a big party or family reunion, with the attendant logistical challenges of bringing large groups of people together. It will be exciting, gratifying, and sometimes difficult. The best weekend for a social event is November 18 and 19.

Finance and Success

Jupiter advances into your Fourth House of family and home, drawing you to pour more attention and energy there. As a year-long transit, it suggests changes in your living situation, from moving house to redecorating to adding people to your household. This is also a period of "going inside" metaphorically, as you get in touch with the past or find what stirs you from the deepest part of your being. Now you begin a six-year climb to a new success; although you are "underground" now, you will continue to enjoy the successes of the past as you plant the seeds for new ones.

Rewarding Days

4, 5, 9, 10, 13, 14, 15, 18, 19, 20, 23, 24

Challenging Days

1, 6, 7, 8, 21, 22, 28, 29

Virgo/December

Planetary Hotspots

You're putting an intense amount of energy into your home as the planets bunch up in your Fourth House. A remodel, preparations for holiday visitors, or a big party are all possible. This could also bring out the best or the worst in family members. There can be an energetic spirit of pitching in or a reluctance to do so. Challenges are most likely on December 3, 15, 18, 21, and 25. However, there are harmonies throughout the month permitting resolution of difficulties, particularly on December 7, 16, and 24.

Wellness and Fit

There's a need for lots of physical strength and energy output this month, but you may feel as though you don't have what it takes to do the job. Focus on mental tasks—your forte—when your muscles tire.

Love and Life Connections

Dealings with contractors and partners may be difficult on the challenging dates mentioned above due to carelessness or lack of regard for your needs. You can minimize the impact of these planetary triggers by creating clear contractual arrangements and choosing a good date for signing the agreement.

Finance and Success

Getting overwhelmed is possible around December 5 as Saturn begins its five-month retrograde period. It is especially important that you stay within your physical capabilities, because you could end up doing lasting harm to your body at this time due to stress or overuse. On December 18, Pluto's new yearly cycle signals that it's time for a new set of goals regarding your home and family life. You'll be able to initiate action toward a goal you've put off, waiting for the right time. Although it will still take a few years, you can start moving in that direction now.

Rewarding Days

2, 3, 6, 7, 11, 12, 16, 17, 20, 21, 22, 29, 30

Challenging Days

4, 5, 18, 19, 25, 26, 31

Virgo Action Table

These dates reflect the best—but not the only—times for success and ease in these activities, according to your Sun sign.

	JAN	FEB	MAR	APR	MAY	JUN	JUL	AUG	SEPT	OCT	NOV	DEC
Move	1-3											8-26
Start a class										2-26	18-30	1-7
Join a club						3-28	29-31	1-10				
Ask for a raise						26, 27	19-31	1-12, 23	6-30			
Look for work	22-31	1-28	25-31	1-16	19-31	1-3						
Get pro advice	3, 4, 8	1, 4, 5	3, 4, 27	1, 23, 24	21, 24-26	16-18, 21	14, 15, 18	10, 11, 14	7, 8, 11	4, 5, 8	1, 4, 5	2, 3, 25
Get a loan	6, 7	2, 3	1, 2, 29	25, 26	22, 23	19, 20	16, 17	12, 13	9, 10	6, 7	2, 3, 30	1, 27, 28
See a doctor	22-31	1-28	25-31	1-16		28-30		11-27				
Start a diet	22-31	1-8						8, 9				
End relationship									7, 8			
Buy clothes		3-28	1-4									
Get a makeover								25, 27-31	1-30			
New romance		3-28	1-4	6-30	1, 2							
Vacation	8, 9	4, 5	3, 4, 31	1, 27, 28	5-19, 31	1-23	18, 19	14, 15	11, 12	18, 19	4, 5	2, 3, 29

LIBRA

The Balance
September 22 to October 23

♎

Element:	Air
Quality:	Cardinal
Polarity:	Yang/Masculine
Planetary Ruler:	Venus
Meditation:	I balance conflicting desires
Gemstone:	Opal
Power Stones:	Tourmaline, kunzite, blue lace agate
Key Phrase:	I balance
Glyph:	Scales of justice, setting sun
Anatomy:	Kidneys, lower back, appendix
Color:	Blue, pink
Animal:	Brightly plumed birds
Myths/Legends:	Venus, Cinderella, Hera
House:	Seventh
Opposite Sign:	Aries
Flower:	Rose
Key Word:	Harmony

Your Ego's Strengths and Weaknesses

The paradox of your nature is that even though you appear so nice and refined on the outside, inside you have strong motivations to take action. This is because of your cardinal air nature, Libra. Your life revolves around relationships, both with other people and with concepts and objects. Throughout all, you seek balance and harmony. You have an eye for beauty, spatial relationships, and elegance, in both the physical and the theoretical sense. What others may not understand is how intelligent you are, even intellectual, unless you turn your attention to mathematics or musical theory. These are all qualities of air—the element that seeks to discover the natural ties between things, ideas, and people. Your cardinal quality is a little harder to understand, because you may feel like you wait for others to take the lead, so oriented are you toward getting along harmoniously with those around you. However, you have definite ideas about what you want and will take action to get it. You are very strong-minded when it comes to what you want in your relationships, what kinds of beauty you want to surround yourself with, and how you think the world works. You only have to look at the situations that drive you to take action to see that there are many things in life that trigger your active side—the things you will fight for. You might even say that you're driven to fight for peace. The downside of this is that you want peace so much that you are sometimes afraid to assert your own needs and desires, and you may not want to rock the boat enough to raise the issue. In your fervor to create an environment of cooperation and conviviality, you may lose yourself in the process, asserting yourself on behalf of someone else without regard for your own interests. You can counteract this tendency by making a conscious effort to develop your own autonomy and individuality.

Shining Your Love Light

There's no one who loves being in love more than you, Libra. You thrill to the companionship and camaraderie of partnership, but you also enjoy the challenge of making a relationship work. You enjoy managing your relationships too, but you must guard against losing yourself in them. Only when you maintain your individuality can you create healthy love bonds.

You'll never feel more challenged than when you're with an Aries. Aries is your flip side, the assertive and individualistic part of yourself you need to bring out to be balanced. Taurus is like a more practical "you"—also attuned to beauty but in a commonsense manner, and you see eye-to-eye in many ways. You instinctively "get" Gemini, another air sign. Together you can explore the realms of mind and culture. You may not understand the importance that Cancer places on feelings at first, but there's much you can learn from this sign, while lending your own objectivity to the exchange. Leo loves life, lifting your spirits and inflaming your passions in a way that pulls you out of your usual coolness. Don't be fooled by Virgo's sense of duty and organizational skills—they mask a yearning to be loved the way you know how to love. You won't be able to outsmart another Libra. If you fight, it will be over who's nicer and more harmonious. You'll be a great couple! Scorpios may seem too intense for you, with your smooth and cultured ways, but once you see that they have as much interest in human nature as you do, you'll be endlessly fascinated. Sagittarius will lead you far and wide to explore people, cultures, and subjects you've never seen or known before. You'll find common ground with Capricorn by exploring the beauty of history and government, and will add pragmatism to your intellectualism for an unbeatable combination. You and fellow air sign Aquarius make a breezy couple. You'll be at every social event and party until dawn. You'll love Pisces's sweet and gentle side—this sign brings a healing touch and emotional softness that responds well to your sense of harmony and beauty.

Making Your Place in the World

Your people skills recommend you for many positions in today's world. You do well in any customer service position, from retail to specialized training and technical support. Your insights and natural interest in human nature will keep you endlessly fascinated in psychological or spiritual counseling positions, as well as in unofficial counseling roles like hair stylist, fashion consultant, or interior decorator. These positions are especially apropos because they use your creative talents as well. To satisfy your more serious and intellectual side, you may be drawn to mathematical, musical, or linguistic theory. And with your drive to create harmony and justice around you, you could find yourself studying or practicing law. Of course, work in the pure arts is your forte. With training and practice, you'll excel in traditional forms like painting, sculpture, or calligraphy, or in more modern forms like computer graphics, special effects, or fashion design. Tapping your sense of beauty, you can also choose a career in building architecture, landscape architecture, or set design in stage or film.

Putting Your Best Foot Forward

Libra, you are so intent on balancing all that is around you, especially in your relationships with other people, that you can leave your own individuality underdeveloped. You are the gentle artist of balance and harmony, whether in your personal relationships or in the aesthetics of your surroundings. You can speak with authority about the lives of others because you listen attentively and absorb what you hear. However, when asked about yourself you may have less insight into your own ideals, goals, dreams, and identity. Knowing your own mind and heart is just as important as knowing those of another, because without self-understanding your life goes out of balance, and no amount of external beautification will bring you back into equilibrium. You have to do things alone sometimes to cultivate your own nature. You enjoy companionship, but time alone allows you to physically develop your own center without reference to someone else in the room. This opens the door to pursuing your own goals and dreams—the first step in building yourself from the center out. The more you cultivate your own nature, the more you exemplify the true balance you seek.

Tools for Change

Your social skills are awesome, Libra, but you will benefit from learning to take a more direct approach in your interactions. Even though you truly care about other people, sometimes it's harder to care about yourself. This means that you could try to get other people to do things for you by doing something for them that will prompt a specific response. This is primarily because you don't consciously know what you want, or because you feel awkward bringing up your own needs and desires. It's far easier to go with the flow and make the other person think that it's what he or she wants to do.

However, being more direct is healthier because you are more likely to get what you want, it requires you to know yourself, and it keeps the relationship in balance.

It's important to get in touch with your own self a little more. One way to do this is to test your comfort boundaries. This you can do by going on an adventure, which can be anything you have never done before. Trying to stretch beyond what you've already done teaches you what you're capable of and results in self-knowledge. Exploring new realms of the outdoors, the halls of learning, emotions and creativity, or spirituality all reflect you back to yourself and show you your strengths and weaknesses, and your character traits and the way you express them. Activities that require physical fitness bring double benefits in that they also get you in touch with your physical body and increase its strength, flexibility, and resilience. Given your penchant for creative pursuits, you can also develop your self-knowledge by pursuing a hobby—especially a skill-based one. As you develop more proficiency with your pastime, you will again see yourself in the mirror of your creative expressions.

Centering is important for Libras, whose symbol of the balance scales suggests the process that is constantly taking place inside you. Meditation that focuses on building your awareness of your chakras (major energy centers along the spine) and the main central energy channel are especially helpful. Tai chi also helps develop an awareness of balance, focusing on the hara points and building pools of energy in each one. Breathing practices are useful, and so is yoga—especially those postures which focus on developing balance.

Affirmation for the Year

I am managing reasonable risks to achieve worthy goals.

The Year Ahead for Libra

You start the year with Jupiter in your solar Second House, Libra—a great place for building resources. However, the resources you need to accrue right now are not necessarily monetary; you may need to build skills as well. You will be bringing things of value into your life, and this often results in spending rather than saving money. In fact, in order to fulfill the dreams you hatched last year, you'll need to invest in turning your vision into reality. Consequently, you could see more cash going out than coming in while Jupiter is in Scorpio. You're laying a foundation for the next ten years, so it's important to take a reasonable risk to signal to the universe that you are confident you can fulfill your plans. When Jupiter enters Sagittarius and your solar Third House on November 23, you'll enter a more social period. You'll be out and about, perhaps spreading the word about your new venture or laying the mental foundation for it by getting new training. The more you focus on activities involving mind and communication, the more you establish your new path. This energy will continue through most of 2006.

Saturn is in Leo and your Eleventh House again this year, giving you a chance to fulfill the activities you began last year. The focus is on groups and organizations, from family ties to professional alliances. You've taken on new responsibilities since mid-2005, and you need to stay with those duties this year if you want them to be a stepping stone to something better. Even if the politics or interpersonal conflicts become difficult, you will benefit from outlasting them.

Chiron stays the course in Aquarius and your Fifth House. You're becoming more aware that you keep yourself from being happy by sacrificing your own needs and desires for others. By always placing others before yourself, you don't have to think about what it would take to make you feel fulfilled. It's dawning on you that it isn't enough to seek happiness through the successes of those close to you—you have to reach for your own dreams in your own right.

Uranus reaches the middle degrees of Pisces and your solar Sixth House, nearing the halfway point of its transit. This means that you're three years into an awakening in that most mundane area of your life—the rhythms and routines that get you through the day.

This includes health practices, and a positive lifestyle change now will head off health difficulties later.

Neptune is in Aquarius and your solar Fifth House once more, shrouding and mystifying issues of self-expression and creativity. You may be struggling with a romantic involvement, asking yourself, "Why do I always attract the same type of lover?" Or your children could require a sacrifice from you. Your style and forms of creative expression are going through a slow, subtle change as well. If this is a major part of your life, the effect will be profound.

Pluto remains in Sagittarius and your Third House, renovating the way you view the world. You may do this through contact with new people or educational venues, through personal study, or in a structured classroom. Think of ways you can empower yourself, especially with a win-win approach and a positive attitude.

The eclipses move into Virgo and Pisces, your Twelfth and Sixth House axis, with the lunar eclipse on March 14. This adds emphasis to the process of reorganizing your life and health routines. Doing service for others adds to your fulfillment through a feeling of contribution. Don't expect to be recognized for what you are doing now—it's all on the inside.

If you were born between September 26 and October 18, Saturn in Leo is contacting your Sun from your solar Eleventh House. This puts the focus on groups, from family to social to professional. You have responsibilities here—possibly new ones that are taking you down unfamiliar social roads. You have a goal in mind, something you want to accomplish, a quid pro quo that is involved in any volunteer work. You may find yourself in the midst of a difficult situation due to political or interpersonal conflict. If so, only you can decide if it is worth it to stay. You may find that groups with which you have an ongoing relationship may not satisfy new-found needs. You're looking for new sources of support to match where you're headed next. Over the next year, you'll be able to peel away the social encumbrances that no longer suit you. This could include, in your personal life, a decision to associate with a different "crowd". If the old crowd's pastimes undermine you, you have to let go. These issues will arise near January 27, February 19, April 5 and 24, June 20, August 7, November 16, and December 5.

If you were born between September 29 and October 8,
Uranus in Pisces is contacting your Sun from your solar Sixth House.
You have noticed a growing chaos around you over the years, and
now it's time to figure out how to simplify your life. Esoteric studies
teach us that an organized life creates an organized (healthy) body.
The modern spread of Chinese feng shui emphasizes this fact. Your
health routines—what you eat, how much you sleep and exercise,
how you respond to stress—need to change. The same goes for your
lifestyle patterns, from how you drive to how you relax to how clut-
tered your home is. It's time to clear out and get rid of what you don't
need, not so much as a catharsis but to streamline your existence.
The goal is greater spirituality. Your health in all areas of your life
now stems from within, and the more you can do to root out the
nefarious sources of chaos in your own nature—the more you can
find peace within—the more you can create peace around you. Surprising events related to this cycle will occur on or near March 1,
June 5 and 19, September 5, November 19, and December 2.

If you were born between October 7 and 12, Neptune in
Aquarius is lending its support to your Sun from your Fifth House.
Now is the time to take your dearest dream and create a vision of
your life that puts you in the feature role. Set your sights high,
because this is the best opportunity you'll have to see clear to your
soul, where your inner truth lies. You'll respond most profoundly to
plans that correspond to your notion of your life purpose. Discovering this will involve some exploration and experimentation if you
are unsure of where you're headed. In fact, you may feel confused
now. Never mind: you've got a year, even longer, to sort it out. The
fog will clear as this year passes, and you'll be more aware of what
you want in life as a result.

You are likely to idealize romantic partners undeservedly. It is
important to be both pragmatic about your expectations in love and
cautious about investing trust until you've known your partner for a
while. Neptune will pervade your experiences around January 27,
February 5, March 15, May 10 and 22, August 10, October 29, and
November 9.

If you were born between October 15 and 20, Pluto in Sagittarius presents opportunities to you as it contacts your Sun from your Third House. The key to dramatic change in your life comes from within, now. Pluto gives you the opportunity this year to completely reform the way you see the world. Every experience you have in your life is both colored and precipitated by your attitudes and beliefs about the world and what it has to offer. By examining your thoughts and questioning their validity, you can discover whether they are supportive of your life and truly reflective of the world as it is. Additional education or training, especially in communication skills, will be helpful in furthering your goals. This could include psychological counseling to help you as you change the way you see life. Your immediate environs are likely to be in upheaval, whether it's a nearby road under construction or your next-door-neighbor's home. Your extended family will also go through changes, and they may require more support from you in the coming months. Pluto's energies will be felt most on March 17 and 29, June 16, September 4 and 16, and December 18.

If you were born between September 22 and 25 or October 21 and 23, none of the major planets are contacting your Sun this year. This is no reason to feel left out: other planets in your chart may be activated, and they will bring plenty of events and guide you as you find your path through the year. Without the outer planets' contact to your Sun, you will feel less challenged, however, and your path will have more familiar signposts. You will have the chance to relax a little more, to complete tasks previously started, and to engage in activities of your choosing rather than those that are thrust upon you by life's circumstances. It will give you more time to play, as well as to choose projects and activities that you enjoy. Altogether, it should be a relatively peaceful year.

Libra/January

Planetary Hotspots

A fixed grand cross is reflected in events that hit your sense of security. Money is at issue as additional expenses arise, but there may be an opportunity for additional income that comes up suddenly, perhaps as an emergency, and if so you'll have to act fast in order to respond. Seeds for what's happening now were planted last fall, and now you get your chance to move forward—but not without obstacles. Key dates are January 15, 18, 23, and 27.

Wellness and Keeping Fit

You're likely to neglect your need for fun during this intense period. If it's absolutely necessary to dip into your reserves, make sure that you at least combine pleasure with work by listening to music, taking frequent breaks, and eating nutritiously. This is not the time to skimp on sleep.

Love and Life Connections

Disagreements are likely in your home life as Venus tracks backward through your Fourth House. This may be the time to hold firm on an important rule or decision, even though others don't understand or agree. If you need to adjust your position, now is a good time to do so. All relationships go through an adjustment period this month, with improvements to follow.

Finance and Success

On January 27, Jupiter contacts Neptune, highlighting the efforts you've been making toward creating a more meaningful life for yourself since 1997. This is the time to take stock and adjust your course if necessary. The key is to go for fulfillment, not just what is easy. You're entering a four-year formative period upon which the following eight years of success will be based.

Rewarding Days

1, 2, 10, 11, 15, 16, 20, 21, 25, 26, 29, 30

Challenging Days

5, 6, 7, 12, 13, 14, 27, 28

Libra/February

Planetary Hotspots
The heavenly dynamics of January continue through February 6 with intensity and remain with you through the rest of the month in a more background role. You'll get the chance to complete more of your work without disruption now. Venus returns to forward motion on February 3, permitting your home life to settle into a new normal. On February 5, a new cycle of creativity and spirituality starts when Neptune's yearly dance with the Sun begins.

Wellness and Keeping Fit
Continue your efforts to improve your well-being through the program you've been following. This is also a good time to plan a health-enhancing vacation for this year.

Love and Life Connections
Your family life has been challenging since the holidays, but the obstacles to harmony have been cleared for the time being. If something remains unexpressed, wait for an opportunity to discuss it—don't just let it go thinking that the problem will disappear. If allowed to remain underground, it will fester rather than heal. Think about a proposal for positive change that you can make to bring the family together.

Finance and Success
Your extra expenditures at the beginning of the month are for a good cause, if you don't overdo. Remember, you can wait to buy some things until you need them, unless availability is an issue. Beware of get-rich-quick schemes or bargains that seem too good to be true now and for the rest of the year.

Rewarding Days
6, 7, 11, 12, 16, 17, 21, 22, 25, 26

Challenging Days
2, 3, 8, 9, 10, 23, 24

Libra/March

Planetary Hotspots

Work is emphasized as the planets move through your Sixth House, and shocking events could occur on March 1, 11, and 14, as Uranus is activated by the Sun and Mars and a lunar eclipse highlights the same area. Mercury retrogrades over the eclipse point on March 8, bringing logistical problems to the surface that will be resolved by April 11.

Wellness and Keeping Fit

Your health may be affected by all work and no play. Take the usual precautions, and do something extra to relieve the stress on March 1, 2, 11 to 14, and 29. Travel could expose you to illnesses that you have a hard time resisting on the mid-month dates.

Love and Life Connections

With all your work-related commitments and financial demands, you may have sacrificed your social and romantic life. Without going overboard, this is a good time to give yourself some slack and do inexpensive things that you enjoy. You get some life-changing input from someone else on March 29, which enables you to move forward with your plans. A partnership may be in the offing.

Finance and Success

You've been wanting more freedom and variation in your work since 2003, when Uranus entered your Sixth House. As Uranus's cycle starts on March 1, it's a good time to set your next set of related goals for the coming year. Events on March 11, 14, and 29 propel you forward with your plans. Your expenses leave you a little shorter than usual as Jupiter comes to a standstill in your Second House. This condition will persist for four months as you pour your extra cash and time into creative projects that will bear fruit in the future.

Rewarding Days

5, 6, 7, 10, 11, 12, 15, 16, 17, 20, 21, 25, 26

Challenging Days

1, 2, 8, 9, 22, 23, 24, 29, 30

Libra/April

Planetary Hotspots

You set your sights on higher, social goals last July and have been working against the wind to further a good cause. April 5 is a turning point in your efforts, when Saturn returns to forward motion after five months. For the most part you enjoy what you're doing and feel committed to it; now it gets easier, too.

Wellness and Keeping Fit

Venus passing through your Sixth House of health makes this a good month for you in terms of overall well-being. Make pleasure a part of your fitness routine to get the most out of it, or you may feel Venus's lazy side. It will also help to work out with a friend.

Love and Life Connections

As the Sun and Mercury make harmonious contacts on April 16 and 19, those you are closest to empower you with key insights to help transform the way you communicate in personal and public interactions.

Finance and Success

New work comes in to pump up your bank account on April 20 as Venus harmonizes with Jupiter. However, you encounter obstacles on April 9 that can be worked out over the duration of the month, with key events on April 13, 18 to 20, and 30. This situation ties in with what you experienced on March 11. Pressure at work increases at mid-month, with a disruption that could throw you off balance on April 18. Give yourself the time you need to figure out what's going on instead of responding in a knee-jerk way. There's a bigger issue that follows an event thread that started March 1.

Rewarding Days

2, 3, 6, 7, 8, 11, 12, 13, 16, 17, 18, 21, 22, 29, 30

Challenging Days

4, 5, 19, 20, 25, 26

Libra/May

Planetary Hotspots
With Mars, Jupiter, and Uranus trine each other, your finances get even better than before as you capitalize on business projects early in the month. Your ability to respond to others' emergencies turns a handsome profit, or at least earns brownie points that turn into a promotion and an increase in pay at some point. This brings a welcome respite from the care you had to take late last year and early in this one. The situation you faced in January is repeating on a new level, easier to manage now with your interim effort. It may help to think of your current circumstances as a step in the prosperity cycle you began in May 2000. This will get you back to thinking in terms of your long-range goals so you create what you really want.

Wellness and Keeping Fit
If you make "fitness dates" now, you'll be sure to stay on the road to well-being, because you never stand up a friend. It's something to look forward to and becomes extra relaxing due to the social interaction that is so important to you.

Love and Life Connections
Disagreements with a friend or partner could mar your day on May 23, but you could just as easily use this energy to build excitement in the relationship if you tend it as you would a garden. Generosity and consideration won't overcome a deep-seated conflict, but they go a long way toward letting someone know you care.

Finance and Success
There is a potential for cash-flow shortage, but it's because you're busier, especially around May 4. Challenges arise from May 4 to 22, but then you get the breathing room you need to let the dust settle and see where you stand.

Rewarding Days
4, 5, 9, 10, 14, 15, 18, 19, 27, 28, 31

Challenging Days
1, 2, 3, 16, 17, 22, 23, 24, 29, 30

Libra/June

Planetary Hotspots

There's plenty of planetary tension to go around in June, as the fixed grand cross re-establishes itself from June 4. This time the emphasis is on resolution, so even though the issues of January, February, and May reassert themselves, solutions are more readily at hand. Even though your activity level will be intense, the feeling of completion and integration will bring a sigh of relief. Some situations will require more massage in the months to come, but the load definitely feels lighter after June 22.

Wellness and Keeping Fit

If you've been ignoring health matters that need attention, they will give you a reminder as Uranus begins reverse travel on June 19. This will tie in with events on March 1 and 12, April 8, and June 5. You have five months to clear the imbalance, with another peak event around September 5.

Love and Life Connections

Situations with siblings and neighbors that require refocus and change become more urgent around June 16, permitting you the opportunity to tip the balance in favor of healthier interactions. New insights come to you, and you realize that sometimes you just have to back off and let events take their own course.

Finance and Success

Finances may be a bit squeezed as you enter the active period from June 4 to 22. Some difficulties may be avoided if you make sure you get the bills paid on time. On the whole, this period, for all its drama, will be good for your pocketbook. Try to avoid giving handouts on the basis of a hard-luck story.

Rewarding Days
1, 2, 5, 6, 7, 10, 11, 14, 15, 23, 24, 27, 28, 29

Challenging Days
12, 13, 19, 20, 25, 26

Libra/July

Planetary Hotspots

Disorganization results in communication problems in career and business all month long as Mercury travels backward from July 4 to 28. It may seem at first as if the problems that arise are going to be big and complicated, but they will reveal themselves to be relatively harmless and straightforward to solve after July 10.

Wellness and Keeping Fit

You'll do yourself a world of good if you take a vacation, or at least a few days off, this month. Even though there's a high level of activity in your life right now, sometimes to keep it in perspective we need to get away. This is your time to draw back. Circumstances will bring peak events on July 5 and 14, so you may want to plan accordingly. After July 22, there's a part of you that wants to get away from other people and do things that are more personally satisfying. This could be the right time to get away, whether it is to complete some home projects, take a spiritual retreat, or visit faraway lands.

Love and Life Connections

Parties, meetings, events—you want to go to them all, and there are plenty of them available to you now. However, personal issues, perhaps with children or romantic partners, hold you back around July 30. These challenges tie in with events last month and on July 5. It's a good time to go with the flow.

Finance and Success

Financial matters take a turn for the better after Jupiter returns to forward motion on July 6. For four months, you've been trying to squeeze more out of your budget, and the squeezing is almost over. Now the benefits of your efforts can start rolling in.

Rewarding Days
2, 3, 4, 7, 8, 9, 12, 13, 20, 21, 25, 26, 30, 31

Challenging Days
10, 11, 16, 17, 22, 23, 24

Libra/August

Planetary Hotspots

The emphasis is on your obligations to groups and organizations as the fast-moving planets trigger Saturn in your Eleventh House from August 7 to 26. You'll confront the same type of challenges you've been dealing with all year, but now you have more wiggle room to push things forward through negotiation and creativity. Key dates are August 2, 7, 17, 20, 22, and 26. The annual cycle of success through hard work starts when the Sun and Saturn connect on August 7. It's time to think about how you can work within groups to further your own plans, as well as to serve them in return.

Wellness and Keeping Fit

The inner tension you feel now is related to your need for freedom and variation in your work routine. You're feeling especially confined around August 13, and this could lead to illness unless you respond to your need for time away from the grind.

Love and Life Connections

Relationships with colleagues or anyone else in a group setting can be set on a new course this month. You've made many sacrifices for others, and now it's time to bring some balance back. It will take time to develop the right form, but you can start by talking about it.

Finance and Success

In spite of your restlessness, your work efforts result in extra rewards around August 29. You display exceptional ingenuity in solving problems, which eases your tension and increases your interest in the job you have. Keep working toward the new job you want to create for yourself, even though this month goes well.

Rewarding Days
4, 5, 8, 9, 16, 17, 18, 21, 22, 23, 26, 27, 28, 31

Challenging Days
6, 7, 12, 13, 19, 20

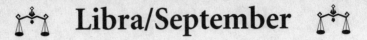

Libra/September

Planetary Hotspots
The hidden issues that came to the surface last month around August 13 and 29 are the source of challenging events from September 3 to 9 as Pluto returns to forward motion and Uranus gets triggered by the Sun and the lunar eclipse. This invigorates your creative process at work, but it also makes you more restless. Your communications with the outside world have a powerful impact now.

Wellness and Keeping Fit
Your energy level gets a boost when Mars enters your sign on September 7. However, illness is also possible if you overextend yourself on the crest of this wave. Circumstances may seem to demand it as your workload peaks. The simplest thing is to set aside some of your pet projects for other required duties so you have time to maintain your regular health routines.

Love and Life Connections
You could become overly eager to accomplish your own personal goals for your relationships now, and push others beyond their readiness, especially after September 6. If you insist on indulging your impatience, you'll push your relationships back instead of forward. Opportunities for gentle, natural growth occur on September 15 and 23.

Finance and Success
If you've worked hard, executed a plan, and been consistent in applying yourself since the beginning of the year, you're experiencing the fruits of your labors now in the form of increased income. As September 24 approaches, you become aware of how well this plan is matching your ideal of what you want to be doing, and especially as to how it fulfills your need to be creative. You'll have a chance to do Phase Two of your plan next year to get even closer to your goal.

Rewarding Days
1, 5, 6, 13, 14, 17, 18, 21, 22, 23, 26, 27, 28

Challenging Days
2, 3, 4, 9, 10, 15, 16, 30

Libra/October

Planetary Hotspots

Your life assumes a more peaceful tone as the planets enter harmonious interconnections in the first half of the month. Romance, or at least fun, is in the air, and you have time to indulge in health and beauty treatments. Issues with romantic partners and children that arose in mid-May recede after October 29 as subtly as they came into your life. After October 22, your activity level rises once again, so enjoy the break while you can.

Wellness and Keeping Fit

Relaxation is a fine art that you should practice this month during the planetary break. Take those long, luxurious baths. Get a massage treatment or go to your favorite day spa.

Love and Life Connections

New romantic connections are possible through October 15, but there are obscuring factors that may make it hard to judge if the new prospect is for real due to Mercury's impending retrograde. You'll have to give it time to know if you can trust the person, at least through November 17. It may be wise to delay intimacy, no matter how much you want it. Children's demands for new toys and pastimes could put the pinch on your budget later, even though you're feeling flush now. Thinking ahead will help you avoid difficulties later.

Finance and Success

Your cash on hand is good right now after a year of good fortune. You may feel inclined to spend it on extras for yourself and your children. When Jupiter moves out of your Second House on November 23, you won't be feeling so flush; you'll have new opportunities to generate prosperity, but they won't be the same as the ones you had over the past year. Third-house opportunities often bring long-term prosperity rather than immediate results.

Rewarding Days

2, 3, 10, 11, 15, 16, 20, 21, 25, 26, 29, 30

Challenging Days

1, 6, 7, 12, 13, 14, 27, 28

♎ Libra/November ♎

Planetary Hotspots

The planets highlight your Second House of resources and permit a retrospective on how the past year has gone. Jupiter is completing its year there, ideally a time for developing the ideas you had in fall 2004. There have been many obstacles to surmount, but they have dovetailed with your goal of having a freer, more creative work life. This becomes apparent as work projects and tasks are more to your liking this month—a trend that will continue.

Wellness and Keeping Fit

You have been working with a health-improvement program since the spring, and the benefits are becoming increasingly evident. After November 20, you'll be able to maintain the routine with less conscious focus and forced discipline.

Love and Life Connections

There is a focus on money in a relationship now. You may need to negotiate a way to handle money that both of you can agree on. Setting common general goals is the first step; then establish a budget and basis for spending that will permit you to accomplish your agreed-upon goals. When both of you are headed in the same direction, it is easier to maintain a similar set of spending patterns. This may bring some surprising revelations about each person's values, but it is necessary to bring them out to reach common ground.

Finance and Success

You can extend your goal-setting focus to those you established about a year ago, when Jupiter entered your Second House. Now it's time to take stock and adjust your plan. Once Jupiter enters Sagittarius and your Third House on November 23, you'll shift to a new direction to create what you want in life—one designed to gain knowledge and perspective in order to help your dreams grow.

Rewarding Days

6, 7, 8, 11, 12, 16, 17, 21, 22, 25, 26, 27

Challenging Days

2, 3, 9, 10, 23, 24, 30

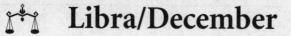

Libra/December

Planetary Hotspots

You've got mail! Or at least paperwork, books, and learning opportunities all around you. The planets are clustered in your Third House, harmonizing with your sign. If there's a project you want to launch to accomplish your goals, this is the time to do it. You've been working on empowering yourself through attitude, communication style, and understanding of the world since 1995. This could include finding ways to communicate with others, such as writing or teaching. Your latest project will fit into this context.

Wellness and Keeping Fit

You feel the way that chaos undermines you and your health this month. It throws you off-center and can even lead to injury, whether due to distraction or tripping over something.

Love and Life Connections

Ties with siblings and extended family are highlighted now, and this could create a houseful of relatives. You're busy preparing, from organizing to shopping to cleaning. There's a deep sense of fulfillment as you experience this, even though there are some rough spots to get through. You've got extra group responsibilities starting December 5, as Saturn's five-month period of backward motion begins. This could be related to a project or organization where you've taken on new duties.

Finance and Success

This is a good time to complete old projects, clean up paperwork, and manage details. An organized office makes for an organized mind. The more you can start your new projects with a clean slate, the more focused you'll be and the more profound will be your success. Get what you can completed by December 27, when the energy shifts to a focus in your home.

Rewarding Days

1, 6, 7, 13, 14, 15, 18, 19, 23, 24

Challenging Days

4, 5, 8, 9, 10, 20, 21, 22, 27, 28, 31

Libra Action Table

These dates reflect the best—but not the only—times for success and ease in these activities, according to your Sun sign.

	JAN	FEB	MAR	APR	MAY	JUN	JUL	AUG	SEPT	OCT	NOV	DEC
Move	3-22											27-31
Start a class	1-3											8-26
Join a club						29, 30	1-3, 25	11-27				
Ask for a raise							25, 26	12-31	1-5	1-22		
Look for work		9-28	25-31	1-30	1-4	3-27						
Get pro advice	6, 7, 10	2, 3, 6	2, 5-7	2, 3, 25	22, 23, 27	19, 20, 23	16, 17, 20	13, 16-18	9, 10, 13	6, 7, 10	3, 6-8	1, 4, 5, 27
Get a loan	8, 9	4, 5	3, 4, 31	1, 27, 28	24-26	21, 22	18, 19	14, 15	11, 12	18, 19	4, 5	2, 3, 29
See a doctor		9-28	25-31	1-30	1-4			27-31	1-30	1		
Start a diet		9-28	25-31	1-16					7, 8			
End relationship										6, 7		
Buy clothes		3-8	5-31	1-5								
Get a makeover									12-30	1-22		
New romance			25-31	1-5	3-28							
Vacation	10, 11	6, 7	5-7	2, 3, 29	19-31	2, 23-30	1-18, 20	16-18	13, 14	10, 11	6-8	4, 5, 31

SCORPIO

The Scorpion
October 23 to November 22

♏

Element:	Water
Quality:	Fixed
Polarity:	Yin/Feminine
Planetary Ruler:	Pluto (Mars)
Meditation:	I can surrender my feelings
Gemstone:	Topaz
Power Stones:	Obsidian, amber, citrine, garnet, pearl
Key Phrase:	I create
Glyph:	Scorpion's tail
Anatomy:	Reproductive system
Color:	Burgundy, black
Animal:	Reptiles, scorpions, birds of prey
Myths/Legends:	The Phoenix, Hades and Persephone, Shiva
House:	Eighth
Opposite Sign:	Taurus
Flower:	Chrysanthemum
Key Word:	Intensity

Your Ego's Strengths and Weaknesses

Although you tend to hide it, Scorpio, you're full of feelings, sensations, and impressions reflecting the life around you. This is related to your fixed water nature. You tend to bury your feelings because you feel it gives you an advantage in dealing with the outer world—it's a survival instinct. By not revealing yourself, you refrain from showing your hand before you're ready. It also allows you to maintain the status quo, which is the objective of all the fixed signs. Your job is to preserve things the way they are, unless change is proven to be good and timely. You test everything and reserve judgment until you are thoroughly convinced. This makes you resistant, even stubborn, in others' eyes, but it could also be called loyalty or perseverance if wisely applied. Taken too far, you can dig in your heels and obstruct change. You may appear unresponsive to others while you are working out what to do inside yourself. Even though Scorpio is the sign of transformation, you may be uneasy with change. Once you are convinced of something, however, you will follow it through to its end. You are actually good at coping with, even thriving on, the constant changes that affect the world. This is because of your watery side. It gives you the flexibility to move through and around obstacles without changing your own form, making you the master transformer that you are. It also makes you empathic: you pick up on the feelings of others, and you are sensitive to deep feelings and energies that can be developed into the psychic senses. Your greatest weakness is the potential to take what you feel and sense from others personally rather than viewing that knowledge objectively, which would immediately reveal that the energies are not directed at you.

Shining Your Love Light

You are a tender and passionate partner once you break down the barriers, Scorpio. However, it takes time for you to get to know someone well enough to open up. Once you do, it's because you've tested the relationship and broken down your own defenses, choosing to get close. For this reason, you're not one to switch loyalties easily. You prefer to stay with a partner long-term because it is too much work to start over again. You'll overlook many flaws and weaknesses in order to maintain what you've built.

Aries is a challenge for you, but one you enjoy because it brings out your joyful, competitive side. Taurus is your complement, supplying the constructive impulses you need to complete the transforming processes you trigger in yourself and others. Gemini cajoles you into lightening up, but you get to take your airy friend into the mysterious depths of consciousness. Fellow water sign Cancer creates a nest to make you feel right at home, and you'll feel secure together sharing your emotional world. Leo's enthusiasm may trigger cynicism in you at first, but you'll learn the value of optimism and faith in yourself. You are comforted by Virgo's steadiness and dedication, making it easy to trust and build a lasting bond. Libra may seem insincere, but has just as much interest in an intimate relationship as you do, and will work at making it succeed. Sagittarius will test your limits, asking you to cover ground faster than is your nature; you'll be able to help this sign deepen the experience of life. Capricorn shares your serious perspective, adding breadth of vision to your depth for a meaningful experience together. Together you'll explore the outer world and its trappings, perhaps building structures of great relevance to humanity. Aquarius can be the thorn in your side, until you realize that this sign is just trying to get you to let go of your attachments, which don't do you any good anyway. You'll respond especially well to Pisces, another water sign, with whom it is easy to drop your defenses. It gives you the chance to express your own feelings without fear.

Making Your Place in the World

One way to think of transformation is as a healing ability, and many Scorpios are involved in healing in some form, however remote from its obvious manifestations. This can be expressed through healing people in conventional ways, such as the medical arts, but it can also be directed toward healing the planet or helping animals. The mind can be the focus, through psychological counseling or psychiatry, or the body, through conventional or naturopathic medicine. You could also engage in psychic or spiritual healing. If you choose to heal the planet, you can become an ecologist, chemist, organic farmer, toxic clean-up specialist, geologist, or geophysicist. With your interest in the mysteries of life, you may be drawn to life as an investigator. Scientists investigate the phenomena of the world around them, while in law enforcement investigators solve crimes. Writing crime novels, or narratives about science's mysteries, could also suit your style.

Putting Your Best Foot Forward

To be at your best, Scorpio, you must express your feelings. There's no denying that you're a deeply feeling person, but you feel vulnerable when you express those feelings. You may feel that revealing who you are inside compromises your strength. You are aware of the forces that can upset the delicate balance of humanity in its environment, and of just how tenuous our grip on life is. For this reason, you carefully deliberate before taking action; you are constantly thinking about what could go wrong and what you would do if it did. Your reticence is the finest example of holding energy, which creates stability and builds internal power. The player who holds his cards close to his chest is less likely to lose. However, taken to extremes, such holding becomes withholding. Others will withdraw from you because they don't understand what's happening inside you. If you can't be expressive with your intimates, they can mistake your attitude for coldness. By remembering to be open with those you trust—and building trust with those who deserve it—you'll add to your strength because of the network you develop with other capable people.

Tools for Change

Although you feel proud that you can maintain an even keel in the most ravaging storm, you can improve your experience and achieve more fulfillment if you cultivate your ability to let the boat rock a little with people you trust. Communications training will assist you in developing the skill of putting words to your feelings and teach you ways to deal with conflict without overreacting. You can also benefit from studying psychology—not just to get insight into what makes other people tick, but to get in touch with your own feelings and motivations. It may be helpful for you to keep a journal as well, which can give you a reflection of your sometimes intense emotions and help you develop more objectivity, which is essential in resolving conflicts. Remembering to express your feelings a little at a time goes a long way too in heading off disagreements before they occur.

Your deep feeling nature can also be expressed creatively. The arts provide a variety of methods for you to keep the energy moving through and out of your body in a positive way. In particular, writing about life's more challenging situations, or using visual media to express yourself in a nonverbal way, will support your Scorpio side. You can also benefit through travel, especially to foreign locales. New ideas, opinions, and perspectives will also support your goals.

You have a marvelous gift for sensing the feelings of others around you—one that can come out as psychic ability but also can leave you feeling uptight. You can cleanse yourself of these extra energies in many ways. You can use physical exercise. It helps if the exercise is one that induces a meditative state—an individual activity rather than one that involves other people. Yoga, pilates, martial arts, hiking, swimming, and skiing, to name a few, fit into this category. Of course, meditation is another way to achieve peace and clear your energy field. Breath-oriented practices are especially cleansing. Since you are a change specialist, learning about how changes occur—and how they are induced through our actions, attitudes, and beliefs—will assist you in fulfilling your function as a Scorpio. The Chinese Book of Changes (I Ching) will help you tune in to this subtle world.

Affirmation for the Year

I am expanding in new directions without fear of change.

The Year Ahead for Scorpio

This is your year, Scorpio! A vision of the future is developing within you, and, if you dare to have faith in yourself, you can create it over the next twelve years. Your timing is right because Jupiter is in your sign and your solar First House of new beginnings, and you've had the Midas touch ever since October 25 last year, when it entered Scorpio. You're being flooded with ideas, and the possibilities seem endless! There are more options than you can fulfill, but you get three years to sort them out by testing and trying them. During this year, your vision of the future will be clearer than usual. You'll feel inspired and optimistic—so much so that you could be tempted to take greater risks than usual. Just remember that your rosy outlook must be tempered by patience and common sense, and you'll find the middle road between caution and gamble. On November 23, Jupiter enters Sagittarius and your solar Second House, when you will naturally shift to putting your plans into motion, your dreams into form. You will first need to collect your resources and lay the right foundation for your new endeavors. You will continue to work with this energy into 2007 as well.

Saturn will spend another year in Leo and your solar Tenth House. Your star has been rising, if you've been taking the initiative responsibly over the past ten years. If so, this is a pinnacle for you, a time of promotion, recognition, and leadership. No matter where you find yourself, you'll be working hard and may be given more authority relative to your role in the past.

Chiron is in Aquarius for the second year, your solar Fourth House. Last year, you began to get in touch with your deeper nature. You saw ways in which you could grow, ways in which you hold yourself back. These are tied to your past, especially your childhood and family experiences. You will benefit from uncovering troublesome events and rewriting the lessons learned from them. You can aid your growth process by seeking the support of others in this recovery process.

Uranus in Pisces supports your self-development from your solar Fifth House. Uranus supports the energies of Jupiter, feeding you inspiration. You'll be brimming with ideas! You'll find romances to be highly stimulating as well. If you have children, they will be sources of innovation and startling awareness. They will surprise you with their talent and creativity.

Neptune is in Aquarius for the eighth year, dissolving old ways of dealing with private matters. You've been experiencing a washing away of old attitudes toward home, family, emotions (and their expression), and privacy. Your home could be a source of spiritual peace, and you could enjoy spending time alone.

Pluto inhabits Sagittarius—your Second House. Your resources—such as time, money, energy, and skills—are going through a long-term transformation. You're changing the value you place on these things, and most likely using them differently. You may be considering changing the source for your income so that you can earn more, or reconfiguring your financial portfolio to ensure your future.

Starting March 14, the eclipses begin to trigger the Virgo-Pisces axis (your Eleventh and Fifth Houses). You'll be focusing on social interactions more over the coming eighteen months. This could include having or spending more time with children, a new romance, more social activities in groups, a new hobby—in short, more time doing the things you enjoy the most.

If you were born between October 26 and November 18, Saturn in Leo brings new structure to your Tenth House. If you've used Saturn well over the past twenty years, you're in the midst of a reward period that started last summer. It's a time of success, and others will recognize your wisdom and leadership ability. If you're not in a position to take on a role of responsibility and authority yourself, a new boss or supervisor could enter your life. This is not necessarily a bad thing, but you will be learning new ways to deal with authority figures in your life. Your career will assume a larger than usual role in your life relative to other areas this year. As with all Saturn transits, your steady efforts will be rewarded. If you are in a leadership role, you'll learn to deal with the way others' react to authority figures, because you have become one. You may also have increased contact with your parents, especially your father. Saturn-flavored events will occur on or near January 27, February 19, April 5 and 24, June 20, August 7, November 16, and December 5.

If you were born between October 30 and November 9,
Uranus in Pisces is rejuvenating your solar Fifth House activities:
sports, romance, children, hobbies, and anything you do for fun.
You may find unusual romantic partners highly alluring. Your children may surprise you with a new talent. You could become interested in a unique hobby or sport. The ordinary and humdrum will
not suit you now—you want to break out and assert your individuality. Because this is a harmonious contact to your Sun, it will generally bring pleasant stimulation to the pastimes that give you joy.
However, unexpected events could occur, such as accidents or losses
due to high-risk activities. If you engage in creative pursuits as a
hobby or profession, your style—even your work—could change
dramatically. If you are discontented with your life path, this is the
time to change it. Your direction in life is your most important creative product and source of fulfillment, and Uranus will give you
direction-finding inspiration this year. Peaks of Uranus energy
occur on March 1, June 5 and 19, September 5, November 19, and
December 2.

If you were born between November 8 and 13, Neptune in
Aquarius is challenging you to let go of old ways of dealing with
your home, family, and private matters. You may experience inva-
sions or compromises of your privacy, or a dissolving of unhealthy
patterns of dealing with those near and dear to you. This can be a
blessing if your childhood was troubling or you'd like to make a
clean break. Others may give you feedback that prompts you to look
more deeply inside yourself for the sources of your behavior. You
may have dreams that reveal truths about your childhood, or
through spiritual growth discover a better way of expressing your
feelings. Something at home could require a sacrifice—someone
could be ill and require extra care, or your home could require repairs
or remodeling. Your home could become more spiritual in some way
as a result of your efforts now. No matter the stimulus, you will probably withdraw somewhat from outer-world activities in order to use
Neptune's energies for the highest good. You will experience Neptunian energies the most around January 27, February 5, March 15,
May 10 and 22, August 10, October 29, and November 9.

If you were born between November 16 and 21, Pluto in Sagittarius is making a mild contact to your Sun from your solar Second House. You are making some significant changes where your resources are concerned this year—changes you have felt coming. You may find yourself making a transition to a new source of income. You could decide that time is more important than money and scale back on the effort you put into money-making initiatives. On a deeper level, a quiet transformation in your values is emerging. You're discovering what's really important to you, and these realizations will have an impact throughout your life before Pluto's contact is completed. While you are in the midst of this transitional time, you may decide to cut back on your spending or divert it in a new direction to accomplish different goals. This is also a good time to revamp your financial portfolio to keep up with your changing needs. This is not a good time to take a big risk or get involved in a speculative scheme, but a truly good opportunity to invest in something secure and trustworthy could go very well for you in the long run. The thread of these changes will develop around March 17 and 29, June 16, September 4 and 16, and December 18.

If you were born between October 22 and 25 or November 21 and 23, none of the major planets are contacting your Sun this year. This suggests that you will feel less compelled to follow a particular path or deal with specific issues this year. Your Sun is where you take up new challenges that require courage, so there'll be less need for that this year. You're also less likely to encounter completely unfamiliar situations or go through major changes. You may consider this a "time off," or at least a time when you can choose your activities with more freedom and fewer obstacles. If the major bodies contact your other personal planets—the Moon, Mercury, Venus, or Mars—your year will be more active. Otherwise, you can just put up your feet, take an extended vacation, or do some of those things that you never seem to get to but will make your life more meaningful.

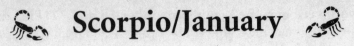

Scorpio/January

Planetary Hotspots

This is your Midas-touch year, with Jupiter in your sign, but there are a few obstacles in your path—a fact which began to emerge in September last year, as the grand cross in the heavens began to form. As this configuration is highlighted, you're looking ahead into what you can create in the next twelve years. Jupiter contacts Neptune on January 27, and you need to factor in what makes you feel most fulfilled—the ideals you hold for your life—because this is the time to take bold steps in that direction. It ties in with a path you started in 1997, and now it's time to renew your pledge to follow that path—or to follow another one that holds more promise.

Wellness and Keeping Fit

With the eclipse points moving through your health houses, it's important to stay focused on your health routines, or problems will be revealed in March and September. Don't let your eagerness to create the future distract you.

Love and Life Connections

Relationships with neighbors and siblings may be rocky this month as Venus proceeds backward through your Third House. Use this time to clear the air. Energies are harmonious for clearing the air and reaching agreements on January 17.

Finance and Success

Peaks of activity will occur on January 15, 18, 23, and 27 in a very busy time for you. This could be a time of great opportunity, however, so stay with the program and use your will to push you through the intense periods. You are equal to the task.

Rewarding Days

3, 4, 12, 13, 14, 17, 18, 19, 22, 23, 24, 27, 28, 31

Challenging Days

1, 2, 8, 9, 15, 16, 29, 30

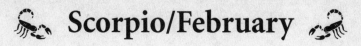

Scorpio/February

Planetary Hotspots

If you're thinking big, you'll find continuing opportunity this month as the planets start moving out of their grand-cross pattern on February 6. Yes, there are obstacles, but if you use them to refine your goals and affirm your determination, you'll gain from those challenges. February 5 brings the start of a new yearly cycle of Neptune, giving you the opportunity to put in motion new expressions of creativity and imagination, as well as spiritual growth.

Wellness and Keeping Fit

You'll enjoy your fitness activities more this month if you partner with someone. Whether it's handball, running with a buddy, or your usual weight routine, friendship makes the work easier and even more fulfilling.

Love and Life Connections

Difficulties with neighbors and siblings dissipate as Venus returns to direct travel on February 3. While the situations may require continued vigilance and care, you're out of the woods. You'll be busy, your focus shifting to your home and family and the projects you have there. Think about what you want to create in your home, because the yearly Neptune cycle, which puts the focus on your home and family, starts on February 5.

Finance and Success

This is a good time to start new educational and outreach programs, as well as projects involving communications, such as writing, classes, and lecture tours. Commerce picks up after February 3, with revenue increases to follow. Your hard work on the job may continue to be relatively unnoticed, but that won't last forever.

Rewarding Days

1, 8, 9, 10, 13, 14, 15, 18, 19, 20, 23, 24, 27, 28

Challenging Days

4, 5, 11, 12, 25, 26

Scorpio/March

Planetary Hotspots
Creative projects reach a blockage this month, bringing a useful delay as Mercury retrogrades through your Fifth House from March 2 to 25. However, with the Sun and Mars triggering Uranus, your innovativeness is stimulated at a deeper level during this pause. The pressure is on to become more productive as Jupiter begins its backward motion on March 4. Four months from now, you'll have made substantial progress if you exert concentrated effort. Your emphasis should be to test and weed out the opportunities that show little promise or are not what you really want.

Wellness and Keeping Fit
Injury is possible if you play sports, especially on March 1, 2, 11, and 25. If your creativity feels stifled, take a play break. This is more in the nature of a day out or an overnight trip than a long vacation.

Love and Life Connections
It's time to trim your sails, and this includes relationships. Those closest to you need more space now, and you need some yourself to focus on personal projects. Your attention is drawn to circumstances at home on March 15, tying in with events around January 27.

Finance and Success
You've been developing your financial strength since 1995, and the next stage of this process begins on March 29 when the subject planet, Pluto, changes direction. This can involve resetting your budget, making new income and expense projections, redistributing your portfolio, or taking out a loan. Events and information critical to this process also stimulate action on March 14 and give clues to what you'll experience in this area for the next five months.

Rewarding Days
8, 9, 13, 14, 18, 19, 22, 23, 24, 27, 28

Challenging Days
3, 4, 10, 11, 12, 25, 26, 31

Scorpio/April

Planetary Hotspots

Impediments to your forward progress are removed on April 5 as Saturn returns to forward motion. Career and business can now reach the peak you've been working toward for fifteen years. There are three more months before you can add your current project to the mix, but that's really only icing on the cake. You can see a period of intense activity coming up, the fruits of your labors, so now is the time to make preparations. This could mean anything from cleaning up old projects to hiring new employees to taking a vacation so you emerge refreshed and ready to roll.

Wellness and Keeping Fit

You need to have a bit of fun now—it's the best way to take care of your body and reduce stress—but in a healthy way. That means running on the beach, not partying all night. Treat yourself to a massage series, and get back into those team sports with your friends. Golf and other companion sports could bring business gold as well.

Love and Life Connections

Children or romantic partners can be the source of financial challenges, which arise around April 8 as Mercury, Mars, and Pluto cross paths. The situation can be resolved harmoniously around April 19 and 20 as Mercury and Venus harmonize with Saturn and Jupiter.

Finance and Success

This month is not a good time to take unusual financial risks, as your likelihood of loss is very high. This stems from the Mars-Pluto face-off on April 8, which is triggered the rest of the month by Mercury and Venus. If you must help someone out financially, do so only within the realm of what you can afford to give as a gift, rather than as a loan. Key dates are April 13, 17 to 20, and 30.

Rewarding Days

4, 5, 9, 10, 14, 15, 19, 20, 23, 24

Challenging Days

1, 6, 7, 8, 21, 22, 27, 28

Scorpio/May

Planetary Hotspots

You reach the halfway point in your "Midas touch" year on May 4, as the Sun opposes Jupiter, which is in your sign. You've had to work hard this year, but it's a turning point, and your past efforts have been coming together to make your future look bright indeed. Two more months, and you'll be settled in at a new plateau where your talents are being better used and rewarded. It's also the right time now to weed out opportunities that don't fit the direction you want to follow. If you're not sure yet, stick with it. You'll still have time to decide, although the more you can streamline your efforts toward fewer initiatives, the more focused, peaceful, and successful you'll be.

Wellness and Keeping Fit

Your health is good and your vitality is in balance as Venus transits your Sixth House of work and health. You'll be serene in spite of the activity bubbling around you, because you know that all is truly well at the deepest levels.

Love and Life Connections

You'll get feedback, especially from May 4 to 11, that will help you to redirect your forces more beneficially. You may not like all that you hear, but you'll recognize its value.

Finance and Success

Money flows around May 26 due to your consistent hard work. It's possible that someone puts in a good word that brings in a contract. May 7 is a big day as a grand trine comes to a peak that involves your sign. The sky's the limit now as circumstances converge to support your plans and dreams. This goes back to May 2000, when your current prosperity cycle began.

Rewarding Days

1, 2, 3, 6, 7, 8, 11, 12, 13, 16, 17, 20, 21, 29, 30

Challenging Days

4, 5, 18, 19, 24, 25, 26, 31

Scorpio/June

Planetary Hotspots

More tests of your new plans appear on the horizon at the beginning of June as the grand-cross planetary pattern reassembles on June 4. Some of these challenges come in the form of feedback from someone whose opinion matters very much to you. The added perspective proves invaluable, because it energizes you with new inspiration and drive to succeed. You'll need this energy to fuel your outreach effort, which is the weak point in your skills and plans.

Wellness and Keeping Fit

You can combine well-being and pleasure by doing your fitness activities with a friend. You'll benefit from the lightness this adds to your mood, and socializing brings optimism and diffuses your intensity.

Love and Life Connections

Partnership is highlighted this month as Venus travels through your Seventh House and triggers Jupiter. The peak date is June 6, but there'll be activity here through June 22. Some of what you experience will be part of a learning process, as you get to see your relationships from someone else's perspective in a gentle way.

Finance and Success

The outer world demands your time more urgently through June 22, and you'll feel forced to neglect home and family again. Touching base with them will help ease the situation as others fill in for you. Financial changes reach a climax on June 16 as Pluto reaches the culmination of its yearly cycle. This could bring in a large sum of money for past work, or it could require a large payment. Either way, it's something you've been working with since March 29.

Rewarding Days

3, 4, 8, 9, 12, 13, 16, 17, 18, 25, 26, 30

Challenging Days

1, 2, 14, 15, 21, 22, 27, 28, 29

Scorpio/July

Planetary Hotspots

With Jupiter returning to forward motion in your sign on July 4, you'll experience a corresponding change in direction of your own fortunes. You've been working hard toward the goals you identified late last year and early this one. If there's been little to show, it's mostly because it's still early in the process. However, now you get the first signs that something is happening. You can see which of your ideas are the most fertile and develop them accordingly. You may end up discarding some of the notions you had, but that means you can put more energy into the ones with real potential.

Wellness and Keeping Fit

The planets are giving you a break now, and your attitude is more relaxed. Take advantage of this time to engage in restorative activities. Go dancing instead of trying to outdo your best time on the stationary bike. Double your pleasure by taking a friend—or more—along. If you take a vacation this month, expect the unexpected. Mercury is retrograde from July 4 to 28 in your "vacation" house. This doesn't kill the fun if you can be flexible—it just makes you more aware that travel is truly an adventure where anything can happen. Remember, the vacations where something unusual happens give you the stories you tell for the rest of your life.

Love and Life Connections

Your relationships move ahead this month, too. As your path clears in other areas, your love life also opens up. Don't overreact to things said around July 30.

Finance and Success

Career issues take a back seat after July 22 for a change. Challenges arise at work around July 5 and 14, and they could become more strident next month if you ignore them.

Rewarding Days

1, 5, 6, 10, 11, 14, 15, 22, 23, 24, 27, 28, 29

Challenging Days

12, 13, 18, 19, 25, 26

Scorpio/August

Planetary Hotspots

Your creative side expresses itself in all its glory all month long if you give it free rein. This involves spending money to get the equipment and supplies you need to "play" with your ideas. What you discover can be the foundation of future successes, and at the very least you will fuel the fires of happiness. The peak date for this is August 29, but you'll feel the inspiration from the start of the month.

Wellness and Keeping Fit

Socializing is a good way to relax this month—a way to get away from the stresses of work and home life. Exercise with a friend; eat out with a group. Avoid unusual types and levels of physical activity, because you could suffer accident or injury, especially around August 13 and 29.

Love and Life Connections

The work vs. home dilemma hits again, and it requires focus to maintain your balance all month. You'll notice that the tension is greater during the last two weeks, as your ability to handle critical situations is tested. Key dates on the home front are August 14, 17, 21, and 27.

Finance and Success

Inspiration feeds enterprise feeds success—at least, they will if you follow through on the ideas you have now. On August 7 the start of the yearly Saturn cycle makes it time to launch new plans for career advancement based on your innovative concepts. You'll see what is going on in the workplace with exceptional clarity, and it will spur your plans. Others are likely to give you recognition for past accomplishments now and in the coming year.

Rewarding Days

1, 2, 3, 6, 7, 10, 11, 19, 20, 24, 25, 29, 30

Challenging Days

8, 9, 14, 15, 21, 22, 23

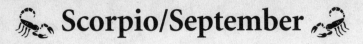 Scorpio/September

Planetary Hotspots

You get one more chance to check in with your ideals for personal fulfillment around September 24, when Jupiter and Neptune make the last of three contacts. You're much closer to your goals now than you were in January, but this is only the start of eight years of expansion, so it stands to reason that some aspects of your plans are yet incomplete. Now you can move ahead with less interference and fewer obstacles as Jupiter spends its last three months in your sign.

Wellness and Keeping Fit

You feel an urge to withdraw a little after September 6, and this dovetails with your need to replenish your chi forces as you get caught up on overdue work at home. Completed work brings inner peace, but don't forget to actually take some time for things you enjoy doing. A vacation, extra time improving your fitness, a massage, or acupuncture treatment are all ways you can pamper yourself.

Love and Life Connections

If those in your workplace are not receptive to your new ideas, the people in your network of friends and colleagues are more encouraging. Your creative process will be stimulated by the perspectives that others bring, so the more you can open yourself to the suggestions of those you trust, the more relevant and valuable your ideas become. This process is especially fruitful early in the month.

Finance and Success

The ideas you have come up with this year are new, and they must be time-tested to prove their worth. They will begin to prove their usefulness next year, when the planets are in a more harmonious configuration, and they'll produce results you can put in the bank.

Rewarding Days

2, 3, 4, 7, 8, 15, 16, 20, 21, 25, 26, 30

Challenging Days

4, 5, 11, 12, 17, 18, 19

Scorpio/October

Planetary Hotspots

This has been your year, with Jupiter in your sign, but now that period is drawing to a close. It's time to take stock and make the best use of the time until Jupiter enters Sagittarius on November 23. You can make considerable headway until then, but there's a flaw in the way you are perceiving things, or something that needs fixing before you have the firm foundation you want. Mercury's retrograde, starting on October 28, will reveal the weakness and lead you to the correct solution to the problem.

Wellness and Keeping Fit

You can avoid a stress-induced cold or flu by taking preventative measures early in the month. By doing a cleansing based on diet and herbs, you may be able to boost your immune system. Plenty of sleep is also essential now.

Love and Life Connections

This may be a good time to speak thoughtfully, as Mercury begins its retrograde through your sign. Since it is a Scorpio quality to withhold your point of view, perhaps until it is too late, letting others know in a low-key way what your needs are could be a good start in a new communicative direction for you.

Finance and Success

Mercury's retrograde gives you a last chance to rectify situations and relationships that have been damaged by conflict before the planets move on. This doesn't mean that you have to take a direct approach—in fact, it is probably better not to. Indirect kindness or support will be felt by those who misunderstood your intentions. Any actions you take during October and November will support this cause, but the best dates are October 10 and November 2, 14, and 22.

Rewarding Days

1, 4, 5, 12, 13, 14, 17, 18, 19, 22, 23, 24, 27, 28, 31

Challenging Days

2, 3, 8, 9, 15, 16, 29, 30

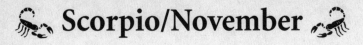 Scorpio/November

Planetary Hotspots

Jupiter moves from your sign into Sagittarius on November 23. The ideas you have now are seeds that must still be planted in order to grow. You now have the task of picking the right seeds—the ones you like the most—and cultivating them. There's no rush; you have the next eight years to bring them to fruition.

Wellness and Keeping Fit

Influences at home could undermine your health. Make sure that toxins and fumes are well managed. Key dates are November 1, 8, and 11.

Love and Life Connections

Relationships are going well now, but something needs clearing up. Mercury is retrograde until November 17, and it will bring to the surface underlying unspoken issues and questions. Being willing to talk about what's going on will deepen your bond and help you understand yourself better as well. A solid relationship may enter a new level of commitment, or you'll clarify an existing commitment to both members' satisfaction.

Finance and Success

Once Jupiter enters Sagittarius on November 23, you are empowered to expand your resources. You have been working on this process since 1995, and whatever your path is, you will receive a boost in pursuing it. New opportunities in alignment with your focus will arise, including some that would lead you astray—perhaps in a wonderful new direction. It's up to you which you follow; the danger is in overcommitting your current resources in order to reach for the greener pastures you see, creating later financial hardship. Everything looks rosy under Jupiter's glow, and it is if your response is tempered by common sense.

Rewarding Days

1, 13, 14, 18, 19, 20, 23, 24, 28, 29

Challenging Days

2, 3, 8, 9, 15, 16, 30

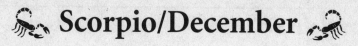 Scorpio/December

Planetary Hotspots

You're entering a wealth-building period, Scorpio, and what happens this month reveals a great deal about what is to come. To build wealth, you have to be willing to invest in something, and that's what you're looking at doing now. What you invest in should be tied to the long-range plans you launched last year. As Saturn turns on its heels to start its retrograde period on December 5, you'll feel an intensification of career/business responsibilities. This is the beginning of five months where you'll be working diligently toward your ultimate goals. It also ties in with the efforts you put forth last year, except that this year income is attached.

Wellness and Keeping Fit

You are energized and rejuvenated after the disciplines of the last two months—and a good thing, too. You're wanting to put your regimen on autopilot, which is fine as long as your habits are good.

Love and Life Connections

Once again, you need to put more focus on your career, putting your home and family life on the back burner. It's essential that you communicate your overall intentions and appreciation to your loved ones. That way, they'll be comfortable making sacrifices so that you can do your work, because it's for them too, and they'll feel included in the process.

Finance and Success

This month you feel an impulsive urge to get going with your recently hatched financial plans, but that may result in hasty decisions. If you're just finalizing decisions that you've been considering for a long time, you'll have the courage and optimism to execute them.

Rewarding Days

6, 7, 11, 12, 16, 17, 20, 21, 22, 25, 26

Challenging Days

2, 3, 8, 9, 10, 23, 24, 29, 30

Scorpio Action Table

These dates reflect the best—but not the only—times for success and ease in these activities, according to your Sun sign.

	JAN	FEB	MAR	APR	MAY	JUN	JUL	AUG	SEPT	OCT	NOV	DEC
Move	22-31	1-8										27-31
Start a class	3-22											
Join a club								25, 27-31	1-12, 20			
Ask for a raise								23-25	6-30	24-31	1-16, 18	
Look for work				16-30	1-19		1, 2	11-27				
Get pro advice	9, 12-14	5, 8-10	3, 4, 8	1, 4, 5	1-3, 24-26	21, 22, 25	19, 22-24	14, 15, 19	11, 12, 15	9, 12-14	4, 5, 9	2, 3, 6, 7
Get a loan	10, 11	6, 7	5-7	2, 3, 29	27, 28	23, 24	20, 21	16-18	13, 14	10, 11	6-8	4, 5, 31
See a doctor				16-30	1-19				12-30	1-26	18-30	1-7
Start a diet				16-30	1-4					7, 8		
End relationship											4, 5	
Buy clothes		9-28	25-31	1-30	1, 2							
Get a makeover										2-26	18-30	1-7
New romance		9-28	25-31	1-30	2, 29-31	1-23						
Vacation	12-14	8-10	8, 9	4, 5	1-3, 29	3-28	19-31	1-12	15, 16	12-14	9, 10	6, 7

SAGITTARIUS

The Archer
November 22 to December 22

♐

Element:	Fire
Quality:	Mutable
Polarity:	Yang/Masculine
Planetary Ruler:	Jupiter
Meditation:	I can take time to explore my soul
Gemstone:	Turquoise
Power Stones:	Lapis lazuli, azurite, sodalite
Key Phrase:	I understand
Glyph:	Archer's arrow
Anatomy:	Hips, thighs, sciatic nerve
Color:	Royal blue, purple
Animal:	Fleet-footed animals
Myths/Legends:	Athena, Chiron
House:	Ninth
Opposite Sign:	Gemini
Flower:	Narcissus
Key Word:	Optimism

Your Ego's Strengths and Weaknesses

As the mutable fire sign, you are a true will o' the wisp, Sagittarius! Your fast pace and quick mind take you from one experience to another like an arrow racing to its mark. Your mutability gives you a flexibility that becomes volatile when it is combined with your fire element. Your mind moves toward wholeness, seeking to see the big picture. Whether you are exploring the universals of human consciousness through psychology or exploring the unifying drives of humanity by visiting foreign cultures, you are weaving a tapestry of understanding out of the threads that you spin from each experience. This mutability keeps you on the move, but that can prevent you from staying around long enough to build a foundation of worldly success—and although you tend to define success in non-material ways, accomplishment has its benefits.

Because you are a fire sign, you have the spark of life and insurmountable inspiration that make you a winner. Your world is lively, and your energies spread in many different directions because you are so excited by the potential you see. You can motivate others toward a goal because you can see the end product so clearly. You have high ideals and ambitions—a reflection of the fact that fire moves upward. This gives you a natural buoyancy, so no obstacle or problem keeps you down for long. On a deeper level, you crave transcendence. You experience deep understanding as uplifting and integrating, as if it lifts you above the clouds. However, your love of movement and thirst for new knowledge may lead you to burn through situations and circumstances so fast that others can't keep up. You may need to remind yourself to exercise sensitivity when dealing with others' feelings, and employ the pragmatism necessary to fulfill your basic responsibilities.

Shining Your Love Light

You have a roving eye, Sagittarius. This doesn't mean that you're less faithful as a partner, but it does mean that your partner has to be ready and able to keep up with a constant stream of adventures. The best partner makes your life an adventure of discovery both inside and outside the relationship. You love to travel and explore new realms of awareness together, whether it is through extreme sports or meditation.

Fellow fire-sign Aries shares your joy in life's challenges and will even give you a run for your money. Taurus can bring you down to earth and remind you that managing your finances carefully gives you more freedom, but you can't expect this sign to take care of all the practical matters. Gemini loves to explore as much as you do—and Gemini's preference for culture and civilization could even tame the wild beast within you. Home-loving Cancer may be a reluctant adventurer, but you both appreciate the qualities of human nature and enjoy observing other people in their daily lives. Leo's fire makes a faithful and ardent lover, whose joy for life fits well with your lively spirit and sense of humor. Virgo has a sense of duty and responsibility that you could grow tired of, but this sign wants to create a better world just as much as you do. You'll get along famously with Libra, whose airy charm and grace offset your brash honesty. Scorpio's intensity can feed your passion for life, while you lighten the Scorpion's seriousness. A fellow Sagittarius is a great companion as you travel through life, as long as you develop a give-and-take when deciding whose road to follow. Capricorn can build upon your ideas and ideals, while you get the satisfaction of seeing your concepts come into concrete form. Aquarius's wry humor and sense of irony suits your humorous take on life: you'll be able to laugh your way from one experience to the next. Pisces can see into you, even through you, to your soul. You'll appreciate each other's spiritual side, the desire to experience oneness with all existence.

Making Your Place in the World

Sagittarius, your desire to learn and to spread knowledge can be applied in many disciplines. If you are a kinetically oriented Sagittarius, you will revel in the world of sports, physical fitness, or health and nutrition. You prefer helping people become healthier (or maintain their health) in such fields as personal training, sports training, or physical or sports therapy. You may also enjoy working with or treating horses in one of the many ways they are employed in human endeavors. If you are the more intellectually oriented type, you can become the quintessential professor, steeping yourself in your academic studies, devising new theories, and teaching rooms full of impressionable young students. You could also become a travel writer, a photographer, or a reporter on foreign affairs.

Given your facility with languages, you can take up a career that requires bilingual capabilities, from roles in international business to translation to providing tour services for vacationers from far-away places.

Putting Your Best Foot Forward

The grass is always greener on the other side of the fence for you, Sagittarius—or at least that's a potential expression of your nature. You have a great gift for developing a vision of the big picture. You first explore the phenomena of the world around you, looking deep within each for unifying principles. You study things that are different, foreign, and unique to ensure that the outliers are included in your analysis. Then you create a hypothesis of what each factor has in common with the others and test it. This is how wisdom is created. In order to do this, you have to roam from place to place and experience to experience. However, this prevents you from laying a foundation, from cultivating the long-term ties that result in rewards, unless you vary your pattern and develop anchors in your life. You may move on before others get to know you, before you move into the complete stages of a cycle, where the benefits accrue, in your zest to cover new territory. While you value process over product, a certain amount of product will make creating the process easier and more fun. Develop anchors in your relationships. Of course, relationships require that you become consistent with those you love. This should not be a chore, because it is a two-way street.

Tools for Change

You're the best when it comes to seeing clear to the heart of a situation and finding its core principle and underlying truth. Your constant movement permits you to observe life in all sorts of circumstances, but you can benefit from returning to your center. Your home is a form of your center—a nest that, even if you move it frequently, can be an anchor in your life. Decorating your home and filling it with the things you enjoy, whether books, travel brochures, or sports equipment, will make it more attractive to you, and you will want to spend valuable restorative time there. Relationships can also be a hub around which you revolve, and building ones that last provides you with a vital emotional, mental, and spiritual resource. To maintain those relationships, you should try to resolve disagreements rather than avoid them or burn your bridges altogether. Conflict resolution training could be helpful, not just in your personal ties but also as a business skill. Staying grounded is another challenge for you, with your drive toward moving onward and upward. You're always looking for the next challenge! However, taking care of pragmatics such as finances, and getting your home organized, are structures that provide a springboard for your next adventure. Getting a little training in organizational skills may be helpful and inspiring.

With your drive toward transcendence, you are already attuned to the spiritual realms. You can use meditation and spiritual practice to anchor you as well. Specifically, bringing your energy into your lower chakra centers (the heart and below) will keep your feet on the Earth and also help you avoid accidents. It will also help you stay in the moment instead of working ahead of yourself as you so naturally do. Keeping a pet will warm your heart and your hearth, making your home a more welcoming place. A dog is a good travel companion, while a cat mimics your independence. Establishing a regular schedule is another way to create more consistency in your world. Don't stick with it slavishly, or you'll feel confined; instead, develop a balance between structured routine and free-choice time so you manage your adult responsibilities but don't feel burdened by them.

Affirmation for the Year

I enjoy taking time to rest and restore myself.

The Year Ahead for Sagittarius

This year will bring out your spiritual side, Sagittarius, and lay the groundwork for making some overdue changes. Jupiter in Scorpio and your solar Twelfth House draws you inside yourself more than usual, but it is not a place unfamiliar to you. What most people don't realize is that Sagittarius is not just a go get 'em fire sign. You also thrill to the inner landscape that reveals the mysteries of life and leads to the transcendence you crave. Your spiritual path and practices may become more significant to you while Jupiter is in this house, and even if spirituality is not your style, you'll have other pastimes that encourage you to contemplate life. You will soon discover how vast the inner landscape can be, especially if you are confined in any way. If you are ill or otherwise confined, inner journeys will calm you and release the expansive feelings that give you joy.

Once Jupiter enters your home sign, Sagittarius, on November 23, you'll feel like someone's spiked your drink. The giddy feeling of Jupiter's creative urge results in a burst of new ideas and inspirations. It's a seed-planting time, so sow as many as you like, keeping in mind that you will have to weed some of them out over the following two years. This starts a twelve-year cycle of enterprise, education, and expansion.

Saturn gives you support for a second year as it makes its way through the latter half of Leo and your solar Ninth House. The systems and structures of the world support your efforts at climbing the ladder of knowledge and success. Now is the time to put final touches on the preparatory cycle you've been in for the last six years, because you'll be reaching an apex starting in September 2007.

Chiron shares supportive insights with you, becoming a true messenger of the greater gods as it goes more deeply into Aquarius and your Third House. You're more sensitive to the needs of others now. You may feel inspired to take a more healing approach in your communications, or even get some training in healing techniques. Your long-term devotion to raising group consciousness will be well-served by this five-year transit.

Uranus continues its path through Pisces and your solar Fourth House, disrupting those forms that are no longer relevant so you can remove them. The focus will be on your family and private life, and your past—particularly your childhood. You will benefit greatly by paying attention to this area of your life, because it holds the key to a great awakening process for you.

Neptune is in Aquarius and your solar Third House, where it has been since 1998. You've been experiencing a long-term process of subtle change, where old ways of thinking are simply dissolving away. Old hurts, old wounds are nearly forgotten, and it is easier now to forgive—especially yourself. Continue to let go as you raise your consciousness to greater understanding.

Pluto once again inhabits your home sign and First House, so you get yet another year to wring more transformation out of your life. By now this may seem ho-hum, but remember that this is your golden opportunity to make deep changes to last the rest of your life. Your life is fluid now in a way that others envy.

The eclipses begin to support the process of change by making a challenging contact to your Sun from your Fourth- and Tenth-House axis and the signs of Pisces and Virgo. Once this process begins on March 14, you'll experience climactic events about every six months that will help you turn the corner on renovations in home and career.

If you were born between November 26 and December 17, Saturn in Leo is contacting your Sun from your solar Ninth House this year. You've been preparing for six years for a new high point in your life, and you have twenty-one months left before that door opens for you. You may be impatient to bring it on sooner, but patience is what got you this far, and it will carry you the rest of the way—for steady, patient, and consistent application of effort is what creates Saturn success. Saturn's influence will be robust and rock-steady, so stick with your task. Because of Saturn's harmony to your Sun, you are already beginning to garner some success, but the effects will build as you continue to work toward your biggest goals. You may find yourself fitting in a few more classes to build skills or focusing more on outreach, travel, or publishing as a springboard for your rise. If you have not used these energies well in recent years, it's not too late to start. The benefits will not be as great because they have not been built over a long time, but you will still progress. Saturn will give clues to how well you're progressing on or near January 27, February 19, April 5 and 24, June 20, August 7, November 16, and December 5.

If you were born between November 29 and December 7, Uranus in Pisces will awaken you to new potentials as it connects with your Sun from your solar Fourth House. Your family and home life may be unsettled or even chaotic now. Whatever its source, it's causing you to focus more attention there, to feel more tension. You may want to break free, but you'll benefit if you use the stimulus as a source of insight into your past—especially your childhood. You may find that challenges now are directly related to experiences you had before you were seven. It may help to bounce your insights off someone else, such as a friend or counselor. The more willing you are to face the roots of your current issues, the more benefit you will get from this transit. Someone else could be at the core of the increased tension at home. If so, it may be necessary to set boundaries or take even more dramatic measures to make your home safe, secure, and peaceful. If you are sensitive to your environment, you don't have to wait until events take over your life. Action taken early in the cycle, which begins March 1, can head off greater difficulties later. Other dates of peak Uranus energy are June 5 and 19, September 5, November 19, and December 2.

If you were born between December 7 and 12, Neptune in Aquarius and your Third House is making a supportive connection to your Sun. You've been going through a long, gentle cleansing of the way you perceive the world. This could be due to an educational process you've signed up for, from formal courses to therapy to spiritual training. The communicative impact of visuals, from photographs to sketches, could be on your mind, and you may be using or studying symbols. Stories are more compelling than facts now, as is poetry over prose. If you are a writer, your style may contain more visual images and symbols, or it could be more spiritually oriented in some way. Most important, however, is a shift in the way you think about the world. You may be more acutely aware of the gray areas of an issue, where once before you saw things in terms of black and white. You may also feel confused as you go through these changes, because the old ways of processing information are breaking down as well. As old thoughts dissolve away, it takes time for new ones to take their place. Although subtle, Neptune's energies will be strongest on January 27, February 5, March 15, May 10 and 22, August 10, October 29, and November 9.

If you were born between December 15 and 20, Pluto in Sagittarius puts transformation front and center in your life from its position in conjunction with your Sun. You've felt this coming for at least a couple of years, and now the time is ripe for the impending changes to occur. Any stagnant situations that carry a lot of tension are out of balance and will be rectified this year. The focus will be on self-empowerment—on doing what's right for you. It's time for you to figure out where you've been giving your energy and power away to others, and to take it back so you can use it for your own fulfillment. It's not enough to live through others anymore. Although you typically avoid issues, it's time to meet them head-on. The changes you make won't be complete in a day, or even a year, so don't sell yourself short by going for too little. Dare to go for your wildest dreams and work from there. Attitude is everything, so keep your mood upbeat. You'll be moving into psychologically unfamiliar territory, and that can feel uncomfortable and at times distressing as you move into new mental and emotional realms. The thread of these changes will develop around March 17 and 29, June 16, September 4 and 16, and December 18.

If you were born between November 22 and 25 or December 21 and 22, no major planet is contacting your Sun this year. This may be a welcome respite from the high level of planetary connections you've been dealing with over the past few years—a breather. You can review and integrate what you've learned, putting the finishing touches on the changes that may still be incomplete. If other personal planets—the Moon, Mercury, Venus, Mars—are being triggered by the slow movers, this will still be an active year. Even so, you will find your circumstances less challenging, with fewer obstacles, than if the Sun were involved. This year promises to be a bit more relaxed.

🏹 Sagittarius/January 🏹

Planetary Hotspots

A fixed grand cross continues an alignment that has existed since October of last year, bogging you down in details and old situations that you would like to leave behind. There are situations that require completion, and if you want a clean slate next year when your new Jupiter cycle begins, you need to prepare now by taking care of these leftovers. You may find yourself vulnerable to stress, as you have less control than usual over what happens each day. Peaks of activity occur on January 15, 18, 23, and 27.

Wellness and Keeping Fit

Your health may suffer from the lack of control you have over the events in your life now, as this creates stress to which your body may react. Your best bet is to get away periodically from the fray, which you can do by going for a run or walk, taking a quick drive, or meditating. Giving yourself some space is the most effective way to reduce stress quickly.

Love and Life Connections

If you've made mistakes in managing your resources, let others know and make amends. If others' actions cost you money, you can forgive, but don't let them off the hook. Relationship renegotiations this month will involve different plans for managing your finances as well as other resources.

Finance and Success

There may be a hiatus in your financial flow this month as Venus backs up through your Second House. This could create disagreements with others, whether they are creditors who receive delayed payments or loved ones who receive less of your time. This is fine, as long as the belt-tightening is fairly distributed and you take responsibility for your role.

Rewarding Days

1, 2, 5, 6, 7, 15, 16, 20, 21, 25, 26, 29, 30

Challenging Days

3, 4, 10, 11, 17, 18, 19, 31

🏹 Sagittarius/February 🏹

Planetary Hotspots

The planets give you a break after February 6, and you can get back your life. You'll gain insights into issues that persisted in January as a result of new information received through February 5. You have a dream project in mind as the month opens—something involving writing, teaching, or communicating—that is part of a years-long development process in this area. This ties in with the annual Neptune cycle that begins on February 5.

Wellness and Keeping Fit

Accidents, inflammations, and viruses are more likely to be a part of your life through February 16, and even surgery is not out of the question. The key is to take care of yourself.

Love and Life Connections

Starting February 17, relationships demand more attention as Mars enters your Seventh House. You may notice more angry responses from others; if so, keep your cool without letting anyone consistently overrun your turf. Although it's not necessarily the case, these interactions could be reflecting a need for you to be less intense.

Finance and Success

Your financial fortunes begin to move forward again with Venus, as it returns to direct motion on February 3. It may take until early March to get back to normal, so remain disciplined. You'll gain even more benefits if you can make this new level of self-control a habit. Career issues continue to pull you away from the other things you find satisfying, but it is for a good cause. If your career is already fulfilling, this is a time of immense happiness for you because of the pinnacle you've reached. If you chafe under the load, you need to find ways to enjoy your profession more or move to a position that makes it easier.

Rewarding Days

2, 3, 11, 12, 16, 17, 21, 22, 25, 26

Challenging Days

1, 6, 7, 13, 14, 15, 27, 28

Sagittarius/March

Planetary Hotspots

This month is a turning point this year, when your decisions and responses to your experiences determine in large part what the rest of the year will bring. The Sun and Mars stimulate change in your home environment when they contact Uranus on March 1 and 11. This is reiterated by Mercury, which travels backward through your Fourth House from March 2 to 25. This may bring to the surface necessary repairs involving water and gas, which can be avoided if preventive measures are taken. Key dates are March 1, 2, 11, and 12. The lunar eclipse on March 14 also has a powerful impact, emphasizing change in your home and professional life over the next six months.

Wellness and Keeping Fit

You need regular time away from people this year as Jupiter moves through your Twelfth House. This will help you cleanse yourself of energies to which you are vulnerable now. You become more aware of this need and find a more effective way to satisfy it around March 4.

Love and Life Connections

You want more freedom in your family life, and your inspiration regarding what to do about it will be running high on March 1 as Uranus begins its yearly cycle. You can make the most of this by focusing on positive innovation rather than denying the need and holding on to the past. Changes at home affect your work life and vice-versa on March 8, 14 and 29.

Finance and Success

Your finances are in balance, and work is no longer overwhelming you, which is good since so much of your focus is directed homeward. Actions you take at work in response to events around March 29 will have far-reaching effects.

Rewarding Days

1, 2, 10, 11, 12, 15, 16, 17, 20, 21, 25, 26, 29, 30

Challenging Days

5, 6, 7, 13, 14, 27, 28

Sagittarius/April

Planetary Hotspots

You've been working hard to acquire new skills and understanding to apply in your chosen life path, and as of April 5, when Saturn returns to direct motion, something falls into place and you reach a new plateau. This could apply to college, independent studies, or personal growth. If traveling, your adaptations to the foreign culture take a quantum leap now, too. Although there are still three months to go to complete your current process, you've definitely turned the corner.

Wellness and Keeping Fit

If your activities are curtailed due to your situation or that of a loved one, look for ways to express yourself within the confines you are faced with. You are inclined to want to retreat now, and if you can get away, do so. If you can't, take "mini-retreats" inside your head. This can be accomplished through meditation, or you can simply get in touch with that center inside. Take your exercise away from people—in the woods or countryside.

Love and Life Connections

With Uranus being triggered in your Fourth House, your home and relationship life is a major focus now as disruptions interrupt your planned activities. It's best to give them your full attention, because they need solving. If you carry on as if nothing is happening, the situation will grow into a problem. If it's too new to know what to do, just pay attention to what's going on until your purpose becomes clear. Key dates are April 8, 13, 17 to 20, and 30.

Finance and Success

The planets support putting work and career issues on the back burner so you can deal with personal matters. Wait until next month to expect people who owe you money to pay you back.

Rewarding Days

6, 7, 8, 11, 12, 13, 16, 17, 18, 21, 22, 25, 26

Challenging Days

2, 3, 9, 10, 23, 24, 29, 30

Sagittarius/May

Planetary Hotspots

You're not in the direct line of planetary fire now, so that gives you a chance to get caught up. The fixed grand cross pattern of January is repeated this month, with these planets highlighted through May 22. This focuses in your houses of integration and completion, so you'll be managing paperwork and clearing many lingering projects and predicaments from your life. This integration process is important, because through it you'll feel whole and more energetic. It will clear the way for new enterprises that you already have in your head.

Wellness and Keeping Fit

Health matters could rise to the surface now, and it's a good time to get a check-up, as tests will show what's really going on. Do not ignore symptoms now: they could signal deep-seated imbalances that if treated early will dissolve without harm. Key dates are May 4 to 15 and 22, with special emphasis on May 15. Injury during sporting activities is possible around May 26.

Love and Life Connections

Disagreement over the course of a romance could arise on May 26, as Venus and Mars clash. Children could also make a request that would make life difficult. In either scenario, compromise can provide a solution.

Finance and Success

Around May 26, someone in your personal life will reveal a way to spend your money, but that doesn't mean that you have to acquiesce. There are other ways to solve the problem than the one first proposed. If you follow your intuition, you'll find an easy solution based on something you learned early in the month. If the expenditure is based on true need, explore the options yourself rather than relying on the other person to do it.

Rewarding Days

4, 5, 9, 10, 14, 15, 18, 19, 22, 23, 31

Challenging Days

6, 7, 8, 20, 21, 27, 28

Sagittarius/June

Planetary Hotspots

Pluto reaching the halfway point in its yearly cycle means that you reach a peak in the process of reinventing yourself that started last December. As you approach this crescendo on June 16, you'll feel yourself go into hurry-up mode so that you can reach your current benchmark. You'll be unfolding a new part of your nature after that point through which you will take back control of areas you've given over to others in the past. This could come as a result of a dramatic interaction with someone you are close to.

Wellness and Keeping Fit

Stress can be relieved this month by seeking the support of those whose healing abilities you trust. It's a good time to treat yourself to a weekly massage or acupuncture treatment. Make sure you get away periodically, and don't neglect your need for sleep.

Love and Life Connections

As Uranus's retrograde period begins on June 19, your attention is drawn homeward. You feel like you want to break free from a restriction there, but there are others to consider. If you can resist the urge to react on June 19, you'll have the chance over the next five months to create your way out of the stricture and make a smoother transition to what you want.

Finance and Success

Work becomes all-consuming as the fixed planets contact each other in unison once more, bringing flashbacks of what you experienced last fall and in January, February, and May. The key now is completion, as conditions are now set for some long-term situations to give way and morph into something more workable. The intensity begins on June 4 and continues through June 22.

Rewarding Days

1, 2, 5, 6, 7, 10, 11, 14, 15, 19, 20, 27, 28, 29

Challenging Days

3, 4, 16, 17, 18, 23, 24, 30

Sagittarius/July

Planetary Hotspots

You feel less trapped now by your circumstances, and you can see the light at the end of the tunnel as Jupiter begins to move forward in your Twelfth House on July 4. This has been a big restorative period for you, which began last October 25. While there are still five months to go before you emerge from your cocoon, you can feel yourself breaking free. Don't rush things, because the cycle isn't ripe yet. However, you can continue to dream and plan.

Wellness and Keeping Fit

Health matters also take a turn for the better now with Jupiter's change in direction. You have more energy and optimism—you'll be back to your old self. This is a good month for a vacation, so plan ahead and let others know ahead of time so they can manage without you. It's best to go before July 22.

Love and Life Connections

Relationship hiccups occur around July 5 and 14 that presage what could occur next month if you don't give enough attention to them now. In the first instance, the circumstances will be about career; on the second date, your relationships—both work and personal—will be involved.

Finance and Success

Mercury's retrograde, which starts on July 4, falls in your house of other's money. This means that monies you ordinarily get from others may not come through in the usual timing, or that others may demand more from you than usual. This could come from those to whom you owe debts or from your partner. However, this retrograde is not going to create hardship—just a little curtailment of your plans.

Rewarding Days

2, 3, 4, 7, 8, 9, 12, 13, 16, 17, 25, 26, 30, 31

Challenging Days

1, 14, 15, 20, 21, 27, 28, 29

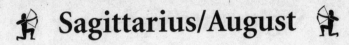 Sagittarius/August

Planetary Hotspots

Energy floods your world and your system as Mars interacts with Uranus on August 13 and Pluto on August 29. This highlights your personal-growth issues as they are expressed through career and home life. You're called on to respond to more than the usual number of critical situations around these dates, and you'll feel as though the inner lessons you've been working on are being tested. You'll have the opportunity to head off the situation at the end of month with actions taken around August 17.

Wellness and Keeping Fit

You're more accident-prone than usual this month, especially around August 13 and 29. On August 13, such an event would be unexpected and occur in your home or because of something at home; on August 29, it would be because of something you've known about but haven't been able to take care of yet. You can reduce this potential by doing one thing at a time and staying focused on that thing around those dates.

Love and Life Connections

This is an ideal time for a vacation, even though you can think of plenty of reasons to stay home. Take others with you—you'll have more fun—and go to places where there are people rather than rural or solitary spots. You may especially enjoy touring spots where there are remnants of ancient civilizations.

Finance and Success

Saturn's new cycle starts on August 7, making that date a good time to set goals for the coming year. These should be related to preparations and projects to help you reach the career pinnacle you'll get to in another year's time. You will even be able to enjoy some of this success this year, if you're open to the possibilities.

Rewarding Days

4, 5, 8, 9, 12, 13, 21, 22, 23, 26, 27, 28, 31

Challenging Days

10, 11, 16, 17, 18, 24, 25

🏹 Sagittarius/September 🏹

Planetary Hotspots

Critical events early in the month draw your attention to the balance of career and home. As Pluto returns to forward motion on September 4, another stage in your personal empowerment process is near completion. It helps you maintain your perspective and self-assurance when dealing with the home/work situation, which arises from September 5 to 7. Events now tie in with those in March, June, and August 13 and 29. What happens now clarifies your course of action over the next three months.

Wellness and Keeping Fit

Team sports and social exercise, such as dance, hold more appeal this month, and so do fitness activities you can engage in with a companion. They take you out of the house or workplace and allow you to decompress.

Love and Life Connections

People in career or business give you feedback that helps you adjust your approach to home and family, especially early in the month. These events coincide with the lunar eclipse on September 7 and give you insights that spur you into action with the solar eclipse on September 22. You have already seen the potential benefits as well as the necessity of change, and now you realize with even greater conviction that you were correct.

Finance and Success

Your quiet pursuit of personal and spiritual development has led you to spend more time in solitude over the past few months, and you're beginning to see the fertile ground you're creating for next year's expansion. Continue to work with your unseen reality, because you will be able to see with increasing clarity what your next path to fulfillment will be over the course of the month.

Rewarding Days

1, 5, 6, 9, 10, 11, 17, 18, 19, 22, 23, 24, 27, 28, 29

Challenging Days

7, 8, 13, 14, 20, 21

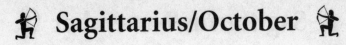

Sagittarius/October

Planetary Hotspots

The planets ease up early in the month, and opportunities for pleasurable social contact come your way. You'll get more than enjoyment though, especially if you're involved in commerce or selling; you'll get business from your contacts too. The importance of hidden factors becomes evident by the end of the month, when Mercury begins its three-week retrograde period in your Twelfth House. See if you can sort out what's really going on October 5, 15, 22, and 24. There will be a knotted-up thread of understanding that will need unraveling in November.

Wellness and Keeping Fit

You've been through a lot in the last few months, and it's time to retreat. Go on a short road trip, or at least get away for a day. If you can take a spiritual retreat or focus on inner work, so much the better.

Love and Life Connections

Family are more conciliatory now, especially early in the month, so leap on the opportunity to heal wounds if it presents itself. There'll be a process here that plays out over October and November, with key dates of October 10 and November 1, 8, 14, and 22. By seeing it as something that takes more than one encounter to heal, and by allowing the other parties to see the truth for themselves, you are responding in the best possible way.

Finance and Success

Writing, communicating, and publishing have played a major role in your career path since the year started, and you may have felt trapped in the role. The planets will shift in two months to a more generally harmonious pattern for you, and you'll feel released and relieved. You don't have to finish everything now, but you will feel an urge to complete whatever falls in rhythm with this year's cycle.

Rewarding Days

2, 3, 6, 7, 15, 16, 20, 21, 25, 26, 29, 30

Challenging Days

4, 5, 10, 12, 17, 18, 19, 31

⚹ Sagittarius/November ⚹

Planetary Hotspots

As the month starts, you feel the "hush" before Jupiter starts rejuvenating your life. You may even experience flashes of insight that show you the possible futures that can be fulfilled over the next twelve years. When Jupiter enters Sagittarius on November 23, you'll be thrust into that energy field and flooded with Jovian optimism. This is the time to see, dream, and plan your future. Jupiter gives you the vision, but doesn't make it work for you—Saturn does that. How you apply yourself in the coming years will determine how deeply you'll be fulfilled.

Wellness and Keeping Fit

To activate the new cycle, you have to drain and clear and cleanse your life. Cleansing the body is part of that process. Although you can work with this energy all month, the best time is through November 17, while Mercury is still retrograde.

Love and Life Connections

You have had plenty of lessons since 1995 about the give and take of relationships with Pluto in Sagittarius. You've learned to be sensitive to the power you hold and how to stop giving it away unconsciously. When Jupiter enters your sign on November 23, it will magnify this process and all that you have learned through it. It will expand your power, and you will be challenged by others if you misuse it. If there is a great task that you wish to undertake, don't be afraid to go for it. You've been preparing for this for many years.

Finance and Success

If there is anything you can do to tie up loose ends, this is the time to do it. You want your desk cleared by November 23, so that you can begin your new cycle of enterprise with a clean slate. It's worth setting aside other projects to get this done.

Rewarding Days

2, 3, 11, 12, 16, 17, 21, 22, 25, 26, 27, 30

Challenging Days

1, 6, 7, 8, 13, 14, 15, 28, 29

🏹 Sagittarius/December 🏹

Planetary Hotspots

You've got more energy than you know what to do with as the energy planets come together in your sign. You're full of inspiration and eagerness to act, with opportunities to match ideas. Others are as excited as you are about your vision of things to come, and they are willing to lend their support. Your new cycle of personal empowerment starts on December 18, when the Sun conjoins Pluto. This is the time to firm up your plans for the coming year. One of those plans should be to develop the long-range goals you have for the new twelve-year cycle that started November 23.

Wellness and Keeping Fit

Injuries and accidents are possible this month, especially on December 3, 11, 18, and 21. This is due to your eagerness to be ahead of yourself. If you can pace yourself and stay in your center, you will prevent this from occurring.

Love and Life Connections

You can trim the sails of your impatience by using your great sense of humor to laugh at circumstances, as well as yourself. Otherwise, you could end up taking it out on others and dampening their enthusiasm for your plans. In your leadership role, it is up to you to set the tone.

Finance and Success

There are some past plans on which you've been following through that seem as though they will hold you back in fulfilling the new ideas you've dreamed up. What you're feeling is Saturn's retrograde, which starts on December 5. For five months, you need to invest extra time in this seemingly less productive project. In the long run, it will amplify your new plans and pay off in its own right, even though now, it feels like an obstacle.

Rewarding Days

1, 8, 9, 10, 13, 14, 15, 18, 19, 23, 24, 27, 28, 29

Challenging Days

4, 5, 11, 12, 25, 26

Sagittarius Action Table

These dates reflect the best—but not the only—times for success and ease in these activities, according to your Sun sign.

	JAN	FEB	MAR	APR	MAY	JUN	JUL	AUG	SEPT	OCT	NOV	DEC
Move		9-28	25-31	1-15								
Start a class	22-31	1-8										
Join a club									12-30	1, 19-21		
Ask for a raise										1-23	17-30	1-5, 18-20
Look for work					5-31	1, 2		27-31	1-12			
Get pro advice	10, 11, 15	6, 7, 11	5-7, 10-12	3, 6-8	4, 5, 27	1, 2, 23	20, 21, 25	16-18, 21	14, 17-19	10, 11, 15	6-8, 11	5, 8-10
Get a loan	12-14	8-10	8, 9	4, 5	1-3, 28	25, 26	22-24	19, 20	15, 16	12-14	9, 10	6, 7
See a doctor					5-31	1, 2				2-26	18-30	1-27
Start a diet					5-19						4, 5	
End relationship												4, 5
Buy clothes				16-30	1-28							
Get a makeover											17-30	1-27
New romance			29, 30	16-30	1-31	2, 24-30	1-18	11-31	1-5, 17			
Vacation	15, 16	11, 12	10-12	6-8	4, 5, 31	2, 27-29	25, 26			15, 16	11, 12	8-10

CAPRICORN

The Goat
December 22 to January 19

VƧ

Element:	Earth
Quality:	Cardinal
Polarity:	Yin/Feminine
Planetary Ruler:	Saturn
Meditation:	I know the strength of my soul
Gemstone:	Garnet
Power Stones:	Peridot, diamond, quartz, black obsidian, onyx
Key Phrase:	I use
Glyph:	Head of goat
Anatomy:	Skeleton, knees, skin
Color:	Black, forest green
Animal:	Goats, thick-shelled animals
Myths/Legends:	Chronos, Vesta, Pan
House:	Tenth
Opposite Sign:	Cancer
Flower:	Carnation
Key Word:	Ambitious

Your Ego's Strengths and Weaknesses

You've got drive, ambition, and energy, Capricorn—the perfect combination for accomplishment. This is the trademark of your cardinal earth energy. As a cardinal sign, your vitality runs high, in spite of your earthy side. Ideas spring forth from your mind effortlessly, and taking action is just as natural. You like to be on top, because when you're in control you know things will be done right. You're good at pushing and motivating, delegating and overseeing, but you're not a follower. You're also not the best at follow-through: you leave that for others to manage. You like to run with the ball when it's your idea, but if someone else comes up with a good notion, you're not quite as enthusiastic—at least until you use your considerable reasoning capabilities to overcome your ego.

As an earth sign, you are very practical. Your earthiness slows you down, making your actions more effective. This also broadens your vision: you like to look at the whole picture, with breadth and depth. You want to know the history of a situation, and you may even be a student of history because of the way it enables you to predict the trends of the present and future. You are interested in the grand things in life, from fine architecture to the institutions of society. Your taste runs toward the classics, and you prefer a sturdy older piece of equipment to a shiny new gizmo which may not last as long. You have the ability to build, but you are more likely to build something which stands on the hidden structures of society, like a government system or law, rather than a physical building. The downside of your nature is the tendency to accept that the ends justify the means. In your eagerness to reach the top or accomplish your goals, you may step on toes—not because you mean to, but because you don't pay attention to the niceties along the way.

Shining Your Love Light

You're an ardent lover, Capricorn, as long as you're in charge. Sensual, warm, and committed, you are a devoted partner in the time you have to spend with your beloved. That's the key: time. Your relationships could suffer from neglect if your excitement over the work you're doing overshadows your love life. An ignored relationship soon dies, despite all your good feelings and faithfulness. To you, going to work is a way of expressing your love, but you have to remember that others need more direct demonstration of your feelings. This is not your strong point, but you would do well to cultivate an ability to express your feelings.

You'll feel a competitive edge with Aries and enjoy playing the game of who's best and first. Taurus's methodical approach to life is reassuring. Together you can sustain a balanced drive toward your goals. You wonder what makes social gadfly Gemini tick, until you recognize that this sign has as much appreciation for expressions of culture as you do. Cancer expresses the feelings you hold inside, while you give Cancer a reassuring structure. Leo may vie for the top spot with you, because Lions like to lead as well, but once you recognize that your styles are different, you can lead together. You love Virgo's technical skills and efficiency—you'll get so much done as a team. Sociable Libra's objectivity and your pragmatism make you a great team with a varied perspective. Scorpio shares your serious take on life—you won't have to convince this sign of what's really important. Sagittarius has the principles to guide your actions, while you provide a place to express ideals in concrete form. Another Capricorn automatically understands your perspective and will work alongside you on your grandest plans. You may get a little political with Aquarius, as you become aware of the balance of responsibility and freedom both at home and in the world. You have a soft spot for Pisces, because this sign never lets you forget your feeling side, and so appreciates the structure you bring to life.

Making Your Place in the World

Any position where leadership qualities are important is one you'll be comfortable in. You'll fit right in at the office of a large corporation, especially if you can call some of the shots. You love seeing the positive impact of your ideas at work. You also have a sense for handling finances, especially the big-picture side, which makes you a good treasurer, managing accountant, or chief financial officer. Managing stock portfolios, being a broker, or handling real estate transactions will also tap your potential. You do best in an environment where you are challenged, and if you are not too risk-averse you will excel at managing your own business: you have the entrepreneurial spirit, a knack for structuring your company, and the ability to think big. Other careers in which you can use these skills include managing a branch office or working in government, especially on the legislative side.

Putting Your Best Foot Forward

You're a professional, Capricorn, no matter what you do. You love nothing better than to put on the uniform of your chosen field and "wear" the role that you have learned to fulfill. You've worked hard to develop your expertise, and now you work hard to live up to your responsibilities. Your gift is your professionalism and the leadership ability that stems from your talent for keeping personal feelings out of the way while you weigh the decisions set before you. However, these fine qualities can be taken too far. If you forget to take off the business mask when you come home from work and let the warm, fuzzy you come out with those you love, you run the risk of missing out on the best part of close relationships—the loving interaction you can share. You also have to give yourself and those around you quality time to enjoy life. When the walls stay up, you deny yourself the nourishment that others can give you. It may help to schedule time with those you love, at least until fitting the personal side into your life becomes its own reward.

Tools for Change

Capricorn, you see so much to be done in the world that you never want to rest. However, to be a well-rounded person and enjoy life, you need to play. The first thing you can do to keep yourself in balance is to reduce the amount of responsibility you have. You can enlist the help of others in completing the tasks you see before you by delegating or asking for help. You can also work smarter yourself: find ways to be more efficient or eliminate tasks that you do only out of habit. Staying organized is essential, and if you need some help getting there you can hire someone or get training in organizing skills. Once you do this, you'll have more free time.

Given your constructive nature, you can turn any playtime activity into work. To avoid this, take up activities that have no reward other than the joy of doing them—certainly they should provide no income! It's also important to spend time doing nothing. You should also enhance the element of spontaneity and surprise in your pastimes by going someplace unexpected or breaking your routine.

Much of your emphasis is on the outer world, so you may ignore your inner world. Another way to balance your character is by developing an awareness of your inner health. It's important first of all to know what you're feeling. Sorting through your emotions and understanding how to deal with them will make life more rewarding for you. You can cultivate this side of your nature by studying psychology or astrology, and even getting counseling if you need help opening yourself up. You will also benefit from taking a psychic development course, although you will find the gifts that emerge easier to manage and more enjoyable if you focus on psychological and spiritual development at the same time. All of these approaches will tune you in with more sensitivity to the processes and energies that pass through you or reside within you.

Affirmation for the Year

I am increasing my success by enlarging
the circle of my acquaintance.

The Year Ahead for Capricorn

You've just completed a year of high activity reaching for a pinnacle of success, Capricorn. Now it's time to reap the rewards! Jupiter is in Scorpio, your Eleventh House, until November 23. The Eleventh House is where you contact others who can be of outerworld benefit to you, such as in your career or business. Group markets and audiences will be your greatest source of growth and strength during this time, so the more people you can meet and get to know, the more benefits will come to you. Of course, it helps to be selective and not overly eager—a Jupiter danger—or you will put people off. Use your usual discretion and allow them to lead. You are likely to receive recognition for past efforts this year as well, whether in the form of awards, a raise, or a promotion. Groups to which you belong may also recognize you by giving you a role that will increase your standing in the organization. Once Jupiter goes into Sagittarius and your solar Twelfth House, you'll begin a one-year period of consolidation and completion. You may have a big project that takes you out of the public eye, or you may just need some chill time. Your space will be expanding inward with spiritual undertones. While you are on retreat, you will have time to gather energy for a new twelve-year period of expansion, as Jupiter moves into your Sun sign in 2007 and 2008.

Saturn spends its second year in Leo and your solar Eighth House. You are in the midst of a restructuring of your financial base—most particularly your personal resources. This could mean that you reevaluate and reapportion your financial portfolio, changing insurance coverages, buying and selling stocks and bonds, or changing your sources of income.

Chiron is in Aquarius and your Second House. This provides the impetus for your Saturn–Eighth House actions. You have decided that the way you handle your resources needs some repair, or perhaps a complete overhaul. You want to create greater stability and power in your personal resources, from your finances to your property to intangibles like skills and time. Underneath all this is the realization that you've had your priorities wrong. Now you can get them right, and Chiron gives you five more years to do it.

Uranus is in its fourth year in Pisces and your solar Third House. You're undergoing a pleasant awakening process that nonetheless has its surprises. This is the gentlest way to go through change. You don't have to have direct experience to learn: it is enough to observe others and take the lesson to your own heart. Coursework, interpersonal interaction, or spiritual training could provide the stimulus for this joyful growth.

Neptune continues to travel through Aquarius and your solar Second House, where it has been since 1998. Like Chiron, it is reshaping your financial picture. It is no longer enough for you to just earn money (lots of it) any way you can. You are now concerned with enjoying the way you are earning it. Bringing your ideals to bear on your world makes you feel more fulfilled, and this is as important to you now as the money you put in the bank.

Pluto remains in Sagittarius and your solar Twelfth House, where it has been since 1995. At that time you started a long-term spiritual transformation process that has been opening your mind and heart to new awareness and greater sensitivity. This process will continue in 2006.

The eclipses enter Virgo and Pisces, your Ninth and Third Houses, on March 14. This will emphasize the shift in consciousness that you are already experiencing and make it possible for you to actualize some of your dreams. Whether it comes through travel, higher education, or spiritual practice, your life will change in pleasant ways.

If you were born between December 25 and January 16, Saturn in Leo contacts your Sun from your solar Eighth House. This is the time to get your financial house in order. From your investment portfolio to your insurance protection, a reevaluation is essential right now. This is also a good time to consider how you want your affairs handled after you die (your will or living trust). Now is not the time for investing in high-risk or short-term ventures, because they will not succeed while Saturn holds sway in this area. Instead, look for the long-term, steady, and secure places to place your wealth. The mysteries of life will also grab your attention now. You will be fascinated by what makes the human psyche tick, and find ways to explore it that suit your style, whether through psychology or occult studies. It pays to look at the long-term picture, because this is part of a slow, steady rise to the top that you have been working on for the last ten years. With four more years until you reach the top, make plans that will permit you to maximize your results then. Saturn events will occur on or near January 27, February 19, April 5 and 24, June 20, August 7, November 16, and December 5.

If you were born between December 28 and January 6, Uranus in Pisces is connecting with your Sun from your solar Third House. Your mind is in a rejuvenation period this year. From the news on TV to a new class you're taking to something new your sister has gotten into, you're getting it from all quarters. All these are conspiring to give you a new way of seeing the world, even a new way of thinking itself. Your intuition is stronger, your mind working more quickly. Yet, you're not accessing information in the same way. You are not just recalling facts you've learned, you're deriving insights from the wisdom you've accrued. Don't be surprised if the knowledge is not right at your fingertips. It may take time for the right answers to percolate to the surface, but you'll learn to be more patient with this new and more satisfying way of knowing. Your brothers, sisters, and neighbors may be a source of surprises as well, and don't be surprised if there is a disruptive influence near your home, such as a construction site or a new sewer system being put in on your street. This cycle begins March 1, with additional dates of peak Uranus activity on June 5 and 19, September 5, November 19, and December 2.

If you were born between January 6 and 11, Neptune in Aquarius is boosting your ideals from its position in your solar Second House. You are tired of making money without meaning. You want to imbue your activities, and your sources of income, with more spiritual meaning to you and more impact on others. You are also willing to make a sacrifice for your ideals, and that could mean taking a cut in income to do something you feel passionate about. Take care to be realistic about your needs so you don't get yourself into the financial red while your making your transition to a new state. Your goals should be as professional and realizable as before, only cast in a new vision of what the possibilities are. Only you know what you are capable of, but you should temper your dreams with a dose of realism—a Plan B in case Plan A doesn't work as you think it will. Confusion and illusion are possible side effects of a Neptune transit. Don't take actions hurriedly or when you are unclear about what to do, and accept the advice of only those with whom you have built a relationship prior to this time. Your imagination will also be strong, and it is possible to fulfill your dreams under this contact, if well-managed. Neptune's subtle energies will be strongest on January 27, February 5, March 15, May 10 and 22, August 10, October 29, and November 9.

If you were born between January 12 and 16, Pluto in Sagittarius is working its way through your solar Twelfth House. You've been feeling changes coming, but now is the time to take action. This year you will become aware of subtle, hidden influences in your life that have a large impact on the way you approach the world. You may be uncomfortably aware that something is not right, but not sure what to do. Pluto will bring all the relevant issues to the surface in the coming year—which will be a relief, because then you can deal with them. There may be problems with someone close to you who requires a sacrifice. You may be limited, even confined, by the powerful needs of others, or yourself. Sometimes long-term illness plays a role when Pluto makes this kind of contact. There are many other things that limit us, and you will be finding out what those things are. The best way to approach this is as a spiritual transformation. If you actively pursue that transformation, you will be able to manage it better than if you wait for events to occur. This is not something that will take your full focus or bowl you over, but rather it will lurk in the background and emerge periodically. The benefits come from becoming more sensitive to hidden influences in your life. Pluto events will emerge into your life around March 17 and 29, June 16, September 4 and 16, and December 18.

If you were born between December 22 and 25 or January 17 and 19, the major planets are not contacting your Sun this year. This does not mean that your year will be uneventful, especially if other personal planets—the Moon, Mercury, Venus, or Mars—are being contacted. However, with your Sun out of the loop, you will feel less challenged and more comfortable with what comes up. You will not be treading an unfamiliar path, nor will you need to tap your inner strength and courage so deeply. You may be able to take some time off, relatively speaking. It may be a good time to take an extended vacation or enjoy life more. You can also use this year to take up a project that you've had to put on the back burner during more active periods. You will not feel pushed by circumstances as much, so it's good to be clear about what your goals are. If you want to accomplish something big, you'll need to push yourself.

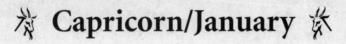 Capricorn/January

Planetary Hotspots

The four planets squaring off in the heavens this month are triggering your finances and sense of well-being. You've taken on temporary belt-tightening measures to accomplish goals that are part of a larger mission. You'll feel the squeeze more acutely this month as you find more places to activate your plans. Social contact and creative output is emphasized. Important dates are January 15, 18, 23, or 27.

Wellness and Keeping Fit

With Venus retrograde in your sign, your makeover could extend to changes in your health regimen as well. There's no better time to make over your nutritional and fitness plan to ensure that your beauty changes happen from the inside out. By the time Venus goes direct on February 3, you can have your new habits well established.

Love and Life Connections

It's time to take a good look at your relationships and figure out what needs to change. Venus is retrograde in your sign, and major changes could take place in your personal ties. Even if no big moves are called for, all your close connections will be renegotiated in some ways. All will be resolved by February 3. This is also an excellent time for a personal makeover. A revision in style, from fashion to hair to ways of presenting yourself to others, is timely now, and you'll be especially focused and inspired.

Finance and Success

Consolidating your successes of the past is an important part of sustaining positive results. As Jupiter triggers Neptune on January 27, entering the closing phase of the thirteen-year cycle that began in 1997, dreams you hatched then come to fruition. Now it's time to begin building them as the platform for your next round of enterprises, while making sure they will benefit you for years to come.

Rewarding Days

3, 4, 8, 9, 17, 18, 19, 22, 23, 24, 27, 28, 31

Challenging Days

5, 6, 7, 12, 13, 14, 20, 21

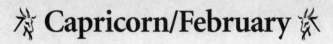 Capricorn/February

Planetary Hotspots

Your life gets a lot easier after February 3, when Venus returns to forward motion in your sign. The past six weeks have brought extraordinary personal lessons, perhaps revealing the need to be warmer and less disciplined than before. After so much self-scrutiny, these new qualities are more integrated into your basic nature and require less attention on your part. Neptune's new cycle, which starts on February 5, draws your attention to spirituality and tunes you in to your dreams for greater fulfillment. Incorporate them into your plans for the coming year, and you'll be richly rewarded.

Wellness and Keeping Fit

Venus in your First House could have affected your health, but you're more likely to have become aware of ways in which you could improve your style. Continue to experiment with new clothes, hair styles, and wearing a more optimistic attitude. If new health routines are called for, this is a good time to incorporate them into your life.

Love and Life Connections

Venus signals changes in your love life as well. If your primary relationship didn't go completely south, you've at least renegotiated how it is working in your life. This probably involved a change in perspective and self-image on your part, perhaps some behavior changes as well. Keep up the good work, and don't believe for a minute that it's all your responsibility.

Finance and Success

The focus turns to your finances and use of resources around February 5: What do you want to create? What do you want to support with your investments? These are the questions to answer as Neptune starts its new yearly cycle in your Second House. Outreach efforts started after February 8 will be more effective.

Rewarding Days

1, 4, 5, 13, 14, 15, 18, 19, 20, 23, 24, 27, 28

Challenging Days

2, 3, 8, 9, 10, 16, 17

Capricorn/March

Planetary Hotspots

Old ideas are discarded and new ones unsettle your perspective as Mercury tracks backward through your Third House from March 2 to 25, with critical turning points on March 2, 8, 12, and 25. You're inspired around March 1 as Uranus's yearly cycle begins, giving you new creative impetus. Jupiter's change of direction on March 4 signals a change in your interactions within groups and organizations. It may be time to cut back on obligations and social outings in order to curtail expenses.

Wellness and Keeping Fit

Mars in your Sixth House suggests the possibility of surgery or other medical procedures this month, although if possible it is good to avoid them around March 11. It's a good time to revamp your fitness routine, and you'll be extra energetic, but injuries are possible if you overdo it.

Love and Life Connections

You feel compelled to makes changes in your home and family life around March 29, when the last Aries solar eclipse of this series occurs. This is your last chance to complete a transition you began in October 2004. Siblings and neighbors surprise or even shock you around March 1 and 11.

Finance and Success

Discoveries you make while working further spur your innovative spirit to action when Mars makes contact with Uranus on March 11. The changes you've been making in order to fulfill your dreams reach a turning point on March 4, with a significant event around March 15, as Jupiter contacts Neptune for the second of three meetings. Turn your doubts into solutions and a firmer resolve. Travel could prove difficult around March 14.

Rewarding Days
3, 4, 13, 14, 18, 19, 22, 23, 24, 27, 28, 31

Challenging Days
1, 2, 8, 9, 15, 16, 17, 29, 30

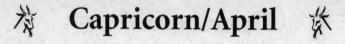 Capricorn/April

Planetary Hotspots

You seem placid on the surface, but there's lots going on behind the scenes for you. With Mars opposing Pluto in your Sixth and Twelfth Houses on April 8, there's a hidden factor that emerges into prominence then. It could have to do with health, work, the sacrifices you make for others, or simply "karma." It will create busy-ness in your life for the rest of the month as Mercury and Venus trigger these planets.

Wellness and Keeping Fit

You are more vulnerable than usual to illness or injury with the Mars-Pluto interaction on April 8. You can avoid this by not over-exerting yourself, either at work or in your fitness routine. Staying grounded and focused during physical activity are also good preventive techniques. Just as important is taking breaks during stressful periods and getting plenty of sleep.

Love and Life Connections

Your attention is drawn home, where you've got several spring projects in the works and not a few books you're looking forward to reading. Although other activities pull you elsewhere, this is your source of pleasure this month.

Finance and Success

Financial restrictions you've placed on yourself are relieved somewhat on April 5, as Saturn returns to direct motion. However, this is just the end of Phase One of your complete plan, so maintain your resolve. Now you're beginning to see results. Contacts you make for the next three months will eventually feed your income, but not right away. Don't let the lack of fast response cause you to lose faith in your efforts.

Rewarding Days

1, 4, 5, 9, 10, 14, 15, 19, 20, 23, 24, 27, 28

Challenging Days

11, 12, 13, 25, 26

Capricorn/May

Planetary Hotspots

Matters relating to your financial independence are highlighted as Chiron and Neptune change direction in your Second House on May 15 and 22. This brings a new understanding that you must improve your portfolio, but it may require considerable change, and you're not sure at this point how to accomplish it. Since this is only the beginning of the process, you can gather information and advice to factor into your decision-making process. You have five months to work this out and get your new situation established.

Wellness and Keeping Fit

You can abate the potential for injuries by staying focused, keeping your stress level down, taking inflammation-reducing supplements, and getting plenty of sleep. This energy peaks on May 26.

Love and Life Connections

Others behave more aggressively toward you as Mars travels through your Seventh House, but that comes with benefits. If you can listen to what they say, you can learn some important lessons to use in your social life, with positive implications for business. Energetic pursuit of social contacts through May 9 will generate results both immediate and long-term. Conflict that arises at home on May 23 can be resolved to everyone's advantage over the following three days.

Finance and Success

Your long-term goal of financial independence requires budget-cutting now but will bring you great reward later. This year and the next are a turning point in the implementation of your plan, as Jupiter and Saturn move through your money houses. With Jupiter at the halfway mark in its yearly cycle on May 4, visible progress is evident.

Rewarding Days

6, 7, 8, 11, 12, 13, 18, 19, 20, 21, 24, 25, 26

Challenging Days

2, 3, 9, 10, 22, 23, 29, 30

Capricorn/June

Planetary Hotspots

Business and finance come into the foreground as the planets return to their grand-cross pattern in your money houses from June 4 to 22. The weakest link in your life is how well your earning capacity fits with what you really enjoy doing. You began a long process of shifting emphasis back in 1998, and you continue moving toward that new goal.

Wellness and Keeping Fit

Your ability to function efficiently could show signs of serious erosion around June 16, when Pluto reaches the peak of its annual cycle. This could happen if you make a habit of ignoring your body's signals and consistently cutting back on sleep, exercise, or nutrition. This drains the energy stores in the body, which take a long time to build up again. Coddle yourself, and let others do the same from time to time.

Love and Life Connections

Your love life looks good through June 22, if you can find the time for social activities. Dating will be especially pleasant, and romance is in the air. You may also meet prospective romantic partners at group events throughout this time, though there are likely to be obstacles to long-term relationships now.

Finance and Success

Since July of last year you've felt increasingly that it's time to fish or cut bait. Sooner or later you have to take the plunge and surrender to the new process you've initiated. This month brings welcome results from your efforts but creates a new logistical puzzle to solve, which comes to a head on June 19.

Rewarding Days

3, 4, 8, 9, 12, 13, 16, 17, 18, 21, 22, 25, 26, 30

Challenging Days

5, 6, 7, 19, 20

Capricorn/July

Planetary Hotspots

Misunderstandings are possible all month long as Mercury retrogrades through your Seventh House. It's a good time to sharpen your listening skills and make sure you are clear about what others are saying. The key issue for you is likely to be your ability to listen to others, because they will have plenty to say, even if they are not saying it. Try to be receptive, and draw them out if someone needs encouragement to speak. If you are on the receiving end of an accusation or dispute, bring in a mediator to lend an objective viewpoint, because your "opponent" may be too emotional to hear you if you are on your own.

Wellness and Keeping Fit

The planetary contacts on July 14 give you get a chance to check in on the health imbalances you've been working to overcome. Don't ignore symptoms now, or you'll have more to deal with next month, which could be considerably less pleasant. Responding to your body's needs now will be easier and require only mild and preventive remedies.

Love and Life Connections

It's a good time to go out and have some fun, to take your mind off your problems. You'll be in a festive mood after Jupiter begins its forward path on July 4. There may even be something to celebrate. Business opportunities arise at meetings and social gatherings, but you don't always have to work the room even if it's a business event.

Finance and Success

Disruptions in work flow occur around July 5 and 14 that must be straightened out. The problems are likely to be electronic, and communications may be involved. Don't let this situation slide, because next month real difficulties will occur if it is not attended to now.

Rewarding Days

1, 2, 5, 6, 10, 11, 14, 15, 18, 19, 27, 28, 29

Challenging Days

3, 4, 16, 17, 22, 23, 24, 30, 31

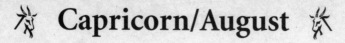 Capricorn/August

Planetary Hotspots

Links that you have with the greater financial world—stocks, bonds, insurance, etc.—require attention this month in a big way and spur you to restructure your portfolio. This is part of the ongoing process you've been working on to increase the level of meaning in your life and to pursue greater success. You've been waiting patiently to make these changes, and although they are not yet in the final form you would like, you'll make substantial headway this month.

Wellness and Keeping Fit

It's time to get away from your immediate surroundings for your health and fitness routines and do atypical things. This can mean going to a new international restaurant, or hiking in the country instead of visiting the fitness center. Getting away will give you a broader perspective and allow you to reprioritize the long list of things you want to accomplish.

Love and Life Connections

The other people in your life may not be as cooperative as you'd like in making the financial changes you need—in fact, they may the source of some of the difficulties that have moved you in this direction to begin with. The potential is high right now for you to come to agreement with them about future plans.

Finance and Success

An opportunity comes your way from a colleague or social contact around August 17 that leads you in precisely the direction you want to move. You couldn't be more delighted, because it is more than you'd hoped for and gives you the chance to test your new skills as you broaden your mind.

Rewarding Days

1, 2, 3, 6, 7, 10, 11, 14, 15, 24, 25, 29, 30

Challenging Days

12, 13, 19, 20, 26, 27, 28

⚴ Capricorn/September ⚴

Planetary Hotspots

Eclipses on September 7 and 22 highlight education and long-term goals, bringing a mound of paperwork to your desk. Travel is likely, and a vacation early in the month will bring unexpected adventures. Educational or outreach initiatives that you began around March 1 reach their peak on September 5. You have three months to go before you consider them complete.

Wellness and Keeping Fit

If you stay in the moment and accept circumstances as they occur, you are able to respond more creatively and get something good from your experiences, even if they are not what you planned. Pluto has been teaching you about the self-imposed obstacles of over-scheduling your life—that rigidity breeds stress. You'll be tested on this once again as Pluto returns to forward motion on September 4. Your flexibility will determine how much you benefit.

Love and Life Connections

You meet many stimulating and enjoyable people in your travels, especially early in the month. An unusual romantic connection is even possible. These encounters will thoroughly change your perspective and inspire new ways of seeing the world. Ongoing situations with siblings draw your attention at this time as well.

Finance and Success

Organizations and group meetings continue to be a potential source of business, but you can't approach your contacts directly. This is not the time to push, but rather a time for relationship-building. In December, you can take more direct action, but this will only be as successful as your efforts now at creating general goodwill based on low-key social interaction.

Rewarding Days

2, 3, 4, 7, 8, 11, 12, 20, 21, 25, 26, 30

Challenging Days

9, 10, 15, 16, 22, 23, 24

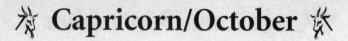 Capricorn/October

Planetary Hotspots

This is an active and fruitful time for you, as the fast-moving planets pour support into your Second House. New business deals and projects come your way, and it's money in the bank. These enterprises fit in with your long-term plans to revitalize and add meaning to the ways you earn money. This is the proof of what you've accomplished since Neptune turned retrograde on May 22. You can retain some of this business and carry it forward into the coming months and years.

Wellness and Keeping Fit

You should remain true to your health regimen. There are hidden factors in your health picture that need constant tending, and if you succeed in maintaining the routine, you will also succeed in improving your health.

Love and Life Connections

You're rethinking the ways you connect with others through your network of friends, colleagues, organizations, and clubs. In the wake of the past year's growth in this area, it's time to take stock of what you want to take with you into the coming Jupiter cycle, which starts November 23. As Mercury retrogrades through your Eleventh House starting October 28, you may reconsider responsibilities you took on and extricate yourself from them. If you can give key people the heads-up before then, your news will be easier to accept.

Finance and Success

Money flows into your wallet now, but this is not a permanent state of affairs unless you make an effort to retain the business that comes your way. These opportunities tie in with the efforts you've made over the past two years, and you're still riding the wave of success. You'll be highly active through October 22 with these projects.

Rewarding Days
1, 4, 5, 8, 9, 17, 18, 19, 22, 23, 24, 27, 28, 31

Challenging Days
6, 7, 12, 13, 14, 20, 21

⚡ Capricorn/November ⚡

Planetary Hotspots

Groups and organizations will consume a great deal of time throughout the month. Not only is Mercury retrograde in your Eleventh House, but the Sun, Mars, and Venus join Jupiter there as well. Volunteer activities, meetings, and conferences absorb your time and attention. With Mercury retrograde until November 17, things will not go as planned, but you will find all the glitches in the system. Taking good notes will prevent you from repeating them another time.

Wellness and Keeping Fit

This is a good time to do a complete clearing and healing of yourself on all levels. For the physical level, redirect your dietary and exercise plan to one that better supports your long-term health. For the emotional level, inner-child work, Bach flowers, and psychotherapy may be desirable. For the mental level, you can work with your attitudes through affirmation and the I Ching. For the spiritual level, meditation, spiritual retreats, and yoga may do the trick. You have until next December 18 to accomplish this task.

Love and Life Connections

It is possible to ruffle feathers more than usual before November 17 in groups and organizations, and it may even be necessary to do so to refocus someone's efforts to what they should be doing. Even when you're busy, people notice when you take the time to appreciate them, and doing this may help you avoid a faux pas.

Finance and Success

All the attention you're giving to organizations should not lead you to ignore your own needs and affairs. The first thing to be jeopardized is your financial stability; be consistent in taking time for yourself, including the time to manage your portfolio and pay your bills.

Rewarding Days

1, 4, 5, 13, 14, 15, 19, 20, 23, 24, 28, 29

Challenging Days

2, 3, 9, 10, 16, 17, 30

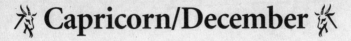 Capricorn/December

Planetary Hotspots

Six planets conjoin in your Twelfth House, emphasizing your internalization processes throughout the month. There is a lot going on beneath the surface and behind the scenes for you, and this could include confining influences, such as illness, a project you're working on in solitude, care you're giving someone else, or a spiritual retreat. No matter what, you'll get the most out of this if you see it as a spiritual experience with lessons to be learned. Your sacrifices now will benefit you in the coming year.

Wellness and Keeping Fit

This is a great time to kick-start your rejuvenation process as the planets highlight your Twelfth House. This is also a good time to plot out the overall strategy you want to follow for the coming year. Put at the top of the list the thing that you feel intuitively is most important or will be most effective in your healing process, then launch your plans this month while so much planetary power is at your disposal. Your power dates are December 7, 16 to 18, and 24 to 25.

Love and Life Connections

After December 11, you feel more like connecting with others, and your charisma is on the rise. If you need to negotiate something with someone, December 19 is a good time to do it.

Finance and Success

Your financial restructuring plan gets a boost from the background work you are doing, and it's one that will see you through the coming five months, when Saturn is retrograde. You're entering a new phase which reduces your available income in the short run, but will increase it in the long run. This could be an increase in the money you are putting away for retirement or a curtailment in one business activity to enhance another.

Rewarding Days

2, 3, 11, 12, 16, 17, 20, 21, 22, 25, 26, 29, 30

Challenging Days

1, 6, 7, 13, 14, 15, 27, 28

Capricorn Action Table

These dates reflect the best—but not the only—times for success and ease in these activities, according to your Sun sign.

	JAN	FEB	MAR	APR	MAY	JUN	JUL	AUG	SEPT	OCT	NOV	DEC
Move			29, 30	16-30	1							
Start a class		9-28	25-31	1-15								
Join a club										2-26	18-0	1-7
Ask for a raise										24-31	1-16, 18-20	11-31
Look for work					19-31	1-27	29-31	1-10	12-30	1		
Get pro advice	12-14, 17	8-10, 13	9, 13-15	4, 5, 9	1-3, 6-8	3, 4, 25	22-24, 27	20, 23-25	15, 16, 20	12-14, 17	10, 13-15	6, 7, 11
Get a loan	15, 16	11, 12	10-12	6-8	4, 5, 31	2, 27-29	25, 26	21-23	17-19	15, 16	11, 12	8-10
See a doctor					19-31	1-27	29-31	1-10				8-31
Start a diet					19-31	1, 2						4, 5
End relationship	12-14											
Buy clothes					5-19, 29	1-23						
Get a makeover	3-22	3-28	1-4			3-27						
New romance				27, 28	5-19, 29	1-23	29-31	1-12				
Vacation	17-19	13-15	13, 14	9, 10	6-8	3, 4, 30	1, 27-29	25, 27-31	1-30	17-19	13-14	11, 12

AQUARIUS

The Water Bearer
January 20 to February 20

≈

Element:	Air
Quality:	Fixed
Polarity:	Yang/Masculine
Planetary Ruler:	Uranus
Meditation:	I am a wellspring of creativity
Gemstone:	Amethyst
Power Stones:	Aquamarine, black pearl, chrysocolla
Key Phrase:	I know
Glyph:	Currents of energy
Anatomy:	Circulatory system, ankles
Color:	Iridescent blues, violet
Animal:	Exotic birds
Myths/Legends:	Ninhursag, John the Baptist, Deucalion
House:	Eleventh
Opposite Sign:	Leo
Flower:	Orchid
Key Word:	Unconventional

Your Ego's Strengths and Weaknesses

With your intellect and interest in current events, you're savvy in the ways of the world, Aquarius. Your fixed air nature steadies your mind and permits you to apply it toward definite goals. Your fixity makes you surprisingly persistent, especially when it comes to ideas: the air side of you. You study a subject and make up your own mind, then defy others to change your opinion. You enjoy a debate and will argue a point just for the sake of it. Like the other fixed signs, you are testing the ideas to make sure they work, and you freely give them up if they don't. This strength of will permits you to develop ideals, rally others to your cause, and follow through to accomplish objectives. However, your fixed nature could lead you to resist necessary changes or prevent your ideas from being adjusted in positive ways.

Because of your airy side, you often direct your efforts toward political or social causes. You're genuinely concerned about peace, poverty, starvation, genocide, and the other problems that plague the modern world, because you see how they lead to the deterioration of conditions everywhere. It isn't enough for you to be intelligent or gifted and use your gifts for yourself. You want to help others with them. You strive above all else to think independently, to shed bias and imbalance in your opinions. You don't want to fall prey to a herd mentality. Out of this independence comes your desire to be on the cutting edge in society's trends. Your social leadership qualities are based in part on your friendliness and ability to treat everyone fairly—qualities that open many doors for you.

Shining Your Love Light

As a lover of all humanity, you have no difficulty collecting people around you. You thrive on group energy, but you also enjoy the company of one special person. As long as you have the freedom to continue your many other social ties, you are happy and loyal in your relationship. However, you need a partner who will understand this—even enjoy it. While you are good at casual relationships, you have to remember to share a special closeness with your partner. Only when you feed your intimate relationship will it grow and thrive.

Aries has a need for independent action as much as you do, and will bring joy to balance your objectivity. Taurus may seem resistant to your ideas, but this sign's rationality will ground you and temper your ideas. You love the way you feel around fellow air sign Gemini—you'll talk till you drop as you enjoy the wonders of culture together. Cancer shares your concern about groups, especially where a familial feeling exists, and brings a rich emotional experience to your life. Leo balances your impartiality with passion and enthusiasm, reminding you of your secret desire to be special. Virgo's love of technology matches your own. Together you can devise ways to support the community you both care about and strive to serve. Libra is another air sign, flowing with you smoothly through parties and cultural events, enjoying the beauty of both art and discussion. You'll feel challenged by the emotional will of Scorpio, who reminds you that feelings are a strong force to be reckoned with, both within yourself and in your partner. Sagittarius prizes freedom as much as you do, giving you guilt-free independence and making each encounter a pleasure. Your mutual travels and adventures will enrich your life. You help balance Capricorn's sober approach to life, while appreciating this sign's worldly savvy. Together you can build progressive structures. A fellow Aquarian will share your social life and make a great teammate in championing the latest political or social cause. Don't overlook the value of Pisces signs: they bring you closer to the spiritual world that inspires you.

Making Your Place in the World

As sociable as you are, it's easy for you to find a niche in the world, Aquarius. Your specialty is group activities and dynamics, and there are many ways that you can use your talents. Teaching is a rewarding way to open people's minds to new concepts, which is something you love to do. You could also go into organizational psychology, the branch that deals with group dynamics. You can apply your knowledge of groups to a business environment, where large organizations need to be able to function well as a team. Team management works well in sales or production, and of course in sports it is vital. Your innovative mind also makes you a natural for research and development, because you firmly believe in new technologies for the betterment of humankind. Any field where the learning process is open-ended—where there's always something new—will delight you, as you quickly become bored with anything rote or routine. Political activism may also attract you, especially with your sense of fairness and your desire to make the world a better place.

Putting Your Best Foot Forward

Aquarius, your gift is your individuality. You have a strong internal barometer that tells you when you are succumbing to the "herd mentality" and losing your sense of freedom and right to be who you are. Because of your fixity, you can react dramatically to anything you perceive as controlling or authoritarian. You're a team player, and you want everything to be on a level playing field. Whether you exercise this marvelous capacity in a political or professional organization, your workplace, or your family, you're sensitive to the dynamics in the group and try to help others find their equilibrium in the group context. However, you can end up achieving exactly the opposite of your desired effect if your exert your powers of differentiation so strongly that reaction becomes rebelliousness. People are turned off by strong reactions, and they lose track of the principles that you are fighting for when their emotions are in play. Instead of hearing you in a receptive way, they are blocking you and experiencing internal resistance. If you speak from your principles without injecting a reactionary attitude, your new ideas will be easier for others to accept.

Tools for Change

Aquarius, you are such a social being, you could go from dawn till dusk without a moment to yourself. Yet this is something that you need in order to keep yourself in balance. As an air sign, you may swing from one extreme to the next without settling in the middle—your center—long enough to get your bearings. You need time to yourself to draw yourself back in and keep from getting so scattered. One of the best ways to do this is to create a work or hobby shop that you can use for tinkering and expressing your technological creativity. You can benefit greatly by letting your inventiveness out—you may even come up with a new gadget that you can market! When you spend time by yourself, it gives your mind free rein to explore the galaxies, reducing restlessness and nervous tension. This is a form of meditation in itself, but other styles of inner practice will also be beneficial. Practices that focus on chanting are especially good, and you may appreciate the vibratory enhancements that come when you use crystals or other meditation tools such as pyramids, incense, or singing bowls. As a mental sign, you may also tend to live in your head and ignore your physical body. You can compensate for this by engaging in a regular fitness routine. You may find it easier to stay motivated when you work out with a friend or group. Team sports could also attract you. Outdoor activities such as hiking, skiing, horseback riding, and gardening will bring you down to Earth, which will help you stay focused and calm. Of course, dance is more your style, satisfying your social, physical, and creative needs. Although you thrive on social intercourse, you may shy away from the emotional expressiveness required in an intimate relationship. There are numerous ways to get in touch with your emotions, but just being interested in doing so is a start. When you realize how important they are to a smooth-flowing partnership, and how rewarding a partnership can be, you'll be motivated to become more aware of your feelings. Communications training or keeping a journal, especially a dream journal, can be helpful.

Affirmation for the Year

I accept greater responsibility, recognition, and reward.

The Year Ahead for Aquarius

You're flying high in 2006, Aquarius! Jupiter wings its way across the top of your chart, moving you toward a crescendo in career, business, and public standing. It is in Scorpio and your solar Tenth House, and the sky's the limit! You feel as if you can accomplish anything or go anywhere, and that may be true if you've built a personal empire over the past nine years. However, Jupiter is the great promiser, but it doesn't always deliver, especially if you haven't coupled your expansionist side with your disciplined, hard-working side (Saturn). If you have done your work, you'll find this to be a true pinnacle with long-lasting results. Your career is in boom mode, complete with increased visibility and standing relative to your previous role. You may be placed in a leadership role. You may receive acclaim or recognition as well. These benefits may be temporary, however, especially if you rest on your laurels instead of seeing these opportunities as another stage in a process where you must keep up the good work. Once Jupiter goes into Sagittarius on November 23, it will light up your Eleventh House of groups. This gives you a chance to consolidate the results of your efforts this year and project them into the community at large.

You'll be challenged by Saturn, which spends a second year in Leo and your Seventh House of close relationships. The feedback you're getting from others may not be all good news. You may be discovering, much to your dismay, that there are flaws in the way you communicate with those closest to you. Weighing what they say with your own insights will permit you to refine your interaction in the best way.

Chiron still wends its way across the wheel from Saturn, in your own sign and your First House. It emphasizes how much growing you have to do to fulfill your image of yourself. Health matters could rise to the surface now, responding better to a holistic approach that recognizes the role your mind and emotions play in the imbalance.

Uranus is in Pisces again this year. Underneath your supposedly cynical view of life lie idealistic values. Now Uranus is teaching you how to get what you ask for. By refining your thoughts, you can develop the ability to create new resources (property and money).

Neptune is in Aquarius for another year, softening your appearance and the sharp edges of your wit. Your approach continues to become gentler as you learn to see the world as shades of gray rather than black and white.

Pluto in Sagittarius populates your solar Eleventh House. Your group and organizational associations continue to be a source of empowerment for you, and you want to continue cultivating them, but in a sincere way. Watch for power plays coming from others, however, because people may attempt to use you in a political game.

You'll feel a shift in emphasis in March, when the eclipses begin to trigger your Eighth and Second Houses, Virgo and Pisces. This places even more emphasis on renovating your financial life—not perhaps so much in rectifying mistaken ways of handling them, although that is possible, but in developing more meaningful ways of earning money.

If you were born between January 24 and February 15, Saturn in Leo is pointing out your interactions with others so you can overcome approaches that prevent you from connecting. You may find that you can't get away with some behaviors you've indulged in for years. Suddenly those around you are giving you feedback that you don't want to hear, but it is very helpful if you can take it in. You may also find that your partnerships require more effort than usual. This may be because your partner needs more from you, or obstacles to a supportive connection must be addressed. Your partner could also have withdrawn, either emotionally or physically, due to travel or additional work obligations. This is a fantastic time to improve your relationships, since you will need to work on them anyway. However, you are likely to feel as if your efforts are futile until much later, since where Saturn is concerned progress appears slow or even non-existent. If you stick with it, progress will become apparent—but remember that sticking with the issue does not require you to remain in a partnership that is unhealthy. You'll feel Saturn most on or around January 27, February 19, April 5 and 24, June 20, August 7, November 16, and December 5.

If you were born between January 27 and February 5, Uranus in Pisces contacts your Sun from your solar Second House, triggering an awakening process. It will send signals to you regarding changes you made seven years ago when Uranus went over your Sun. Then, you felt propelled into a new reality based on the insights you gained at that time. Now, as your insights have matured, it's time to adjust your direction slightly and ground your ideas more in reality. This will involve thinking about finances—both the outlay and the income—immediate or eventual. It's time to lay out a plan or refine the one you already have. Don't hesitate to use the input of others as a resource. Gather around you those people who can help you, because you will need them to bring your grand vision down to Earth. As you push your plans forward, you'll have the opportunity to further them by investing time, money, and effort into their realization. This is the way you prove to yourself that you can make this happen. This cycle begins March 1, with peak Uranus events on or around June 5 and 19, September 5, November 19, and December 2.

If you were born between February 5 and 10, Neptune in Aquarius make a direct connection with your Sun from your solar First House. For a year you'll feel swathed in Neptune's cotton-candy take on reality, feeling more romantic—and perhaps more confused as well. Your imagination will be more vivid than before, and this is great news if you are involved in any creative pursuits. Your ideals will matter more to you, but most importantly your vision of what can be will overshadow the reality you normally see. This is a good time to take note of your insights and give them a place in your life. There'll never be a better time to dream your future. What you see now can be the foundation for the rest of your life's endeavors, the chance for you to create a world that is more meaningful to you as well as more serviceable to others. Allow your visions to become plans and then execute them slowly. This will mitigate the influences that others could have on you during this relatively vulnerable and trusting time. Spirituality is likely to be more important to you now as well. You may find meditation and spiritual practice vital in generating the inner peace you desire. Neptune's subtle energies peak on January 27, February 5, March 15, May 10 and 22, August 10, October 29, and November 9.

If you were born between February 12 and 17, Pluto in Sagittarius makes a harmonious contact with your Sun, revolutionizing your interactions with groups from its position in your Eleventh House. Your interactions with others in the broadest sense both comprise and affect your fate. The influence they have on you, both collectively and as individuals, endows you with feelings of membership or alienation, dependence or freedom, individuality or sameness. It affects your sense of destiny, especially since you are fascinated with, and like to influence, others on a group level. With Pluto in play here, you are acutely aware of the power struggles and politics that often occur in groups. In all likelihood, you are caught up in those struggles or having a hard time avoiding them. Your experiences give you the chance to elevate your perceptions and actions to a higher level. You may take up a cause that serves the public rather than your own needs and concerns. By following the call to action you feel in your heart, you will be making the best of Pluto's contact. You will feel Pluto's energies most around March 17 and 29, June 16, September 4 and 16, and December 18.

If you were born between January 20 and 23 or February 18 and 20, none of the major planets contact your Sun this year. This means that you will not be as challenged as you are when your Sun is triggered, not required to show as much courage or tread a path that is unfamiliar to you. If the other planets in your chart have contacts with the "power-brokers" of the heavens—Jupiter, Saturn, Uranus, Neptune, and Pluto—you'll still find your life very active. However, the changes that come your way won't be as all-encompassing as when the Sun is involved. This could be a good time to relax and enjoy life or catch your breath after many eventful months. Or you could use this time constructively to do something you've always wanted to do but never had the time for. Such reprioritization can add that little spark that makes all the difference.

Aquarius/January

Planetary Hotspots

Your pursuit of high ideals has been being tested since last summer, with an extra layer of challenge starting in October. These circumstances continue as the relevant planets, which have been forming a grand cross, maintain their relative positions all month. However, now the path is clear to resolve some of those issues and move forward. This will require effort to respond to the high activity levels that result on or around January 15, 18, 23, or 27.

Wellness and Keeping Fit

You may be more tired, more dreamy than usual, and you should let your imagination drift as you listen to your body. Getting more sleep will benefit you in the long run. After this month, your health and vitality will rebound.

Love and Life Connections

Others may require more care and sacrifice than usual, with Venus retrograde in your Twelfth House. If there's someone who needs ongoing care, the level of need may be going through changes that require more or less of you than before. If less, then let go and give that person the independence he or she can manage. If more care is needed, it may be time to get more help from others so you can manage your own life.

Finance and Success

You're at a pinnacle in your career or profession, but it may seem that other factors are disrupting you from below. You can use this time to strengthen your position, but it will take persistence. These challenges were here before but previously hidden, so it's best to get them out in the open where they can be resolved. With four years to go in the current cycle, you can continue to reap rewards throughout that time.

Rewarding Days

1, 2, 5, 6, 7, 10, 11, 20, 21, 25, 26, 29, 30

Challenging Days

8, 9, 15, 16, 22, 23, 24

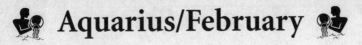 Aquarius/February

Planetary Hotspots

Even though you're doing well in your public life, your private life seems to be suffering from all the recent intense effort you've had to put into your career. This became evident in January, and more will be revealed in the first six days of February—enough to understand more about how to overcome the difficulties. After February 6, you can get caught up and make amends. With Neptune in your sign, the start of its new yearly cycle on February 5 triggers a renewed sense of direction in you that will lead to greater fulfillment. Spirituality, life purpose, dreams, and imagination are all associated with Neptune.

Wellness and Keeping Fit

It's not so much your health but that of others that has had your attention, and this could continue, although in a less demanding way. The key now is to make sure you're taking care of yourself. You'll compromise your own well-being if you deny yourself basic necessities like sleep and exercise.

Love and Life Connections

Someone has required extra care in your life lately, and that need becomes less intense after February 3. This is a good time to spend extra time with your loved ones, or even planning a special trip or outing to celebrate how much you mean to each other.

Finance and Success

After the first few days of the month, January's planetary configuration begins to dissipate, and you get more breathing room at work as well as at home. Financial decisions need to be made after February 7, and a critical event that affects your resources, perhaps triggering unexpected spending, occurs on February 19.

Rewarding Days

2, 3, 6, 7, 16, 17, 21, 22, 25, 26

Challenging Days

4, 5, 11, 12, 18, 19, 20

Aquarius/March

Planetary Hotspots

Career and financial challenges eclipse other concerns in March, as Jupiter and Neptune reconnect on March 15 and Mercury retrogrades through your money house from March 2 to 25. However, contacts of Mars and the Sun with Uranus on March 1 and 11 inspire you to take new approaches to your financial issues, which will bring rewards starting in November if you choose the right way across the rapids.

Wellness and Keeping Fit

Once Venus enters your sign on March 5, others are drawn to you more than usual, and you can enhance your charisma by creating a warm inner glow of health and well-being. While a few beauty treatments and a fresh haircut won't hurt, getting enough sleep and exercise, and eating well, do far more to bring the desired results. You could injure yourself while playing sports, especially around March 11.

Love and Life Connections

Romance could be in the air this month, as your warmth and mystery become more noticeable starting March 5. Don't let the increase in work activity keep you from having fun.

Finance and Success

The responsibilities of your recently reached career pinnacle begin to take a bite out of your life on March 4 as Jupiter changes direction for its four-month retrograde. Your head gets clearer about how to handle the situation after March 15. An unexpected expenditure arises around March 14, when the lunar eclipse highlights your Second and Eighth Houses.

Rewarding Days

1, 2, 5, 6, 7, 15, 16, 17, 20, 21, 25, 26, 29, 30

Challenging Days

3, 4, 10, 11, 12, 18, 19, 31

Aquarius/April

Planetary Hotspots

You get a break from relationship challenges after April 5, as Saturn returns to forward motion. Since November 22 of last year, you've been carrying an extra burden here, and while it's not completely cleared, the pressure is relieved for the time being. This could involve a forming business partnership, where the tasks involved in the start-up have been demanding. Your efforts to boost business will not be completed for another three months, but your ability to see visible progress is invigorating.

Wellness and Keeping Fit

You must continue to take extra care of your health, even if your sensitivity to stress doesn't show right now. Although Neptune isn't currently being highlighted, it suggests the ongoing need for caution.

Love and Life Connections

Your financial challenges are felt by your children or romantic partner, as Mercury, Venus, Mars, and Pluto make challenging contacts starting on April 8. Sometimes talk will only inflame the situation, and this is true on April 13, 17, 18, and 30. By taking a back seat and letting the truth reveal itself, you'll get better results. Indirect or unrelated communications could lead to warmer feelings on April 19 and 20.

Finance and Success

Because of the lack of regularity in your income currently, a little belt-tightening is in order. This situation will not last long—only a month—and savings can see you through if you want to dip into your reserves. Continue to make the most of the current business peak you are experiencing. It will bring in the desired increase in prosperity by the end of the year.

Rewarding Days

2, 3, 11, 12, 13, 16, 17, 18, 21, 22, 25, 26, 29, 30

Challenging Days

1, 6, 7, 8, 14, 15, 27, 28

Aquarius/May

Planetary Hotspots

If you've had questions about your life direction, they come at you front-and-center in May, as Chiron and Neptune slow for their retrogrades in your sign on May 15 and 22. Before this, the grand-cross pattern of January is repeated, bringing back to life threads of events and circumstances from that time, but on a higher, better level.

Wellness and Keeping Fit

Health issues may also arise around May 15, as the wounded healer begins its backward pass. New health patterns are emerging that you have yet to make sense of. This is a good time to explore them more fully and research ways to enhance your health and get yourself back into balance if necessary.

Love and Life Connections

Since last July, it's been your turn to carry a little more responsibility in a relationship's give-and-take, and early this month will be no exception. However, the one you are helping may try to "snow" you, however unwittingly, with a viewpoint that doesn't really represent what's going on. It's your job to figure out what he or she can do and to refuse to fill that gap.

Finance and Success

It feels like you lead a charmed existence with respect to business and finance, at least early in the month, as Mars, Jupiter, and Uranus make a grand trine in your money and work houses. Some of this is unexpected and relates to innovations you've been able to implement quickly in response to a need.

Rewarding Days

9, 10, 14, 15, 18, 19, 22, 23, 27, 28

Challenging Days

4, 5, 11, 12, 13, 24, 25, 26, 31

Aquarius/June

Planetary Hotspots

The emphasis is on surrender from June 4 to 22, as the planets, including Chiron and Neptune in your sign, once more form a grand cross in the sky. You have been learning not to overreact to stimuli that come your way since 1998, and you'll be tested on this again, especially from June 17 to 22 and July 5. Events on these dates are part of a theme that began to play out last summer and was highlighted again in January, February, and May. The surrendering process is part of bringing the ideals you cherish into your life.

Wellness and Keeping Fit

You are more sensitive all month as your First House is highlighted. Avoid impetuous driving or sports to which you are not accustomed, and stay focused. Mild exercise is harmonious with the level of activity you'll have now. It will keep you alert and quick-thinking.

Love and Life Connections

You may experience more than usual aggression from those around you from June 17 to 19 as Mars contacts Saturn, Chiron, and Neptune. Mars highlights buried conflicts, and you may feel less able to view events with your usual objectivity. It does not follow, however, that you are at fault, even though the other person may try to put the responsibility on you. Both parties have a role in creating the situation, but it may be better to keep that in mind rather than to speak it out in the moment.

Finance and Success

You experience a sudden change in fortune around June 19 as Uranus changes direction. Over the next five months you'll have the chance to assimilate this event into your life. This does not mean it is a loss of money, for it may very well be a sudden gain if you have played your cards wisely.

Rewarding Days

5, 6, 7, 10, 11, 14, 15, 19, 20, 21, 24, 25, 28, 29, 30

Challenging Days

1, 2, 8, 9, 22, 23

Aquarius/July

Planetary Hotspots

For the past four months, your career life has been active and intense as Jupiter has backed up through your Tenth House. On July 4, when it returns to direct motion, your goals are fulfilled or nearly so. You feel a sense of relief and release, as well as accomplishment. Now the rewards of your efforts can accrue over the next eighteen months.

Wellness and Keeping Fit

Mercury's retrograde colors the whole month and changes the rhythm of your daily routine. This may come in the form of illness or minor health procedures. These could be voluntary and preventive, such as acupuncture, massage therapy, or even an aromatherapy bath. However, minor surgeries or medical treatments such as a prescription or course of herbs may also be in order. Digestive upsets are also likely, but you can minimize the potential for this by not overeating and by sticking to a good diet.

Love and Life Connections

Relationship issues move onto the back burner, and you feel lighter at heart. Although they haven't completely disappeared, you can contribute more to the process of trust-building by ignoring it for a while. Around July 30, you'll get the chance to get beyond a past hurt. You'll have more opportunity to heal next month, but just let it develop on its own—don't try to create the scenario.

Finance and Success

The first part of the month is a good time for you to get your financial house in order. After July 22, any unfinished business will come to the surface, and may turn into situations that could become unpleasant next month. Pay your bills, balance your accounts, and follow up on lost payments.

Rewarding Days

1, 2, 3, 7, 8, 9, 12, 13, 16, 17, 20, 21, 30, 31

Challenging Days

5, 6, 18, 19, 25, 26

Aquarius/August

Planetary Hotspots

You get a new perspective that permits you to adjust your ongoing process of personal change as the powerful planetary pattern from January, February, May, and June is repeated again throughout the month. You've learned immensely during this time, and now you can move ahead with greater wisdom and certainty. Even if there remain obstacles, you are better prepared to overcome them. A peak where this process is concerned occurs on August 11, when Neptune reaches the halfway mark in its annual cycle. This highlights your ideals and the way you fulfill them this year.

Wellness and Keeping Fit

Take extra precautions this month, as you are more vulnerable than usual to diseases passed by other people. Key dates are August 13 and 29.

Love and Life Connections

It's a good time to start over with situations involving partnerships as Saturn starts a new yearly cycle on August 7. There's no better time to sit down with your beloved or business partner to negotiate where the relationship (or business) is headed and what you want individually and as a couple in both the short and long term.

Finance and Success

If others owe you money, you will not benefit from pursuing them too vigorously now, even though you feel the urge to do so. However, you can pursue new sources of revenue to your benefit, and this is the best way to focus your attentions at the moment. New contracts are most likely to come in around August 17 and 29, but the potential is there all month.

Rewarding Days

4, 5, 8, 9, 12, 13, 16, 17, 18, 26, 27, 28, 31

Challenging Days

1, 2, 3, 14, 15, 21, 22, 23, 29, 30

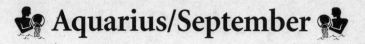 Aquarius/September

Planetary Hotspots

The pressures you've endured off and on during the year find release around September 15 and 23. You've been trying to find ways to adjust to others' need for you to be more structured and responsible over the past year. Meanwhile, your career/business has become both more challenging and more lucrative, but it has taken away from the attention you could give to your personal life. The mid-month release opens the doorway to an opportunity that will take time to build, but it will lead to career options that are more satisfying to you in the future if you pursue it.

Wellness and Keeping Fit

All this talk about meeting someone else's needs and expectations—what about your own? You've been learning how to boost this consideration up the list of priorities, and you are being put to the test throughout September and October. This is the linchpin in your health—to pursue the path that is most fulfilling. It's only when you ignore your own heart that you become scattered and distracted.

Love and Life Connections

Although it seems mild now, someone else's demands on you could rise in the coming months as Saturn moves toward contact with Neptune. Uncharacteristically, you've been inclined to indulge them, but giving them a more realistic idea of what you are willing to do now—setting some boundaries—could alleviate some of the pressure later.

Finance and Success

Energy put into your career this fall is the basis for next year's rewards, including increased income. While you can't sacrifice the rest of your life to the cause, you can put more emphasis there than usual. Pressures to perform are highest on September 24.

Rewarding Days
1, 5, 6, 9, 10, 13, 14, 22, 23, 24, 27, 28, 29

Challenging Days
11, 12, 17, 18, 19, 25, 26

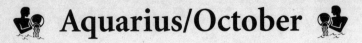 Aquarius/October

Planetary Hotspots

The challenges you've faced in the past year are abating, and the coming year, starting November 23, will be more harmonious—and reaching your goals will be much easier. You should use the next two months to complete the past year's initiatives, and even now the going will be better. You may feel like you've bitten off more than you can chew toward the end of the month as Mercury slows to turn retrograde. You'll face challenges after October 28, but it's all in a good cause.

Wellness and Keeping Fit

You could be injured in the course of fulfilling your career duties after October 27, possibly due to repetitive stress. Varying your activities and taking frequent breaks will prevent this. It's also important to avoid stressing sensitive joints in the weeks prior to that date. A few days away, or even a bona fide vacation, is the best curative. You'll be able to afford the time the most earlier in the month.

Love and Life Connections

With your attention mostly on your career, you could overlook sensitive relationship situations and say the wrong thing, especially as the tensions mount toward the end of the month. Just being alert to others' perspectives will keep your communications in balance. Critical dates are October 5, 15, 22, and 24.

Finance and Success

Opportunities will come early this month, bringing proof of your wisdom in the career and personal choices you've made. More will arrive after Neptune returns to forward motion on October 29. Your dreams are coming true.

Rewarding Days

2, 3, 6, 7, 10, 11, 20, 21, 25, 26, 29, 30

Challenging Days

8, 9, 15, 16, 22, 23, 24

🜄 Aquarius/November 🜄

Planetary Hotspots

Career activities and obligations threaten to overwhelm you through November 17 as the planets cluster in your Tenth House. It's as if all the success you've been shooting for all year gets crammed into seventeen days, with all the pitfalls and minor calamities that entails. It's too late to get yourself more organized than you are because you need to deal with frontline activities. However, others are available to help you, and it will save time if you show them how to do it rather than doing it yourself.

Wellness and Keeping Fit

In spite of all your busy-ness, you need to take care of yourself, or you will suffer long-term health consequences that outweigh the benefits you gain. You should eat regularly, get at least mild exercise, and don't skimp on sleep. You'll be most vulnerable on November 1, 8, 11, and 28.

Love and Life Connections

Relationships at work could get sticky as everyone strains to take on their share of the workload. The atmosphere can take on an emotional charge and inner tensions explode. You can mollify moods and get everyone pulling together by expressing your appreciation for what others are doing. The more you are in charge, the more you can show gratitude with good effect. This can also take tangible form, such as a catered lunch or bonuses for work well done.

Finance and Success

The boom in business this month has a golden lining—it is the gold that is lining your pocketbook. You're receiving substantially more income, or will be soon—in the form of the reward you've been seeking since this time last year.

Rewarding Days

2, 3, 6, 7, 8, 16, 17, 21, 22, 25, 26, 27, 30

Challenging Days

4, 5, 11, 12, 18, 19, 20

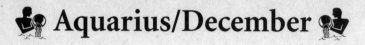 Aquarius/December

Planetary Hotspots

It seems as if you're invited to every holiday party in town—or perhaps you're expected to host them. Either way, your social calendar is full, and it's the way you want it to be. This is where you meet the people upon whom your success depends, especially now that Jupiter is in your Eleventh House. You can maximize your pleasure and your later results if you choose your gatherings wisely and avoid being tied down to just one group. After December 26, you'll itch to retreat into your own space, and that's the right time for it.

Wellness and Keeping Fit

It's hard to exercise when you're tired from lack of sleep and sluggish from too much of the wrong food or drink. If you can limit these disruptions in your rhythms, you'll be much happier with yourself when the holidays are over.

Love and Life Connections

You enter a new stage of development in partnerships on December 5, when Saturn starts its five-month period of backward motion. This is part of Stage Two of a process you began in July 2005. If you've been facing what's real since then, this year will be easier than last. There is the chance for deep transformation, even if it seems like change is impossible. Keeping yourself open to the possibilities will permit you to improve your relationship life in ways you'd only dreamed of before. After December 26, a week's retreat vacation with the companion(s) of your choice fits your mood.

Finance and Success

Contacts made now are seeds planted for the new year, as well as for years to come. You can make a lasting impression without effort. Media attention is possible, especially if you give them a nudge.

Rewarding Days

1, 4, 5, 13, 14, 15, 18, 19, 23, 24, 27, 28, 31

Challenging Days

2, 3, 8, 9, 10, 16, 17, 29, 30

Aquarius Action Table

These dates reflect the best—but not the only—times for success and ease in these activities, according to your Sun sign.

	JAN	FEB	MAR	APR	MAY	JUN	JUL	AUG	SEPT	OCT	NOV	DEC
Move				27, 28	5-19							
Start a class			29, 30	16-30	1-4							
Join a club	1-3											8-26
Ask for a raise			5-31	1-5							17-30	1-10, 18-20
Look for work						3-30	1, 29-31	1-27		2-26	18-30	1-7
Get pro advice	15, 16, 20	11, 12, 16	10-12, 15	6-8, 11-13	4, 5, 9, 10	1, 2, 5-7	2-4, 25	21-23, 26	17-19, 22	15, 16, 20	11, 12, 16	8-10, 13
Get a loan	17-19	13-15	13, 14	9, 10	6-8	3, 4, 30	1, 27-29	23-25	20, 21	17-19	13-15	11, 12
See a doctor	3-31	1-8				3-30	1, 29-31	1-27				27-31
Start a diet	12-14					3-27	29-31	1-10				
End relationship		11-13										
Buy clothes					19-31	1, 2, 24-31	1-18					
Get a makeover	3-22	3-28	1-4									27-31
New romance					27, 28	24-30	1-18, 25	12-31	1-5			
Vacation	20, 21	16, 17	15-17	11-13	9, 10	5-7	2-4, 30	26-28	12-30	1-23	16, 17	13-14

PISCES

The Fish
February 19 to March 20

♓

Element:	Water
Quality:	Mutable
Polarity:	Yin/Feminine
Planetary Ruler:	Neptune
Meditation:	I successfully navigate the seas of my emotions
Gemstone:	Aquamarine
Power Stones:	Amethyst, bloodstone, tourmaline
Key Phrase:	I believe
Glyph:	Two fish, swimming in opposite directions
Anatomy:	Feet, lymphatic system
Color:	Sea green, violet
Animal:	Fish, sea mammals
Myths/Legends:	Aphrodite, Buddha, Jesus of Nazareth
House:	Twelfth
Opposite Sign:	Virgo
Flower:	Water lily
Key Word:	Transcendence

Your Ego's Strengths and Weaknesses

With your mutable water energy, you are the most flexible of the signs, Pisces. You are sensitive to the slightest changes in emotional tone or consciousness at any level. Your mutability gives you the ability to flex and flow as circumstances demand. You naturally look for the wholeness—the connectedness—that exists among all things. You are also an integrator, seeking to bring together separate phenomena into a unified whole, whether it is in the workflow of a hospital or the final stages of a project. You can unite people with your vision and ideals as well as your ability to find common ground. When you feel challenged or overwhelmed, your mutable side may lead you to lose focus and become confused. You may tend to avoid the offending energy or make promises you can't keep to reduce the pressure.

Your watery approach to the world adds to your flexibility but also tunes you in to the "psychic wireless" that all water signs tap. As a result, you attune yourself to inner signals and realities as much as external ones. Your internal states are to you signals of what is happening (or can happen) outside, and this is the source of your visionary approach to life. You can literally see the possibilities, and hold a torch to lead the way to a new future. You can "read" your surroundings, which are full of archetypes, signs, and symbols. It is often easier for you to live for tomorrow, when things will be better, than to deal with today. This can lead to unhappiness if you compare your conditions in the present with those you want to create, and then dwell on what is lacking. Still, you are unafraid to sacrifice your own comforts to create a better world, even if it is only for one other person.

Shining Your Love Light

With your sensitivity, you are a most thoughtful partner. You love the romantic side of love, but you also look for the spiritual. You want a partner who is not put off by your connection with the unseen world, nor by your ability to know things that most people miss. You find it easy to make yourself over in your partner's image, but not so easy to assert your own nature—if you can find it once you have immersed yourself in a new mold. You value spiritual love most highly, and you may find yourself loving someone you can only love in absence because of some obstacle. While pure in form, this is not very fulfilling. Try to concentrate on the here and now.

You're kept guessing in a relationship with Aries. This sign's fun-loving nature and spontaneity brings you joy, but remember to retreat when you need to. You feel comforted and contained by Taurus, reassured by the Bull's steady ways. You'll help this sign develop fluidity and see the subtle side of life. Gemini is as flexible as you are, bringing intellect to your emotional approach, creating a stimulating contrast. You speak the same emotional language as fellow water sign Cancer, who sees the invisible world with a slightly different take. Leo's love of life is infectious, helping you focus your ideals to pursue your heart's desire. Virgo helps you bring into form the inner truth you perceive, demonstrating the link between heaven and earth that you feel. You share a desire to serve others that you can exercise together. Libra brings companionship and impartiality to complement your emotional attunement. You'll appreciate the art and culture that form Libra's world. Scorpio is another water sign, immersed in your world of feelings and psychic impressions. You can flow through life together sharing your perceptions of invisible factors. Sagittarius's rough edges may be hard to take until you realize that this sign shares your idealism about life and means no harm. Capricorn gives you structure and focus, supporting a stable life together. You can relate to Aquarius's eccentricity—a characteristic you share. Aquarius's social skills will rub off on you and you'll bring compassion to the Water Bearer's perspective. A fellow Pisces is sure to delight, as you enjoy wordless communion with each other.

Making Your Place in the World

Your desire to serve others can be expressed in many ways, for so many people are in need in today's world. The medical profession, from nurse to doctor to technician, will permit you to express this urge. With your spiritual attunement, you may prefer healing fields that are more holistic and less mechanistic, such as hypnosis, energy-body healing, or reiki. You may wish to heal a space, as is done with feng shui. You're likely to be able to feel the energies as they move and become still in a household or business. Because of your empathy for others, especially those who are disadvantaged, you may be drawn to working with a nonprofit organization or a program that supports the public welfare. This could come through government, church, or non-governmental organizations. You generally prefer to work behind the scenes, but if your work takes you before an audience, however small, you should take time to restore yourself.

Putting Your Best Foot Forward

You are a visionary and a futurist, Pisces. Your reality is part what you see, hear, feel, and touch, and part the energies you sense flowing through and around you. You are poised between two worlds, the last sign of the Zodiac at one end of the cycle, yet privy to a view far into the future of what has not yet been created in the new cycle. Your natural urge is to respond to what has not yet been revealed. At the risk of being irrelevant, you feel compelled to share your vision with others. However, there's a big gap between the spiritual world you perceive and the physical world that you can be sure that others relate to. It works better if you can find ways to make your vision relevant to those who hear your message. To do this, you need to relate what you see on the inner planes to what others see. Use facts, "real"-world circumstances, and events to show a trajectory toward the outcome you perceive. Logic and practicality are your most powerful supports in this process, and will provide a sure path to clear communication

Tools for Change

Your sensitivity to the inner world is a wonderful gift, but it isn't conducive to dealing with the outer world. Managing the delicate balance between inner and outer is your greatest challenge, and there are many ways to make it easier. The key is externalizing your inner power. It's the way to bridge the gap. One of the best ways to do this is to engage in creative pursuits. Any of the visual arts are good, as well as music, because they are extensions of your watery nature in their nonverbal forms. However, you can extend yourself into less Piscean pursuits such as writing or practical crafts like gardening, ceramics, or sewing. You can redecorate your home, recover furniture, or design a new outfit.

It's also imperative that you follow a regular exercise routine, especially one that develops strength in both core and external muscle groups. Activities which may appeal include swimming, yoga for conditioning, dance, step or regular aerobics, and pilates. However, two approaches that would be especially good for you are martial arts, which will teach you to be more assertive as you develop physical power, and tai chi, which will help you learn to manipulate and balance your energy field.

Meditations that focus on inducing peace and clearing accumulated or stagnant energy will help you be yourself by releasing emotions and thoughts you've picked up from other people. This will be most beneficial when done in the evening. You can strengthen your mind and ability to communicate, another link to the outer world, through education. Higher education teaches analytical skills and induces breadth of perspective. In particular, the study of mathematics and logic discipline the mind, developing the ability to follow a logical progression of thought. Study of philosophy will open your mind to new viewpoints about the world in the broadest sense. Psychology will teach you about the expressions of human nature in the real world—the link between inner and outer being. The area that most reflects your ability to relate to the outer world, though, is your finances. If you focus on learning to manage your finances successfully and consistently, working toward wealth and wise investment, you'll prove to yourself that you can bridge the gap between the unseen universe and the "real" world.

Affirmation for the Year

I enjoy expanding my horizons and accepting new challenges.

The Year Ahead for Pisces

Your life is full of joy and creativity—perhaps even romance—this year! Jupiter is winging its way through your solar Ninth House, where it has been since October 25 of last year. This is your final climb to a peak that you've been working toward for eight years. You can make final preparations for this pinnacle even as you start to see it materialize. The emphasis will be on spreading the word, perhaps through travel or publishing. You will find that your choices are broad, but it's important to stay focused or you'll waste energy. No matter the source, you'll be in greater circulation, in contact with others more than before. You may also encounter new cultures or have reason to brush up on a foreign language. When Jupiter goes into Sagittarius on November 23, it enters your solar Tenth House. You'll enter the peak period you've been working toward since 1998. You'll be front and center, playing a prominent, even public, role. This will be a one-year success cycle for you.

Saturn spends its second year in Leo, your Sixth House. It's time to continue your hard work in support of your long-term goals. It is also a good idea to attend to health and lifestyle issues now. Disciplined application of healthy habits will bring you benefits for years to come.

Chiron is in your solar Twelfth House and the sign of Aquarius. In the Twelfth House, Chiron is a messenger of the spiritual realms. It brings mysterious circumstances, perhaps ailments, to the surface to be healed. You may benefit from using a spiritual perspective to seek the source of blockages in your body or personality.

Uranus is in Pisces and your solar First House. You're in the fourth year of Uranus's travel through your sign. You've been startled awake to new aspects of your own nature, including your boldness and independence. You'll continue on your path of liberation, which may include surrendering your personal interests for a larger ideal.

Neptune is in Aquarius and your solar Twelfth House, enhancing your experience of the spiritual realms. You have become more interested in spiritual reality since 1998, and you may be pursuing a spiritual path with more dedication or bringing your spirituality to the surface. Meditation is key to this process.

Pluto continues its path through Sagittarius and your Tenth House. You've been going through a gradual process of self-empowerment, which has been especially evident in your climb to career success. You've become both more prominent and more public, and you've taken on leadership roles. Because of your rapid changes, you've also had to let go of situations that have outlived their usefulness. By continuing to let go of the old while embracing the new, you will live up the full potential of Pluto's contact.

The eclipses move into Virgo and Pisces, your Seventh and First Houses, come March 14. This opens the door for some of the changes you've felt inwardly to take outward effect, especially with respect to self-presentation and relationships.

If you were born between February 22 and March 13, Saturn in Leo is contacting your Sun from your solar Sixth House. You have plenty to do now, both at work and at home. It's time to get organized, to make substantive steps to restructure your work life, and to move toward the goals you hatched about twelve years ago. You've got a couple more years before you receive the recognition that is truly your due. In the meantime, continue preparing for the time when your more public duties will leave you little time for foundation-building. You can lay some of this groundwork by improving your health. Now is the time to get your habits in line with the person you are becoming. Once Saturn enters Virgo in two years, you'll be more exposed, and you'll want to be able to handle the increased pressures that come from these contacts. A thorough check-up and a course of supportive health treatments such as acupuncture or massage will fill the bill. Self-maintenance routines such as yoga and aerobic training will also go a long way toward increasing your robustness. Saturn's energies will be strongest in your life on or around January 27, February 19, April 5 and 24, June 20, August 7, November 16 and December 5.

If you were born between February 25 and March 3, Uranus in Pisces has reached your Sun from your solar First House. You've felt the changes coming, and the time to enact them is upon you. First you need to sharpen your focus so you know what you want. Write it down and plan it out in as much detail as you can, reworking it regularly. Then you need to keep your attention on what you want rather than what you fear by using affirmations. Keep your supportive friends and colleagues close to you as you make the change, distancing yourself from those who could drag you down. You'll be at your best by tuning into Uranus, acting with ingenuity and resilience as life takes its twists and turns. By next year you'll have landed your jet at a new level, so don't be dismayed if life feels chaotic at times.

Your self-image will go through an awakening process as well. You'll see yourself in a new way as you develop your new path. The feedback you receive from others will reinforce this. You may change your hair, personal style, or even your body shape to match where you're heading now. This cycle begins March 1, with peak Uranus events on or around June 5 and 19, September 5, November 19, and December 2.

If you were born between March 3 and 10, Neptune in Aquarius is connecting with your Sun from your Twelfth House. Since 1998, you've been experiencing the subtle hand of spirituality in your life. This year your process of spiritual growth will intensify. Your psychic sensitivity will increase, as well as your ability to use it—especially through visual methods such as clairvoyance or scrying. You will feel and perhaps see energy exchanges as people interact. You will become especially aware of the tone of group dynamics, which you will learn to trust with experience. Meditation and spiritual development classes will help you understand what is happening and channel the energies. Your new reality may be confusing at times, but you'll adapt to a wider awareness by the end of the year. Your imagination will also be strong and your dream states vivid. You may feel like spending more time alone to be creative and to assimilate all that you are learning on the inner levels. You may also be drawn to sacrifice for others during this time. Neptune's subtle energies are prominent on January 27, February 5, March 15, May 10 and 22, August 10, October 29, and November 9.

If you were born between March 11 and 16, Pluto in Sagittarius makes this your year due to an energizing contact with the Sun from your solar Tenth House. The feeling is intense as you start to take several leaps up the ladder of success. It's been building over the past few years, and if you've been using the energy well, you've built up a good head of steam. The problem this year is going to be how to manage all the activity you've created, to follow through on all the potential successes you've generated. You've been finding, and will continue to find, doors opening to you. This is because others are recognizing your acumen, your mastery in your field. Others see you as an authority now, and it will require you to adjust your demeanor. Some may become envious, or see you as a threat or an authority against which they need to rebel. The result will be power struggles unless you can recognize them early and distance yourself. Eventually everyone will accept you at this new level, and your world will become calmer and more stable at a new high. Pluto's energies are most intense around March 17 and 29, June 16, September 4 and 16, and December 18.

If you were born between February 19 and 21 or March 17 and 20, none of the major planets are connecting with your Sun this year. This gives you more leeway in how you conduct your affairs this year; you could even consider it a year off from a high level of challenge. It's a good time to take a long vacation or take up a project that is dear to your heart but not attached to a goal other than enjoyment. Your life may be just as busy, or you may have time to loaf; either way it will be more your choice than usual. On the other hand, it may be difficult to get out of a rut if you want to. Without solar contact, it may be hard to jumpstart a large effort if that's what you have in mind. However, contacts from the slow-moving planets—Jupiter, Saturn, Uranus, Neptune, and Pluto—can occur to your other personal planets. These connections will trigger events and give you the wiggle room you need to bring about desired changes.

Pisces/January

Planetary Hotspots

Subtle or hidden factors affect your life in all areas, with the greatest impact on the activities designed to fulfill your long-term goals. You're very near the pinnacle of your path, which you embarked on in 1997, and it will be on your mind around January 27 when Jupiter connects with Neptune as part of a thirteen-year cycle. Although you reach the peak next year, you will achieve partial success in the coming months. Use this time to make any course adjustments as you reach for the culmination of your efforts.

Wellness and Keeping Fit

Your extra efforts to complete your work may hit your immune system especially hard this month, as triggers occur to Saturn in your Sixth House. Sleep and regular food are most important to your continued strength, but keeping your objectivity when it comes to the daily challenges of life will also reduce your stress.

Love and Life Connections

With Venus retrograde in your Eleventh House, you'll notice disagreements between those in your social and professional network. These struggles do not have to affect you directly. In fact, you may be able to mediate some conflicts, but only if you are asked. Don't go into rescue mode. You'll have the chance to re-evaluate the organizations you associate with and choose your roles as well as your affiliations. This will help you maximize your coming success.

Finance and Success

With Saturn being triggered in your Sixth House, there's lots of work to do, but that doesn't mean it's good for you to do it all. Prioritize, delegate, and eliminate unnecessary tasks. Just as important, take control of your day by choosing the times you will respond to others. Let the answering machine take messages and call back later.

Rewarding Days
3, 4, 8, 9, 12, 13, 14, 22, 23, 24, 27, 28, 31

Challenging Days
10, 11, 17, 18, 25, 26

Pisces/February

Planetary Hotspots

You're drawn into your inner world around February 5 as Neptune's new yearly cycle begins in your Twelfth House. Use this time to set your spiritual course to achieve greater peace and centeredness, for when you are in this space, you weather every storm without stress. The intensity of last month dissipates after February 6, alleviating the frenetic pace life has taken lately.

Wellness and Keeping Fit

As the planets enter your Twelfth House, this is a good time to retreat from the world and replenish yourself. Stay home and work on a beloved project or hobby, or go someplace where no one knows you and you can experience life without interruption. A short trip, even a vacation, will rejuvenate your energy stores and last for months to come. You don't have to go far (although you can)—just don't answer the phone or read your email.

Love and Life Connections

As Venus goes direct in your Eleventh House, friendships are especially important to you. You will be rewarded by spending time with friends for the perspective and wisdom they bring to you. Even though you crave alone time this month, there will be one or two gatherings that will be especially fruitful for you if you attend.

Finance and Success

Continue to prepare for your next success, even as you maintain your current activities based on previous accomplishments. After a push at the beginning of the month, you can settle into a more routine existence—less exciting but also giving you room for your usual personal pursuits.

Rewarding Days

1, 4, 5, 8, 9, 10, 18, 19, 20, 23, 24, 27, 28

Challenging Days

6, 7, 13, 14, 15, 21, 22

Pisces/March

Planetary Hotspots

Events carry you away in March, since several planetary interactions involve your sign. Mercury is retrograde in Pisces from March 2 to 25, highlighting your relationships and communications. Uranus's cycle starts on March 1 in your sign, giving you new ideas about how to break free from the old you. Mars goads you into action when it contacts Uranus on March 11.

Wellness and Keeping Fit

You could feel overwhelmed this month by demands and interruptions, resulting in stress that ends in viral illness as your immune system suffers. It's time to take preventive measures: boosting your immune system with plenty of sleep, herbal supplements, and good food; doing acupuncture; and keeping to your regular fitness routine. The greatest challenges to your health occur on March 2, 11, 14, and 25.

Love and Life Connections

Around March 11, events at home propel you toward your goals of greater independence and self-expression, even though you have misgivings and are unsure of how you'll accomplish your goals. This may involve your career, but it is as much about your identity and who you are to those you love. You are aware of setting an example as well as wanting the changes for yourself.

Finance and Success

You have the opportunity to make concrete movements toward your goals on March 14 and 29, as the lunar eclipse moves into your sign. This is the beginning of a two-year window of opportunity to bring about the changes you've wanted. Your focused nurturing over the next five months will bring you to a new level by early September.

Rewarding Days

3, 4, 8, 9, 18, 19, 22, 23, 24, 31

Challenging Days

5, 6, 7, 13, 14, 20, 21, 27, 28

Pisces/April

Planetary Hotspots

Challenges to your serenity will arise starting April 8, when Mars and Pluto connect in your Fourth and Tenth Houses, bringing out a home vs. career tug-of-war that you'll have to mediate. Key dates for this are April 13, 17 to 20, and 30. Opportunities coincide with this situation, however—especially those that include travel and teaching themes.

Wellness and Keeping Fit

Lingering health matters move toward resolution as April 5 and Saturn's retrograde period pass. You've still got four months to go to solidify results, but you're seeing substantial progress by now. Maintain the same routines you established last fall and perfected early this year; you'll be pleased with how energetic and fulfilled you feel. Stresses could mount from April 13 to 20, so take it easy on yourself around then.

Love and Life Connections

Any proposals you make toward others this month are likely to go over well, as Venus makes it way through your sign starting April 5. Your requests will be most warmly received from April 18 to 20, as Venus contacts Jupiter.

Finance and Success

You may have felt forced to let work overshadow the rest of your life since November 22, but this will be a thing of the past after April 5 when Saturn returns to direct motion. You're still building toward a wonderful new future, however, so you'll want to continue your focused efforts for the next three months, although with less urgency. This is part of a long gradual climb to success, toward a pinnacle that will come in about ten years.

Rewarding Days

1, 4, 5, 9, 10, 14, 15, 19, 20, 23, 24, 27, 28

Challenging Days

2, 3, 16, 17, 18, 29, 30

Pisces/May

Planetary Hotspots

The process of change that you've been working with since 2003 gets a big boost through May 7 as Mars and Jupiter form a grand trine with Uranus, your guiding star. This comes from foreign places, romantic partners, and your own creative efforts. You may get the chance to publish, teach, or otherwise get your message out to a large audience. Positive media coverage could be possible.

Wellness and Keeping Fit

Chiron and Neptune pull you inward as they begin their retrograde periods on May 15 and 22. It's a good time to gain clarity about your motivations and purpose. It's also a good time to get some healing treatments—especially those that treat the whole person or work on your energy field, such as acupuncture or energetic healing.

Love and Life Connections

Your finances could come up short when it comes to fulfilling the desires of your children around May 26, but don't let that bother you. You can work something out if it's important, and if necessary ask for help from others.

Finance and Success

Communication, commerce, and completion are also in the picture as January's planetary pattern is reiterated. It's time to get more clutter off your desk and clear some leftovers from your to-do list. The planets draw your attention to these matters in the first half of the month, then leave you to your own devices after May 15. You get a chance now to check in on how you're doing with fulfilling the goals you set in May 2000 and to make any necessary course corrections over the coming months.

Rewarding Days

1, 2, 3, 11, 12, 13, 16, 17, 20, 21, 24, 25, 26, 29, 30

Challenging Days

6, 7, 8, 14, 15, 27, 28

Pisces/June

Planetary Hotspots

Action is the keyword this month as both Uranus and Pluto are highlighted in the heavens and make dynamic contact to your Sun. It's time for Stage Two of this year's self-improvement process on June 19, when Uranus starts its backward motion. That starts a five-month period of focused effort on your part to fulfill the dreams you activated on March 1. The halfway point in Pluto's cycle, reached on June 16, brings career and business ventures to a peak. Now you can see the full potential of what you've started. It will play out, requiring only follow-through from you, over the next six months.

Wellness and Keeping Fit

Once again, the amount of activity in your life is dizzying, and calming forms of exercise are called for, as are meditation, sleep, and foods with high nutritional value. You could be injury-prone from June 16 to 19, so take extra care to stay focused then. Carving out some time to play will refresh you more than seems possible and will make your time for work more productive.

Love and Life Connections

This is a good month to enjoy the simple pleasures of life with the people you love. Go with a friend to a museum or the theater. You'll be surprised at how this will fill your spirit and bring you joy.

Finance and Success

Your work efforts are flowering, and you need to respond to the activity you've generated. This means spending a lot more time at work than you like to, but this peak will level off after June 20. You are moving toward a life where you're working smarter, not harder, but this is one of those times when you'll definitely be doing both.

Rewarding Days

8, 9, 12, 13, 16, 17, 18, 21, 22, 25, 26

Challenging Days

3, 4, 10, 11, 23, 24, 30

Pisces/July

Planetary Hotspots

Issues at home that surfaced on March 1 and 11, April 18, and June 19 come to the forefront again around July 5. Do what you can to disperse the difficulty now, because next month it could flare up with more vengeance. Your efforts to create your new self and new world get a boost when Jupiter returns to direct motion on July 6. It harmonizes with Uranus in your sign through mid-September, giving you lots of time to move your plans forward. You'll feel the wind at your back most of this time, so make the most of this time of high energy, optimism, and focus.

Wellness and Keeping Fit

A vacation is one of the best things you can do for your well-being now. It will clear your mind, help you sort out your priorities, and make your efforts more inspired and efficient when you return. You'll actually save time in the long run and increase the quality of your work in ways that cannot be measured. Your workload will abate after July 4 and make it easier to get out the door.

Love and Life Connections

You'll act contrary to others' expectations around July 5, but it's part of the way you're reforming your character and presentation. It's best to introduce these changes now rather than wait until next month, when they'll be discovered under more volatile circumstances.

Finance and Success

Your road to success now involves retracing some steps in the new products and processes you're developing. It's not a complete rethinking of your plans, just a little tweaking. This will be a valuable time when, although you won't make much visible progress, you'll be laying the groundwork for a big leap forward after July 28.

Rewarding Days

5, 6, 10, 11, 14, 15, 18, 19, 22, 23, 24

Challenging Days

1, 7, 8, 9, 20, 21, 27, 28, 29

Pisces/August

Planetary Hotspots

Even though unexpected events are likely this month, you'll feel blessed by good fortune. A beneficial situation develops as the month progresses, culminating on August 29. This could emanate from a general feeling of well-being and optimism that unconsciously brings new opportunities toward you. This "spiritual charisma" feels like magic and can be created at any time when we are tuned to the universe, but it is especially easy this month for you. What stands in your way, however, is the potential for anxiety and tension to overshadow your positive attitude. Such agitation is most likely to occur on August 13 and 29, but if you meet all situations with peace and inner balance, you'll be able to keep the magic with you.

Wellness and Keeping Fit

You recognize the importance of health and fitness now—enough to have a plan. It's time to rework that plan around August 7, to tweak it for the coming year. You can reduce the feelings of tension and anxiety that are likely around August 13 and 29 by maintaining a regular practice of centering exercises and meditations.

Love and Life Connections

If others act more aggressively than usual, it is because they feel competitive, or, perhaps, because they envy you your good fortune. The tensions will rise on August 13 and 29, and then dissipate. If you can skirt the issues rather than confronting them, they will dissipate on their own and can be discussed at a more relaxed time.

Finance and Success

Your plan for the coming year starting on August 7 should include a leaner, meaner workload, so that you are working smarter, not harder. This includes delegating where possible and eliminating tasks that do not contribute enough to the end product.

Rewarding Days

1, 2, 3, 6, 7, 10, 11, 14, 15, 19, 20, 29, 30

Challenging Days

4, 5, 16, 17, 18, 23, 24, 25, 31

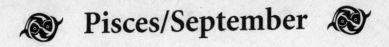 # Pisces/September

Planetary Hotspots

Your life reaches a peak early in the month as several planetary events collide. Pluto's change in direction, Uranus as the halfway point in its cycle, and a lunar eclipse excite your chart and open the door to new possibilities. They'll come through your relationships, whether current or new ones. With your current focus on introducing new opportunities into your life, you are eager to accept them. Events now tie in with those around March 1 and June 19.

Wellness and Keeping Fit

Health could become a concern if you work too long and hard in response to the peak of events. Your vitality is generally good, but if you "get ahead of yourself" you could suffer injury or accident, especially on September 3 or 9. This is also a good time to get advice from health practitioners about how the lifestyle changes you initiated a year ago are affecting your health.

Love and Life Connections

Your relationships are as exciting as your life, and the key word is "unexpected." You'll get some feedback that is a response to your efforts to change your life—another point of view to factor into the person you are becoming. This will come up from September 5 to 7.

Finance and Success

Career-enhancing activities that you began last December reach a turning point on September 4 as Pluto returns to forward motion. You can see the benefits of the projects and initiatives you started in March, as they take on a life of their own. Now it's time to assimilate them more fully into your work life, bringing them to completion as you watch for new ideas to emerge. You feel the impulse to donate to your favorite causes after September 7, but don't be so generous that you sacrifice your financial stability.

Rewarding Days

2, 3, 4, 11, 12, 15, 16, 25, 26, 30

Challenging Days

1, 7, 8, 13, 14, 20, 21, 27, 28, 29

Pisces/October

Planetary Hotspots

You're in the flow now as the planets begin to move into harmony with your sign. On October 1, Mercury enters Scorpio, and that starts a period of greater effectiveness and forward progress that will last through the end of November. However, Mercury will retrograde on October 28, bringing out challenges related to events on October 5, 15, 22, and 24. Even though this could bring a few minor glitches, it will also prolong the harmonious period for you, and you will get more out of the experience than if the retrograde were not happening. During this time, the emphasis is on your plans to create more personal freedom and fulfillment in your life.

Wellness and Keeping Fit

All the ease you're experiencing will release a lot of stored energy, and you'll be very busy. Take care of yourself and make sure to take regular breaks; a short time away from the daily routine will help at mid-month, when there may be a lull in activity.

Love and Life Connections

You've never felt better about your direction in life, and those close to you are behind you one hundred percent. Don't forget to express your appreciation. You've come through a challenging period, and you wouldn't have made it without them.

Finance and Success

You gain the support of others, perhaps even media attention, from far and wide, and this may include financial reward. If it doesn't arrive this month, it is in the works. Opportunities come from your contacts with people in groups through October 15, so this isn't the time to stay home.

Rewarding Days
1, 4, 5, 8, 9, 12, 13, 14, 22, 23, 24, 27, 28, 31

Challenging Days
10, 11, 17, 18, 19, 25, 26

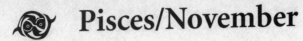 # Pisces/November

Planetary Hotspots

You get results this month as Uranus returns to forward motion in your sign on November 19. However, it will take some effort to get to that point. Mercury retrograde joins the Sun, Venus, Mars, and Jupiter in your Ninth House of exploration and goal-fulfillment. These harmonize with your sign, making this a satisfying time in the long run. You'll be busy, even doing some back-pedaling, through November 17. However, you'll see some forward motion after November 8.

Wellness and Keeping Fit

Although you may feel as though work holds you hostage, you have to break free sometimes. You can satisfy this stronger-than-usual urge now by taking periodic short breaks. Pick one day each week to take a long hike; have dinner with a friend on a regular schedule; do something you love before going to bed each night. A vacation is possible after November 19.

Love and Life Connections

The changes you've been making have necessarily disrupted the flow in your personal relationships. Sharing your successes with those who have lived through them with you is the best way to thank them for being part of the team. You know how important their support has been, and you can let them know by celebrating with them.

Finance and Success

When Jupiter enters Sagittarius on November 23, it begins a year-long expansion of your career and business enterprises. This is a good time to expand in directions you've desired to go since 1995, when Pluto entered Sagittarius. You'll be pulling cherished goals off the back burner now as opportunities arise for you to launch them. Aim high: with Pluto involved, you can shoot for the Moon!

Rewarding Days

1, 4, 5, 9, 10, 18, 19, 20, 23, 24, 28, 29

Challenging Days

6, 7, 8, 13, 14, 15, 21, 22

Pisces/December

Planetary Hotspots

The planets weave a web of intricate interconnections, as last month's cluster moves into Sagittarius and your Tenth House. This invigorates your career, and your attention is focused here almost exclusively until December 19. Although not every experience is harmonious, you are exhilarated by the challenge and excited because a new set of dreams is being empowered. Key dates are December 3, 11, 16, 18, and 21.

Wellness and Keeping Fit

Although there is plenty to get stressed out about now, you are naturally resistant to stress. This is because you are doing what's in your heart. As long as you keep your focus on the events of the moment and act from your appreciation of what the universe is permitting you to do, you will be happy and at peace.

Love and Life Connections

Your very visible role in the outer world makes you less visible at home. You can cope better if you ratchet down your expectations of yourself during the holidays, as well as those of others. Skip the decorations and have someone else address the holiday cards. Better yet, send them in the new year with a newsy note and a photo.

Finance and Success

Pluto in Sagittarius is the indicator planet for your career or business. When its new cycle starts on December 18, you are planting the seeds of the coming year. You can empower yourself by being conscious of what you do around this date, and by setting your intention for what you want to create. This year is especially powerful because Jupiter is also in Sagittarius. It will permit you to build an extraordinary new level of success, one that you've been aiming toward since 1995, even if you didn't know what form it would take then.

Rewarding Days

2, 3, 6, 7, 16, 17, 20, 21, 22, 25, 26, 29, 30

Challenging Days

4, 5, 11, 12, 18, 19, 31

Pisces Action Table

These dates reflect the best—but not the only—times for success and ease in these activities, according to your Sun sign.

	JAN	FEB	MAR	APR	MAY	JUN	JUL	AUG	SEPT	OCT	NOV	DEC
Move					20-31	1, 2						
Start a class				27, 28	5-19							
Join a club	3-22											27-31
Ask for a raise		3-28	1-4	6-30	1-3						17-30	1-10, 18-20
Look for work								11-31	1-12			
Get pro advice	17-19, 22	13-15, 18	13, 14, 18	9, 10, 14	6-8, 11-13	3, 4, 8, 9	1, 6, 27-29	1-3, 23-25	20, 21, 25	17-19, 22	13-14, 18	11, 12, 16
Get a loan	20, 21	16, 17	15-17	11-13	9, 10	5-7	2-4, 30	26-28	22-24	20, 21	16, 17	13-15
See a doctor	22-31	1-18	25-31					11-31	1-12			
Start a diet						28-30		12-27				
End relationship			13, 14									
Buy clothes						3-27	29-31	1-12				
Get a makeover		1-8	5-31	1-5			29-31		6-30			
New romance	22-31					26, 27	29-31	1-11, 23	6-30			
Vacation	22-24	18-20	18, 19	14, 15	11-13	8, 9	5, 6	1-3, 29	25, 26	22-31	1-30	1-7, 16

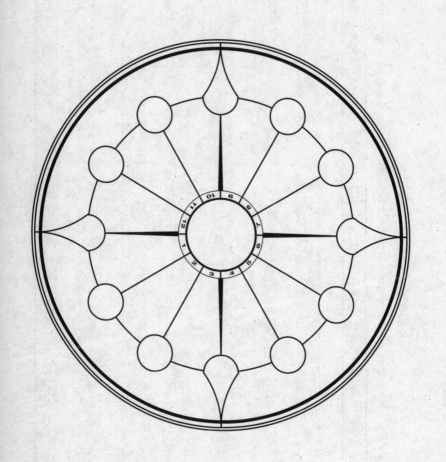

2006 SUN SIGN BOOK

Articles

Contributors

Bernie Ashman

Stephanie Clement

Alice DeVille

Sasha Fenton

Dorothy Oja

Leeda Alleyn Pacotti

Bruce Scofield

Anne Windsor

Astral Intuition
Listening to Your Inner Sign

by Stephanie Clement

According to psychologist Carl Jung, there are two distinct ways of perceiving the world: through the ordinary senses (sensation), and through indirect perception through the unconscious (intuition). Intuition uses the sensations coming from the outside and incorporates ideas and associations from the unconscious. Jung believed that everyone is capable of both kinds of perception, and that each of us prefers one over the other.

Jung also said that psychological balance is important. He indicated that, as we mature, we continue a psychological developmental process that lasts throughout our lives. Sometimes we focus so much on our preferred perception process that we become very strong at using it—so strong that we are overbalanced in one direction. Balanced development involves the cultivation of the less dominant process so that it becomes a skill nearly as strong as the preferred method of perception.

Intuitives are always pursuing the possibilities of what they perceive in the present. They tend to read between the lines, look to the future, and ignore some of the potential that is right in front of them. Sensation types, on the other hand, focus on the present, stick to what is written on the page, and spend little time dreaming about ideas coming from the unconscious.

We all need our ordinary senses to get around in the world. For example, we have to be able to see if we want to drive cars. We have to be able to hear if we want to use ordinary telephones. We need the sense of taste to enjoy food. The ordinary uses of intuition are not as obvious.

Just what are the uses of intuition? As you read this list of traits attributed to intuition, you will notice some that you recognize in yourself and really like. Others will seem less comfortable or familiar.

Characteristics of intuition types

- Seeking sources of inspiration
- Inventiveness
- Seeking opportunities and possibilities
- Seeking something new rather than enjoying what you have
- Inspired leadership
- Initiating and instigating
- Having good test-taking skills
- Creating and understanding metaphor

Characteristics of sensation types:

- Seeking enjoyment in life
- Observing the world around you
- Taking life as it comes
- Staying in the moment
- Enjoying sexual and other physical pleasures more often
- Working diligently on complex tasks
- Creating and understanding metaphor

As you read about the different Sun signs, you will notice that each sign has a particular "take" on intuition. That is, each sign responds to intuitive impulses in a unique way during 2006. As you read about your Sun sign, think of ways you can use this information throughout the year. As you learn to pay attention to your intuition in a new way, you are honoring your own capacity to relate to the world in new, and different, ways. Also, if you happen to know your Moon sign or Ascendant, you can read about them to discover ways to allow your less conscious side to express itself through intuition.

The Intuitive Impulse in 2006

Let's consider the prevailing direction of intuition for 2006. Interest in religion and mysticism has been on the increase for five or six years. Evidence of this includes the fact that, while reading and book buying in general has declined, there have been significant increases in the purchase of books on religious and spiritual topics. People have recognized the interior, even subconscious, forces that guide daily activities and desires. We want to understand ourselves more now than at any time in the past.

Many people see the increasing need to work for social causes and to relate to people all over the planet instead of just in our own families or localities. We are developing a greater sense of empathy for others and a more profound sense of connection to the Earth and its needs. More people seek ways to improve the world, and not just themselves.

A strange paradox has developed in the political scene. On the one hand, we have witnessed increasing secrecy about the way political and foreign affairs are being managed. The secrecy, all by itself, engenders suspicion that we are not being told the truth, or certainly not all of the truth. The feeling of deception makes us squirm. On the other hand, secrets are leaking out. We are finding out about international intelligence scandals and the individuals involved. This period of time must be a political nightmare for world leaders who formerly thrived amid secret negotiations and plots. No secret is sacred now.

For individuals, the vistas are brighter. If you avoid secret liaisons and affairs, and instead direct your energy toward the future, you stand to make striking gains. There are no limits to imagination. Abstract ideas that previously baffled you become clear. Hidden information becomes available, family secrets are revealed, and you feel far more in touch with your personal reality.

As new ideas emerge, they hit you hard. This can be a good thing, even in the midst of your shock and surprise. While new is not always better, more information almost always helps you to make better choices, whereas secrecy prevents you from making informed decisions.

Last but not least, we all can develop our intuition or other psychic powers. There is little doubt that we have such powers, but how can we develop them and use them creatively and effectively? The sections on each Sun sign provide suggestions about how to identify, acknowledge, and encourage your intuitive powers as Uranus continues its progress through the sign of Pisces in 2006.

The Sun Through the Signs

Aries

Intuition can be your greatest source of information and encouragement. You have the potential to grow and develop as an individual, family member, and member of society through your intuitive powers. Naturally intuitive in your approach to life, now you can gain a profound understanding of the psychic currents flowing around and through you.

You find that you are drawn to study new subjects, or to investigate them more deeply than you have in the past. You feel an urge to take a new direction. You read, attend lectures or workshops, and generally open your heart and mind to receive new information.

The metaphor of growth works on both conscious and subconscious levels for you. You may want to select images or stories that exemplify the best potential for growth. For example, your meditation can include visualization of a rosebud opening in bright sunlight to reveal its brilliant color and design to you.

Taurus

Let your intuition choose the places for you to travel for work or vacation. Your love life can benefit from intuitive decision-making, and so can your career. You will be acting more independently, and at the same time you will be paying attention to what is most important for your partner and clients.

If you have an illness or injury, you will find that healing occurs much faster when you focus on your body and its needs. Intuition can guide you to just the right doctor or therapy. Your conversations with your inner self can include guided imagery for healing, conversations with the injured part, and general information about what you need to do to speed the healing process.

You may find that new ideas seem to pop into your head regularly this year. You may even become restless as you consider additional activities or a new direction altogether. Your judgment is generally sound. You have many opportunities, so you have to determine which are the most promising. Get all the facts you can gather, and then listen to yourself.

Gemini

During 2006 you will be challenged to talk about what you are receiving intuitively from the cosmos. You will have sudden changes of mind; for example, you may yearn to move to a new location. Before you jump in the car with your most precious possessions, check out your intuition. Is there a job waiting for you? Will you find a compatible social group to join? Is romance part of the picture? In other words, what's behind the intuitive impulse?

Because your intuition is so powerful now, you need to cultivate your attention skills. Don't allow flights of fancy to distract you from serious work. Pay conscious and close attention to tasks involving machinery or sharp tools. Remember the concept of balance? Be present in the world of sensation when that is required; allow your mind to follow intuitive impulses when that is the best approach. By being clearly aware of both, you will develop new talents in both arenas.

Cancer

You will find that 2006 brings situations in which you are able to go with the flow of other people's activities. You seem to know what is coming up without having to think about it much, and you find simple ways to verify your intuition along the way. If you have any health concerns, be sure to share your intuition with your health care providers. Your insights can help to provide the most successful treatments. Learning the basics of hypnosis and telepathy will be advantageous in all your relationships.

You find you are interested in new subjects and may study them deeply. As you read or attend a class, you find that your intuition is steering you toward the answers almost before you know the questions. Your studies not only offer new knowledge—they help you understand the intuitive skills you possess. You learn which part of your insight comes from logic and which from intuition. This distinction makes you more confident in your decisions.

Leo

When intuition is strong, you find you need to adjust your rational decision-making processes to take this new information into account. The adjustment does not have to involve a huge change. It may be that only a five-degree shift in your mental focus will allow you to take in information and feelings that are well within your sphere of attention.

Career direction and work projects can benefit from this five-degree shift. For one thing, smaller adjustments are easier to absorb. For another, a slight change often delivers spectacular results. After all, you started the project with a lot of good information. It doesn't make sense to junk everything just because one or two pieces don't seem to fit.

Intuition may bring some mental or physical discomfort. Use any discomfort as a measure of your accuracy. Are you right on target? That should feel relaxed and easy. Are you tense? That suggests a slight change of position or mental attitude may be beneficial.

Virgo

Intuition provides you with a golden opportunity to become aware of how you learn about the world around you. Sometimes your knowledge comes from outside yourself. We usually acquire factual information about the world in this way. Sometimes, though, you gain profound insight from within yourself. Some people hear a familiar voice in their heads—a voice that has been with them since childhood. Others make mental pictures that show how to accomplish a task or even portray a place they want to visit. This year you will be able to listen to your inner voice and match it up with what you know about your environment and about other people.

Romance acquires a healthy glow when you apply your inner knowledge to your relationships. Intuition suggests the best romantic activities. Communicating what you feel deep in your heart is one of the best ways to demonstrate your trust in your partner.

Libra

Your desire for harmony and balance in your life benefits from the development of intuition in several ways. First, you use both intellect and intuition to make crucial decisions in your life. This combination of mental processes produces deeper, more accurate insight into any problem. Second, you don't jump to conclusions. Instead you go back and forth, weighing your intuition, perhaps even testing it before you make a full commitment to any action. Third, by practicing a new way to gather information, you exercise your mind in a new way. Mental exercise is good.

Intuition may steer you in the direction of a volunteer position in your neighborhood or church. You find that you have a deep understanding of something that your community needs, and you are able to put some time and effort into making effective changes. You also have good judgment that allows you to fit into a group of like-minded individuals.

Scorpio

Conditions are right for a major change in your life. You will have to take action to make that change happen, and you have several ways to do this. Travel to places you love, engage in focused meditation, and do some research about new products or historical subjects. With each new development, you can use the information or your emotional response as a metaphor for your meditation process, facilitating change.

Your self-healing potential is high because you are aligned in your physical, mental, and spiritual bodies. You can use your meditation skills to maximize the healing power of any treatment you receive. Your internal focus allows you to bring healing power to the site of any problem. Hypnosis is another powerful healing tool that helps you to zero in on a physical or emotional problem, find its metaphorical roots, and develop beneficial alternatives

Sagittarius

Your challenge for 2006 is to deepen your understanding of your personal values. You have discovered that some of your beliefs, while consistent with those of your parents or other people, are not consistent with your inner sense of what is right for you. Now is the time to transcend any worn-out beliefs that keep you from making progress in your career, partnership, or spiritual growth. You will find that old emotional habits fade into the background as you clear up this kind of old business.

Travel or even a major move is possible. Pay attention to the people you meet, but don't tell them all the details of your business. For one thing, they don't need to know. Second, you may change your mind in a big way. Third, a cautious approach to new situations can't hurt you, and can prevent misunderstandings. With a bit of caution, this can be a very good period for new ideas or inventions. Your intuition tells you just what is needed and, sometimes more importantly, what people desire.

Capricorn

Other people come to you with as many opportunities as you can handle. The main question is which opportunities to follow up on. Intuition shows you the future of each possibility. It's almost as if you have a crystal ball that shows you how things will turn out. You also find it easy to do the practical research you need to get supportive facts. Then you will feel more comfortable with your decisions.

You are inspired by the material applications of ideas that once seemed too ethereal to be useful. Your romantic partner may become a business partner, at least in the planning of new endeavors. As you talk over possibilities, the two of you come up with far better solutions than you would have alone. Psychically you are in tune with family and close associates.

Aquarius

You are in the early stages of some big changes in your life. Your intuition is building in strength as you move forward with efforts to make your mark on the world. Social reform is one of your goals, once you have your own financial life in order.

You may experience sleep disturbances or other physical phenomena as your intuition develops. With practice you learn which impulses are meaningful signals and which are more in the nature of side effects to be tolerated, if not ignored. Attempting to follow up on every idea results only in scattered efforts. Your body provides its own set of signals to help you keep on the right track.

A regular program of walking or other exercise helps you to connect your intuition to the practical world. Take your meditation for a walk, or meditate while you work in your garden. Contact with the earth is important to your understanding and your comfort level with the changes you experience.

Pisces

During this period of your life, you undergo many changes. You are ending old cycles in many areas of your life and beginning new ones. This doesn't mean you have to end all your relationships, sell all your worldly goods, and move to an ashram. It does mean that you will be letting go of old attitudes and habits that prevent you from experiencing the depth of love in your relationships, the full value of your material possessions, and the joy of seeing the world in a new light.

Intuition helps you see the future results of today's actions. By knowing a bit about the future, you are more confident in letting go of the parts of your past that no longer provide you with fulfillment or comfort. As you make changes, you may feel restless and ungrounded. Regular meals of natural foods will help in this regard.

For Further Reading

Tierney, Bil. *Alive and Well with Uranus: Transits of Self-Awakening.* St. Paul: Llewellyn, 1999.

Sun Sign Qualities
Finding Your Personal Style

by Sasha Fenton

When I first became interested in astrology, I tracked down the very few books that were then available in British shops and public libraries; then I came across a woman called Sandra Richards who showed me how to put a chart together—by hand, of course, in those days. I went on to make up as many charts as I could and to talk them through with their owners, so in this way I slowly built up a body of knowledge. Eventually, I found sources of books imported from America and I read everything I could lay my hands on. However, there were some forms of "received wisdom" that didn't make much sense—and one of these was the qualities.

The qualities are a division of the Sun signs into three groups. I discovered that before modern astrologers started to call them qualities, they called them the triplicities. I am sure that you have heard of the elements in astrology (fire, earth, air, and water) but you may not know that old-time astrologers called them the quadruplicities. The reason behind these strange names was simple: there are three triplicities and four quadruplicities.

The three triplicities (or qualities as we now call them) are cardinal, fixed, and mutable. Each sign in turn belongs to one of these qualities. Here is the order of play:

Aries	Cardinal
Taurus	Fixed
Gemini	Mutable
Cancer	Cardinal
Leo	Fixed
Virgo	Mutable
Libra	Cardinal
Scorpio	Fixed
Sagittarius	Mutable
Capricorn	Cardinal
Aquarius	Fixed
Pisces	Mutable

Here is another way of expressing the same thing:

Cardinal	Aries, Cancer, Libra, Capricorn
Fixed	Taurus, Leo, Scorpio, Aquarius
Mutable	Gemini, Virgo, Sagittarius, Pisces

The books told me that the cardinal signs initiated things, the fixed signs carried them through, and the mutable signs ended things and allowed them to change into something else. This sounded fair enough—but when I looked at the people I knew and the clients I saw, I could not make any real sense of this. I could see the fixity of the fixed signs all right—who wouldn't see that Taurus, Leo, and Scorpio stuck at things, and even that flaky Aquarius was slow to change its mind—but, dithery Libra and cautious Capricorn as initiators? What about Virgo and Pisces? Did they change direction at the drop of a hat? Not that I could see. It just didn't make any sense.

Eventually I came to two conclusions. The first is that astrology relates to the compass and to geography, and it is this fact that explains many of the terms that we use. For instance, when we look at the angles on a chart; to us, these are the ascendant, nadir, descendant, and midheaven. In reality, the angles refer to the compass points of east, north, west, and south. A horoscope chart is a sky-map, originated by people who lived in the northern hemisphere and who faced southward toward the Sun while looking at the sky. If you think about this for a moment, you will see that the top of the chart—the midheaven—is the place where the Sun shines brightly.

There are twelve astrological houses, and starting from each angle in turn (ascendant, nadir, descendant, midheaven) the three houses within each quadrant are angular, succedent, and cadent. These terms also come from the world of navigation and the compass. But this says nothing about the nature and destiny of people. My second and rather revolutionary conclusion was that the ancient interpretation of the qualities has passed from one astrologer to the next (and one astrology book to the next) without anyone actually stopping to look at them. When I started to look into these for myself, I came to some very different conclusions.

Cardinal Signs: The Catalysts

While it is easy to see Aries as an initiator, it is less easy to do so with the other three signs within the group, so what is really going on here?

Cardinal people think hard about how they want things to be, and they try to change their world to fit their dreams. They don't always pull this off, but often the energy they put into winning on their terms does work for them. They are open to discussion and they can respond to logic, but at the end of the day the only way forward that really matters is *their* way. This may not be immediately obvious to outsiders, because they often present a caring and adaptable face to the world and they certainly do care . . . about their families, their work, and anything else that is of immediate importance to them.

There are always variations within each astrological group, and in this case, Aries and Cancer are more politically inclined than the other two signs. Many Arians are leaders, so some teach, while others are captains of industry or are self-employed. In addition, Aries signs are frequently idealistic, humanitarian, and greatly concerned about outsiders, ecology, public safety, and politics. Many Aries signs become politicians. At one point, about 40 percent of British politicians were born in Aries, and practically everybody in the Cabinet had birthdays in March (Pisces or Aries) or April (Aries). The outcome of the close-run general election in the early 1990s was murder for astrologers who worked in the media, because how could one predict an outcome when the two main party leaders (John Major and Neil Kinnock) had birthdates that were a year and a day apart—and both were Arians!

A glaring exception at that time was Libra Margaret Thatcher. Oddly enough, there were only two other women in high political positions around that time (Barbara Castle and Edwina Currey) and both of these were Libras, with birthdates that were very close to each other's and also to Margaret Thatcher's. Now, we all know that presidents and prime ministers have come under a variety of signs, but the sheer number of Arians, Libras, and Cancers (George W. Bush) who have milled about at or near the top of the political heap made me stop and think.

In personal terms, it is only when we live with a cardinal person or when one is a very close friend that we can see their single-minded purposefulness really clearly. They work out what they want others to do and they then persuade, manipulate, or bully them into doing it. Cardinal-sign people can think up new ideas, but their true talent is in inspiring others to follow these up and turn them into reality. Apart from the open and obvious political arena, they do this in a variety of ways.

Cancers like to run businesses: especially shops and services that fulfill the needs of the public, such as insurance, travel agencies, catering, and domestic things. More to the point, Cancers need to be in charge of their homes and families, and they can make a nuisance of themselves to their children when their offspring are no longer young enough to take direction (or be dictated to).

Capricorns are known for their love of business, too, although they don't always take the top jobs. They enjoy directing affairs from just behind the throne and putting sensible ideas to others in meetings. They hang in their jobs for years and they are often the last of the "old guard" when major shifts and changes come. Old-fashioned industries—such as shipping, banking, and publishing—are full of Capricorns. Indeed, the mind, body, and spirit department of one large British publishing house had ten employees in the 1990s—nine of whom were Capricorns! Many Capricorns are not as quiet and unassuming as astrology books would have you believe—indeed, many are talking machines who have absolutely no capacity to listen. They can have set ideas and they can persuade or push others to follow these to the bitter end.

Libras take a long time to make up their minds, but once they have done so they can be unstoppable. The decision, once made, is stuck fast. Libra is the sign of debate and argument, and Libras can argue the hind leg off a donkey. Many go into the law, arbitration, and sales negotiation, but their real talent for arguing shows itself in the home. They know that they are right and that the other person is wrong, and the partner cannot persuade them otherwise. Libras like to do things their way or no way at all. They will even interfere in something that *you* are doing in order to tell you that you are doing it wrong!

So do cardinal people initiate things? Yes, they certainly do, but the misunderstanding comes in the way that they do it. When reading the old astrology books, we assume this means that they initiate by starting things themselves, but their initiating skills often set others in motion. They are the catalyst or the means of encouraging others to get going. Once this has happened, the cardinal person either moves back to his usual comfort zone or moves on to inspire someone else.

In the early 1980s, I showed what I thought might make some interesting magazine articles on the tarot to a Cancer friend called Anne Christie. Anne looked at them and said, "This won't work as articles; it's a book." I was staggered. Me (moi!) write a book? The girl must be crazy! I became a writer that day. Anne also wanted to write, but it took many more years before she "initiated" herself into doing so—and that mainly at my (fixed sign) insistence, persistence, and nagging.

Fixed Signs: Same Old, Same Old . . .

This is the easiest of the three cardinal types to understand. As one would imagine, fixed-sign people uphold the status quo. They can be stubborn and determined, and they resist change either within their lifestyles or within their own natures. They sometimes stay in difficult situations too long or try to force unworkable situations to work. They have great endurance and they see things through to the finish. When fixed-sign people are driven to the edge, they *will* make changes—often very suddenly or unexpectedly, but only after much thought and agonizing. Once they have made the break, they are unlikely to return to a previous situation. They can put up with a repetitive job or a difficult partner for years and then suddenly reach a stage where they have had enough—walking out without looking back and without regret. This group is closest to the standard astrological description of their nature.

The problem here is that fixed-sign people cannot see all around a problem in the same way that the other two groups can. It is not that they are in denial of the facts—for this implies that they can see what is going on but they do not want to face it. The fact is that they cannot always see the forest for the trees. They decide that a person, job, family, or situation is all right, while not being able to understand why they feel so unhappy. It is only when something truly unacceptable happens that they finally wake up to reality.

Leos are noted for high blood pressure and heart attacks. Is this because they don't notice the warning signs until it is too late? Scorpio is another sign that can become seriously ill with no warning. Scorpios like to be active, to work, and to keep themselves on a metaphorical treadmill until something snaps inside. Aquarians are unconventional and they just don't see the world through the same piece of glass that others do. Nothing will change them. They are open to logic and argument but this doesn't mean that they will change their ways. Taurus signs are notoriously stubborn, but soooo reliable. They are true family folk, who will only leave a poor marriage if a team of horses drags them out. The fact is that they rarely get into bad marriages in the first place, so there is no need for destiny to harness up the steeds of change. Taureans like a job where they can work in a creative way and then stick to it, for life if possible, rarely taking days off. They can withstand boredom better than any other sign. They even take the same kinds of vacations year after year.

Mutable Signs: Facilitators

Mutable-sign people are mightily hard to quantify and to understand. For one thing, they have a reputation for being broadminded and sympathetic. They can be extremely understanding and compassionate when in the right frame of mind, although all of them can switch to being extremely offensive and cutting when the mood takes them.

Traditional astrology tells us that these people are particularly flexible and adaptable and that their job is to bring closure to certain things and then kick-start the process of transformation, but this is hard to see. Unless forced out, mutable-sign people stay in marriages or situations on a permanent basis. They may moan and grumble about their hardships and suffering, but they do little to change them. Some of the men adapt to a poor marriage by having affairs. This is the type of man who looks at his lover with a hangdog expression and tells her that his wife doesn't "understand" him! Mutables require a certain amount of space in their personal relationships, so their jobs take them away from home, and their hobbies and interests involve going out. Some mutable-sign people do make frequent changes, but they do so in the oddest way. For example, some move house frequently or even move from one country to another when boredom sets in. They fondly believe that a change of location will act as a magic wand that solves all their problems at a stroke. When it does not—for the simple reason that they cannot abandon their natures as easily as they leave their homes—their restlessness sets in once again and they start looking around for a new venue.

I have concluded that these people are facilitators who work in fields where people or goods pass through their hands. Consider the Gemini telephone operator or taxi driver whose skill connects people with people or takes folk from one place to another. An astonishing number of Geminis are accountants who meet a variety of clients during the course of a week. I have known highly intelligent Geminis who work as domestic cleaners. Why do that when they could do something better? Their cleaning jobs take them from place to place, so that they don't need to put up with the same people day after day. Their jobs offer flexible hours and plenty of time off. Cleaners move dirt out of houses and into trash bins.

Many Pisceans work in the medical or allied professions and in prisons where an endless stream of new faces come their way. The same goes for all those engaged in complementary therapies, because their clients change hour by hour. You will not see it mentioned in any astrology book, but many Pisceans are excellent sales representatives who go out to visit different customers each day. Some Pisces women lumber themselves with grandchildren after their own children have grown up, but this actually does them a service. It takes them out of the house and brings them into contact with others while they move around the neighborhood taking their grandchildren to their various activities.

Virgos, who write, analyze, or deal with paperwork, do not handle the same project every day and neither do they deal with the same faces each day. Like Pisceans, many work in the medical or complementary medical profession. Sometimes they are part of a large organization and they spend their days among interesting people. They certainly meet many new patients or clients day by day.

My Sagittarian aunt and grandfather were tailors who dealt with new clients every few days, but most Sagittarians prefer to go out in order to call on customers. Many are electricians, carpenters, and other menders and fixers who go from place to place with a bag of tools in a scruffy van. Others are travel reps who pass many people through their hands while they move their clients around the world. Sagittarians work in export and they travel to trade fairs or go to see clients in distant parts of the world.

Even if their lives are completely static, mutable signs often deal with things that pass through their hands. A number of Pisceans work as airport baggage handlers, while others work in television, radio, and the press, where new information comes along all the time. Some are restaurateurs or sales people. All these jobs pass something through a chain from one place to another. Some work in the fishing industry, catching fish in the sea and transporting them to the land. Geminis, Virgos, and Sagittarians are fond of astrology and they may work in the field either directly with clients or via the media. Many Pisceans work as psychic mediums who channel spirits through themselves—they act as a channel that moves (transports or transmutes) information by moving it from one place to another—how mutable is that!

I have known mutable-sign people who work with drains and sewage (think about it) and as prostitutes (think about that one too)! Therefore, the mutable signs do not necessarily live in an unsettled manner, but the people and things that they deal with change, move along, get fixed up, improved, altered, and transmuted while passing through their hands.

For Further Reading

Burk, Kevin. *Astrology: A Comprehensive Guide to Classical Interpretation*. St. Paul: Llewellyn, 2001.

Tierney, Bil. *All Around the Zodiac: Exploring Astrology's Twelve Signs*. St. Paul: Llewellyn, 2001.

Solar Inspiration
Tapping the Creative Force

by Bernie Ashman

Creativity is that elusive expression that resides in all human beings. Sometimes this energy feels so thick, it could be cut with a knife. It may come forward and through us with a presence that is dynamically beyond our conscious mind, and creativity can guide a person to follow the deepest parts of his or her intuition. These invincible forces may eventually (in a painstaking way) weave their magic through our consciousness. When they have had their way with us, the evidence can be found in the world of form.

The ten planets represent unique components of our creative energies. A gifted artist, writer, negotiator, speaker, humanitarian, astrologer, etc., is usually making use of several planetary themes. It is the mastering of these energies that can bring out our best to meet whatever challenges await us.

The Sun

The Sun points to our particular way of falling in love with the creative impulse. It is the willpower to express ourselves. Relaxing into the creative experience can be a challenge; it is like parenting a child. That which is expressed or comes through us can feel like our child, whether it is a book, a new recipe for dinner, or a new way of being. Some individuals must find enough ego strength to let creative vitality come forward. Those with too much attachment to creative impulses may need to learn to let go. We often tap into our greatest willpower when engaged in the creative process.

The Sun is the central force in our universe. Without its magnificent presence, there would be no life on Earth. Just as the Sun plays such a key role in sustaining life on Earth, it has the same big significance as a powerful force in our creative endeavors. It is the planet that shows where we will derive the self-confidence to propel ourselves forward. Taking a risk is another solar theme in astrology. Having the desire to promote your talent is yet another attribute of this fiery planet.

If your Sun sign is Aries you will need to balance patience with assertiveness in discovering your creative talent, and *Adventure and Courage* is your creative theme. A Sun in Taurus requires persistent effort combined with finding some degree of being flexible; *Beauty and Persistence* is your creative theme. Having a Sun in Gemini points to a fondness for diversity, but it's important to learn focus. Your creative theme is *Mental Excitement and New Perceptions*. A Sun in Cancer encourages a need to trust your intuition—and at the same time not fear to show your creative impulse. *Passionate Emotions and Reflective Thought* is the creative theme. A Sun in Leo pulsates dramatically, instilling a roar of creative power, but does need to be tempered with humility. Your creative theme is *Promotion and Dramatic Display*. If your Sun sign is Virgo, you are very aware of the details, but it's important not to lose sight of the forest for the trees; *Quiet Determination and Deep Mental Insights* is the creative theme. Libra Suns are naturally attuned to carefully weighing choices before taking action, yet sooner or later they must jump off the fence and release creative ideas. Their theme is *Social Perception and Balance*. A Sun in Scorpio denotes the need to tap into creative passion and the need to surrender to the full intensity of the creative experience, and *Emotional Intensity and Rebirth* is the creative theme. Having the Sun in Sagittarius stimulates a creative urge that emanates from the desire to seek self-understanding, and from a primal need to light a creative spark in others. *Teaching and Eclectic Reasoning* is the creative theme. A Sun in Capricorn builds creative strength through a very disciplined approach, but sooner or later these signs must leap over a fear of the unknown to wherever creative drives will lead, using *Commitment and Raw Determination* as the creative theme. Aquarius Suns search for creative forces that turn into unique discoveries, and generate the energy to follow through on individual goals. Their theme is *Inventiveness and Mental Ingenuity*. A Pisces Sun yearns to find the faith to totally believe in creative potential, and to gain the inner strength to make a vision become a reality. *Unity and Idealism* is the creative theme.

The Moon

The Moon is symbolic of our intimacy with creative energies—our lunar friend is a key link to our innermost instincts. I remember doing a consultation for an aspiring writer with the Moon in Gemini, a sign heavily connected to communication. The writer had trouble feeling close to the creative experience and enjoying the feeling or process of writing was one of the greatest lessons for her to learn. She began to perceive that she needed to integrate the very intellectual nature of her Moon's sign, Gemini, with the "feeling" side of the Moon. It was important for her to begin to understand that both worlds could have a voice—that they could coexist in harmony.

The Moon is our inner child and is symbolic of the intuitive energies that hold the hand of a child's imagination. Children really need a lot of play time: it builds their brain synapses, helping them to think in a magical way that creates the foundation of a creative inner world, which can be drawn upon throughout life. Even as adults, we all could use a bit of play time, whether it's taking a vacation, going to the movies, or going out to dinner. Our psyche needs to rest!

The Moon is a strong ingredient of the creative experience. Letting our imagination take the lead can be an important step toward exploring creative energies. The Moon represents some of our favorite comfort zones, and there are times each of us needs to leave those captivating, nurturing confines and move into new creative territory. Also, the Moon is symbolic of our home and the sacred space in which we create. For many people, the environment may make a difference in their ability to make a creative idea come true.

Mercury

Mercury, the "winged messenger," represents our mental insight into creative energy. Due to Mercury, there can sometimes be difficulty letting go of an overly analytical conscious mind. Do not dig up the seed before it has had time to grow—we can be well into a creative process before the real depth develops. The conscious mind can distort the reality of the subjective beauty of creative forces as they are finding birth. Mercury can indicate that some mental toughness needs to be learned to penetrate to the core of creative insight.

Venus

Venus symbolizes forming a relationship with creativity. Enjoy the sensuality embedded in the creative process. Let it balance your psyche just by letting go to the dance of these forces. Self-esteem can be bathed by the beauty of moving into situations that are creating greater harmony for you. To stimulate Venus, try to create a balanced creative environment, Wearing clothing or jewelry that inspire your creative urges, or putting possessions near you that stimulate your creativity, can help. Some people connect with the creative process by listening to certain types of music. Being out in nature can also stimulate creative juices. And yet another theme related to Venus can awaken our creative drive: eating tasty food!

Our relationships with others may take on new meaning when we find happiness in creativity. I have witnessed many individuals gain greater clarity about their partnerships through creative success. What's more important, though, is the insight into one's own relating patterns or tendencies. Creative energy seems to stimulate the mind to seek greater clarity in establishing a sense of balance.

Mars

Mars represents the courage to create. It can mean breaking through the obstacles that stand in your way. The warrior planet can help some people become more assertive in the midst of creative processes. Watch out for the "hit and run" game. This is a pattern of not following through, as described in my book, *Astrological Games People Play*. Learning patience is a challenge. When you get your mind lit by this planet's pushy momentum, it feels like being on a caffeine high.

Our competitiveness is linked to Mars. Being competitive is okay—it's becoming too aggressive that needs to be held in check. Or are you lacking assertion? Then it's vital to learn why this is occurring. Sometimes a person needs only to get started to feel the internal fires aroused. It is then that the creative powers will carry us the rest of the way. It is finding the momentum to get started, and not looking back, that can be a challenge.

Creativity can teach us about another Mars theme: anger. The creative process can expose hidden anger, and people with explosive and angry tendencies can find that creative energies help to channel this intensity more productively. An experience of having an old emotional wound healed is another big payoff when exploring the creative process.

Jupiter

Jupiter, the "cosmic gypsy," symbolizes believing enough in the abundance of life that your creativity will come to fruition. A positive attitude combined with some Jupiter humor helps immensely! Faith can miraculously bring a dose of luck. You may read a book or take a class that opens up creative doors. A teacher may inspire confidence and expand creative interests. Traveling on the mental and physical planes can bring out some creative spark.

When I do public lectures, I tend to describe the outer planets' influences in terms of breathing, or what I refer to as "cosmic breath." Jupiter represents taking a deep, expansive, Buddha-belly in-breath, followed spontaneously by an exuberant exhalation, blowing your imagination into the four corners of the world. Your mental forces can get your feet to walk with a sense of wonder. The world just might give in to your contagious enthusiasm. When you are ready to take a chance on an idea or plan in spite of the odds, guess what? You are probably riding the flight of this gentle giant of the sky!

Saturn

Saturn is symbolic of the discipline and concentration that creativity involves. I refer to Saturn as the "cosmic chiropractor," alluding to the adjustments we need to make in the midst of our life journeys. It is important not to try so hard that you lose interest in your creative forces. This planet indicates the power inherent in the commitment to your creativity. It is often fear in the creative process that stops many people from getting started. Taking short, well-conceived, structured steps is the way to get through Saturn problems. The little successes can lead to bigger ones later. It is hard to finish a project without some goal or purpose in mind, but equally challenging is the process of getting started. Create a first step. Just concentrate on this first precious step. Forget about the rest. You may be surprised how easy it is to get going with an initial creative success.

Let's look at Saturn in terms of its particular "cosmic breath." Saturn, like Jupiter, indicates a deep in-breath, but this is a much more deliberate inhalation. The exhalation doesn't happen very quickly. The breath is held cautiously, and held in until the coast seems clear to let it out. This can be a powerful and structured out-breathing, colored with great ambition. This is well-guarded stuff, similar to the actual rings of Saturn. The world will respond when you ride this planet—just be sure to stay mindful of the need for flexibility. If you freeze up a bit along the creative path, remember to lighten up. Speaking of lightening up, scientists say if Saturn fell from the sky, it would be light enough to float on one of our oceans! So balance persistent, grinding-it-out effort with a healthy dose of enjoying the journey!

Uranus

Uranus, "cosmic lightning," denotes forming a friendship with your creative side. This planet, with its objective awareness, offers a great way to balance the excessive emotion and passion that creative forces awaken. Following a creative vision can liberate even more options. Uranus can symbolize the transformational growth in the creative process through expressing unique consciousness.

This planet was discovered in 1781—a time between the American and French Revolutions. This is why Uranus is considered the maverick planet, pointing to ways to explore our individuality. Give yourself the freedom to go beyond societal and peer pressures. Try not to always wait for the support of others before embarking on your creative course; they just might join with your enthusiasm while you're in the middle of your ride. Uranus can indicate that a support group may inspire confidence. Peers may stimulate creative insights.

The "cosmic breath" of Uranus is hyperventilation! The in-breaths and out-breaths are so fast they collide. The exhalations can be fireballs, igniting us into brave new worlds. Doors can open that seemed firmly closed only yesterday. The inhalation is fast because it abruptly launches us into the future—that is, if we are willing to go (even if it's yelling and screaming) into the change. If you feel more mentally alive and fond of new future possibilities, then you are probably making good use of this awakener.

Neptune

Neptune, the "cosmic dreamer," represents merging with your intuitive forces. This planet indicates the need to let go to right-brain energies. This is the spiritual link to your creativity. It is the intuitive vision and faith in something greater than you. The intangible forces lend their magic to your creativity. It is stepping out over the edge with your intuitive impulses that can lead to new paths; there is a transformational potential every time we take a creative risk. Neptune is escaping the ego just enough to capture the presence of the soul in our creativity.

The "cosmic breath" of Neptune is like not breathing at all. This mystical heavenly wanderer fills us with enough intuitive power to move mountains. The exhalation is largely invisible, yet it has the passion to accelerate our artistic sense. This planet blows romantic energy and idealism into us faster than the speed of light! This is a watery planet that flows better if you provide solid groundwork. When you are wanting to experience the world as a place of sense-less beauty, when you commune with your soul, when you have an inner feeling of connectedness to life itself, then, my friend, you are riding the miraculous waves of this heavenly ruler of the oceans.

Pluto

Pluto represents forming a deep psychological bond with what you create. This planet points the way to trusting your creative intensity, and it is symbolic of the personal power that is given rebirth through deep creative expression. Pluto is the death that can be experienced as a greater "you" comes through. I refer to Pluto as the "cosmic composter," because this planet can show us how to take negative tendencies and replant them in more growth-promoting soil. A psychological cleansing can occur due to Pluto's influence that brings hidden fears into the light, and creative intensity can bring out our compulsive and obsessive energies. The passion expressed for your creativity can lead to great growth. Shedding the layers that are holding you back in your consciousness allows a bold new display of self-mastery to brilliantly shine.

The "cosmic breath" of Pluto is a very deep in-breath—an inhalation that penetrates to the core of our psyche. We can hold these in-breaths for months or even years, processing them carefully as though they were our last breaths. The exhalations are powerful—that is, if we allow the inhalations to do their job. These are passionate out-breaths that can transform our world into a bold new place. Self-honesty, and letting our perceptions express our greatest grasp of creative power, can bring the world to recognize our talents. There is a newfound freedom possible if we ride Pluto with an awareness that matches its penetrating search for new self-discovery.

There is no one formula that will arouse our creative forces: each person has a unique style. It is exciting to use astrology as a tool to help tune into creative energies. Creativity has no limits; it can be found in our careers, communication, parenting, business dealings, etc. There are often doors waiting for each of us to enter, but sometimes these doors need an extra push. It can be our own fears or self-consciousness that keeps them a closed mystery. Do you know what happens when you walk through? It is as though you have been on this new side of the door all of the time!

For Further Reading

George, Llewellyn. *Llewellyn's New A–Z Horoscope Maker and Interpreter: A Comprehensive Self-Study Course*. St. Paul: Llewellyn, 2004.

MacGregor, Trish. *Creative Stars: Using Astrology to Tap Your Muse*. New York: St. Martin's Griffin, 2002.

Sun Sign Predictions
Using the Solar Return

by Dorothy Oja

Essentially, the Solar Return is a forecasting technique and a way of looking at the trends for the coming year, starting from the most current birthday. The Solar Return (SR) chart is calculated for the precise time that the Sun returns to the exact place in the sky that it occupied at the time of your birth. Because the length of the Earth's revolution around the Sun varies slightly from year to year, the exact SR may take place on the birthday, or the day before, or even the day following the birthday.

The SR is all the more useful because it takes place every year, unlike some of the other planetary returns. It's an excellent overview that aptly and accurately expresses the themes that you will be required to attend to over the coming year. If you calculate a number of SRs year after year, you begin to see interesting patterns, such as a grouping of years with the same element on the Ascendant. This is most apt to happen if the SR takes place in the same location for a number of years in a row. In this way, the SR is one of several excellent methods for showing stages of maturation in an individual's life.

Because we are speaking of a Solar Return, we are focused on the Sun and all that it means in the chart and in a person's life. The Sun typically symbolizes consciousness, awareness of oneself within the scheme of life, and the ability to forge a place—a creative, vital space in one's life that is recognizable to others, as well as feeling authentic to ourselves. The Sun represents heart, happiness, and the ability to accept and enjoy life in all its fullness.

Typically, the Solar Return begins to manifest its new cycle about three months before the actual date, when the Sun is square the birthday Sun. In fact, those three months are a blending of the end of the previous year's return with the seeds of the new Solar Return. Typically, the last few months and, in particular, the last month, before the birthday are often times of greater confusion or reflection and sometimes melancholy or anticipation.

The Sun is our solar system's "superstar," the center of our astrological universe. In our natal charts, the Sun is the heartbeat, the essential nature and characteristics we are seeking to express and develop. The other planets serve the Sun and help it to fulfill its character. The Sun is the master of our external world, while the Moon governs our inner and emotional life with its constant shifts and changes. And yet, even the Moon is sensitive to the Sun and reflects its light. Given these factors, we can say that the Solar Return is the seed potential and challenge that we face in the coming year.

Like Mercury retrograde, most people with a little knowledge of astrology have heard of the Solar Return. The fact that it is somewhat common knowledge appears to make the Solar Return very important, which it is. However, returns can be calculated for all the planets. As noted above, the Sun's return to its birth location takes place once each year and so is a perfect way to gauge the effects and the themes that are relevant for a short time span. Mercury and Venus travel closely with the Sun and have a more or less yearly cycle as well. If one chooses, Mercury and Venus returns can be calculated. The Moon returns to its birth position once a month, and many astrologers make a habit of looking at Lunar Returns. These can be useful in assessing the conditions of a shorter time frame.

Once we get beyond Venus, the time between planetary returns gets longer and longer, with Neptune and Pluto never returning to their natal position in a person's lifetime, since their full revolutions are approximately 171 years for Neptune and 248 years for Pluto. The Uranus return takes place at age 84, and many people will live to experience that one. Saturn returns happen every 29 years, give or take, while Jupiter takes 12 years to pass through all twelve signs and make its birthplace conjunction. It can be very useful to research other planetary returns and their effects, but we will focus on the Solar Return.

What to Look For

First of all, never look solely at the Solar Return chart for your interpretation. It is always necessary to compare the Solar Return to the birth chart. The SR cannot stand alone and will only work properly if you take into consideration the potential of the natal chart. We can never forget about the natal chart, and all other astrological work springs from the promise of the primary birth chart.

Using an astrology program, the best way to compare the two charts is by setting up a double wheel, using the SR house cusps and placing the natal chart around the Solar Return (see figure 3). The reasoning behind this procedure is because the Solar Return cusps are the most relevant for the coming year. Start with the Solar Return, focus on the conditions that are outstanding, and then begin to compare its placements to the natal chart. When you add the birth chart around the outside of the Solar Return, the themes you have already uncovered will become all the more clear. We'll go step by step for the highlights.

What House Contains the Solar Return Sun? How Does this Compare to the Natal Chart?

Since we have calculated a Solar Return, we must first focus on the Sun's potential message for the year, and so we must assess the Sun's position very carefully as it will tell us the essence of the story.

In the Solar return example for my client's chart, we find that her SR Sun is in the Ninth House (see figure 2), and her birth Sun is in the Third House (see figure 1). She is being asked to stretch her commonly held understandings, her concepts and her ideas, and to

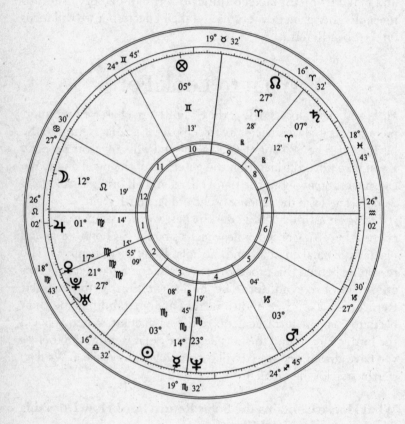

Figure 1

Natal Chart
October 27, 1967, 2:09 AM EDT
Camp Hill, Pennsylvania

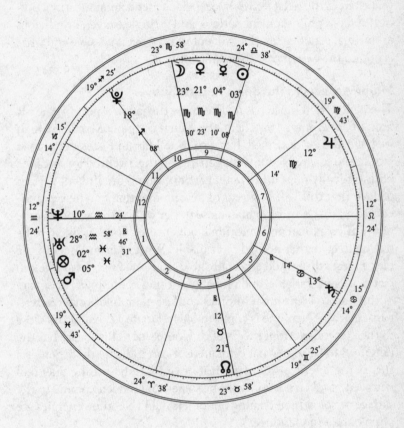

Figure 2

Solar Return Chart
October 26, 2003, 1:33 PM AHST1
Lahaina, Hawaii

evaluate her own communication as well as communication from others. It is a year that will test her current wisdom and will teach her more wisdom, if she is open to that. Her SR Sun is in the house opposite her natal Sun, accentuating the Third/Ninth House axis. Adding to this theme, the SR Sun is conjunct Mercury. This coming year there is the need for wiser, deeper, clearer communication, possibly a more philosophical outlook and attitude, travel, or religious or spiritual experiences. She will entertain what is possible and what is not, to the extent that she can identify it.

Major Aspects to the Solar Return Sun

The next important step is to determine the major aspects to the SR Sun. In our example, my client's SR Sun is conjunct Mercury, which we have already described. It is also trine Mars in Pisces in the First House and square Neptune in Aquarius in the Twelfth House. Since both typically masculine planets (Sun, Mars) are linked, we can deduce that this will be a year of new momentum or a new experience, and that possibly a man close to her will be the agent of some new philosophical and emotional adventure. There is likely to be much energy either needed or available. With Mars in Pisces in the First House, this would especially hold true, and energies are sure to be emotional, variable, and probably at times confusing. The square of the Sun to Neptune reinforces confusion or emotional distress, particularly as Neptune is comfortable in House 12, but also is close to the Ascendant from the Twelfth House side. This square has the potential to be somewhat difficult as it can indicate that there is a surprising event, something not anticipated, and she may feel betrayed or taken advantage of by something hidden coming to the surface or something coming out of left field (Neptune energies are often oblique and indirect).

What House Holds Leo (Ruled by the Sun) on the Cusp?

After evaluating the Sun by house and by aspect, we look to the house that has Leo on the cusp, as that will give us further information about the solar potential for the coming year. In our example, Leo rules the Seventh House and tells us that what we have already interpreted will come through the environment of a close relationship. Neptune hugging the Ascendant is already an indication that interpersonal skills will be required, or negotiation and compromise will be needed, since one end of the horizon axis is heavily influenced by Neptune squaring the Sun and Mercury. The coming year is likely to bring a time of personal confusion about some aspect of a close relationship. However, confusion can easily transform to illumination if the consciousness (Sun) is willing to see beyond ego and pride (Sun) and the obvious, and if the persona (Ascendant) is willing to adjust and be shocked into a higher level of awareness and perception (Aquarius).

The Fifth House

Next, following the theme of the Sun and the solar potential, we must look at the Fifth House, the natural home of Leo, ruled by the Sun. In our example, the Fifth House cusp is Gemini, ruled by Mercury, which brings us right back to Mercury conjuncting the Sun in the Ninth House, and suggests that some portion of the necessary communication this coming year involves Fifth House matters—children, romance, shifts in lifestyle, creative resources, and the state of the heart. Our example shows that Saturn in Cancer is also located in the Fifth House. Saturn always indicates, by sign and house position, what the weighty issue is, or where there is deficiency, real or perceived. Saturn in Cancer in the Fifth House indicates fears of Fifth House matters, which are fears regarding children, blocks in creative movement, or some kind of change in lifestyle. Saturn's position always indicates that work has to be done in that location or life environment.

Other Outstanding Configurations

Now it's necessary to determine what other planetary patterns are dominant that have not already been defined by the previous procedure. We've spoken about the strong angular influence of Neptune on the Ascendant and its square to the Sun and Mercury. There is more! Neptune, we discover, is also involved in a Yod configuration and is inconjunct (150 degrees) Saturn in Cancer sextile Jupiter in Virgo! Jupiter enlarges the Neptune and Saturn issues already discussed. However, the sextile between Saturn and Jupiter, with Jupiter in the Seventh House, indicates the promise or possibility of finding common ground, especially through the accumulated reserves of positive energy from a relationship. The Yod becomes even more complex when we see that Jupiter is square Pluto in Sagittarius in the Tenth House. This pattern indicates that the issue at hand is one that has been building in the subconscious for some time and is now ripe to be brought forth via the square to Jupiter. It also indicates the shock and abrupt energies of Neptune in Aquarius on the Ascendant.

The Yod, often called the "Finger of God," is a very particular configuration—an elongated triangle like the lower part of a kite—and it typifies an issue that is a struggle because it needs much adjustment among many variables either in feeling or resources. With a Yod, something always hangs in the balance, and usually after much deliberation a decision must be made and one of two roads taken. In our example, the base of the Yod, the sextile between Saturn and Jupiter, is more stable, and Neptune, the pointer, is the representative of the soul's purpose. The soul must now decide between a Saturnian conclusion or a Jovian conclusion—or find a way to make peace with both these ends of the sextile.

The Mood of the Year? The Role of the Moon

When we assess the Moon's position and aspects, we find another strong square to Uranus in Aquarius (retrograde) in the First House. Since the Moon rules the emotions—the mother, mothering, heritage, and the home—a strong Uranus square indicates changes in those areas of life, often unexpectedly or suddenly. The Moon conjuncts the Midheaven exactly, right at the top of the chart, and also conjuncts Venus in Scorpio and the South Node. Both the Moon and Venus are weak by sign and both are in detriment (not at their best expression in those signs). The feminine principle is under siege, and deep emotions and strong desires or fears are being stirred in the psyche. This will be a year of great transformation, emotional turmoil included, and the opportunity for growth is immense. Still, all the Scorpio planets indicate that something must die—some pattern must be let go.

Wrapping Up

By just looking at the location of the planets in the Solar Return houses, we see the one most occupied is the Ninth House. The deep

Scorpionic emphasis will benefit from perspective—possibly through travel or some other philosophical outlet.

Putting It All Together

Now that we've assessed the major patterns of the SR, it's time to bring the natal chart back into play. The first question to ask is this: what houses of the natal chart do the SR angles bring to the forefront? Aquarius and Leo correspond to the Sixth and Twelfth Houses in the natal chart—body and soul, work schedules and the details of life, and retreat and recharging. Scorpio and Taurus correspond to the Fourth and Tenth Houses in the natal chart—the domestic front and the career path, as well as the priorities one has defined for oneself and the amount of time devoted to those priorities.

The Double Wheel

Now it's time for the last step in the process of analyzing the Solar Return: the double-wheel chart. Have your computer draw the wheel or place the natal positions manually around the outside of the Solar Return chart. We now have the complete picture, and it is a revelation! What instantly jumps out at us is the natal Moon exactly conjunct the Descendant. Both the Solar Return and natal Moons are highlighted, which increases the emphasis of the feminine and all things Moon-related, as well as the strong emotional impact of the year. The next major condition is the natal Neptune exactly conjunct the Solar Return Moon and Midheaven! There is a deep soul-purpose crisis looming. My client must decide whether to change paths, and to dig deeply into her emotional resources to discover what she truly wants and needs. This digging will bring up her fears. We can also clearly see that this woman is in her Jupiter-return cycle, which always expands issues and our viewpoint, with or without our initiative, and seeks wisdom.

The Dominant Environment

Once you've set up the double-wheel chart and noticed how it all clicks together in amazing ways, take note of which are the most occupied Houses. In other words, when stacked together via the

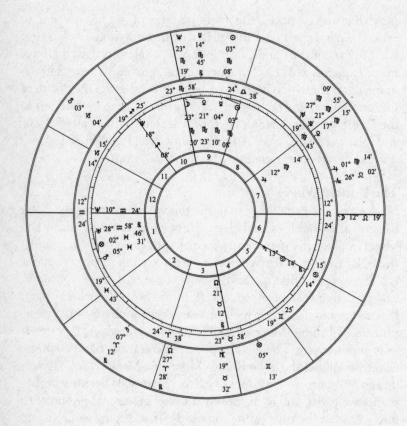

Figure 3

Biwheel Chart

Inner Chart: Solar Return
10/26/2003 1:33 PM AHST
Camp Hill, Pennsylvania

Outer Chart: Natal
10/27/1967 2:09 AM EDT
Lahaina, Hawaii

double wheel, find the House that has the most planets—which will be the total combination of both Solar Return and natal placements. This House is the dominant environment for that birthday year. Be sure to count the Sun only once. In our example, the Ninth House has nine placements, which include the Nodal placements and the natal Part of Fortune. This is by far the House with the majority of planetary energies. This, the environment of traveling and getting out of one's normal routine or myopic outlook, appears to be vitally important. Studying a new philosophy or even some religious/spiritual practices is also a strong possibility or would be an advantage to my client for handling this year's energies.

Solar Return Angles

The angles of the SR chart are very sensitive to transits. In fact, when the Sun crosses the angles, often with Mercury and Venus nearby (before or after the Sun), the promise of the SR will be revealed in some way, and events pertaining to the SR promise will manifest themselves. As the Sun neared the cusp of the Seventh House, the main issue of the year was fully out in the open.

What Happened

Now it's time to tell you the story of what actually happened to this woman and how the SR chart patterns manifested themselves. My client has been married for approximately nine years, but has been with her husband in a committed relationship since 1987. When they married, they both agreed not to have children because they wanted to be free to travel the world whenever they pleased and to have an unfettered lifestyle. They both supported each other to build successful businesses. In the last few years, the husband has been having second thoughts about having a child, which surprised his wife. Although resistant at first, in the last year my client has reconsidered the possibility of bearing a child. Yet when confronted with making a firm decision, both husband and wife have taken turns wavering on the issue. At the end of July 2004, her husband, suddenly and without any real warning, announced to my client that he needed space and was moving out. (In fact, he had already made arrangements for renting an apartment.) He felt that they fought too much and that that was not what a real loving relationship should be like—and he was confused about what he wanted. As you might imagine, the wife was shocked and deeply hurt. There was no other woman involved. The wife has gone on to delve deeply into her psyche and had a profound dream about holding a caterpillar and watching it metamorphose into a butterfly of many colors in her hand. After that dream, she felt that she would be fine. She has dedicated herself to a deeper study and practice of yoga, and has gone on to plan a two-week vacation with her sister. Her husband has also taken some time off to return to his birthplace, visit family, and hunt and fish. The final result of this SR is not known at this time. However, as you can tell from the planetary patterns and from this brief telling of the story behind the chart, certainly the woman involved (and her husband) will be profoundly changed by this Solar Return.

Chart Data
Natal Chart: 10/27/67 2:09 AM EDT Camp Hill, PA.
Solar Return Chart: 10/26/03 1:33 PM AHST Lahaina, HI

For Further Reading
Merriman, Raymond A. *The New Solar Return Book of Prediction*. Bloomfield, Michigan: Seek-It Publications, 1998.

Shea, Mary Fortier. *Planets in Solar Returns: Yearly Cycles of Transformation & Growth*. Glenelg, Maryland: Twin Stars, 1999.

Teal, Celeste. *Predicting Events with Astrology*. St. Paul: Llewellyn, 1999.

Here Comes the Sun

by Bruce Scofield

Any astrology book will tell you that the Sun is special among the points used in astrology. Most books will say that the Sun is the source of life, the point in the chart that confers spirit and vitality, and it is the point that makes us special. It is used to discover meaning and direction in one's life. Such books will also say that the Sun is the source of the astrological energies of the rest of the horoscope. For example, a century ago Alan Leo summed up this view on the Sun very precisely:

> In astrologic study, The Sun gives to every living organism its prana, or life and heat, each individual specializing his own store from the cosmic Prana. Every living thing is plunged into a great ocean of life—God's life; and every organism, whether great or small, appropriates to itself some of this universal life which is ever flowing from the Sun, the vehicle through which the Solar Logos is manifesting. (p. 29)

> [The Sun] is the source of all vital energy, no matter whether coming directly from the Sun or indirectly through the Moon

or the Ascendant. It is the centre of the being, both in body and soul. (p. 68)

> —Alan Leo. *How to Judge a Nativity*. London: L.N. Fowler & Co., 1912.

Leo was saying that the Sun brings forth a great ocean of life from which every organism draws its vitality. He implies that it is the ultimate source of all living energy, even if it gets to us indirectly. For example, it is the Sun's own light that is reflected back to us by the other planets. Many students of esoteric astrology believe that the Sun's rays are the only true rays—they are transmitted to each of the planets, which then, in their own special way, reflect its light back to the Earth. Each planet, then, is a relay station of sorts that focuses and individualizes the pure solar energy. Depending on the time of our birth, many of us become specially attuned to one of these planets and our individuality becomes built around its unique vibration. Astrology teaches that we are ultimately all children of the Sun, but we take in its energy mostly after it has been modified by one of the planets. Just how this happens is not known, but some statistical studies have shown correlations between personality and planets.

How Did It All Begin?

The long tradition of astrology says the Sun is the source of life. Is this true? In order to find out, we must ask the question, "What is life?" and seek to find how it may have originated and how it sustains itself. Now, these are very profound questions, to which most religions offer answers. For the religiously inclined, the simple answer is that God made life and God sustains life. A careful reading of Alan Leo's quote above would suggest that he thought there was a close connection between God and the Sun. For some people, this may be enough. But in this article, I'd like to take a more exploratory and inquisitive approach and leave the symbolic world of astrology in order to enter the highly complex worlds of biology and chemistry to seek our answers.

Today, scientists are still very uncertain about exactly how life began on Earth. A lot has been learned about this topic during the past century, however. We know that crucial organic substances can be formed in a primitive Earth atmosphere that receives sunlight and lightning flashes. We also know that life formed on the Earth about 3.8 billion years ago, not that long after the Earth cooled down from a molten state. But exactly how it all happened is unclear. The current theory is that some kind of self-replicating strand of chemicals got started in a primeval pool of organic "soup" that was being agitated by the extreme lunar tides. Back then, the Moon was much closer to the Earth and was orbiting it much faster than it does now. The early seas must have been like an enormous washing machine, or, more accurately, a mixing bowl. Many scientists believe that the first organisms were a kind of bacteria that fed on the organic chemicals floating all around them. One idea that has been proposed many times is that life was brought to our planet on a meteorite or by a comet. Once it landed in pool of rich organic material, it grew and evolved. This may be possible, but it still doesn't answer the larger question of how life got started in the first place, wherever it came from.

The Original Solar Collectors

Nobody knows what these first lifeforms might have been like, but we do know that the most important life on our planet was thriving by at least 3.5 billion years ago (and maybe even as early as 3.8 billion years ago)—which puts them in the front row. These organisms were definitely bacteria and they got their energy from the Sun. Today we call them cyanobacteria and we owe our existence to them. These tiny organisms found a way to use sunlight to drive chemical reactions that produce the energy needed to grow and reproduce. They devised complex chlorophyll molecules that look like tennis rackets—ovals of carbon and hydrogen atoms with a single magnesium molecule in the center—and hook up by their "handles" to form a solar power station of sorts. These early cyanobacteria dominated the early Earth and grew in huge colonies along the shores of ancient oceans, much like coral reefs do today. They lived in layers, the top ones intercepting photons from the Sun and those under them producing large mounds over thirty feet high. Regardless of whether their predecessors lived without the Sun, these cyanobacteria were the real foundation for life on our planet. They were the first photoautotrophs, the first light-using, self-contained organisms.

Cyanobacteria made and continue to make the air we breath. The early Earth's atmosphere lacked oxygen, but a long, long time ago, cyanobacteria began to make a difference. As they split carbon dioxide out of the Earth's ancient atmosphere and water from the seas, oxygen was released. By about two billion years ago the atmosphere began to hold enough oxygen that certain bacteria learned how to use it to generate a lot more energy than had previously been possible. The "oxygen revolution" was the event in the history of life that made large organisms like ourselves possible, and cyanobacteria made it happen through their use of solar energy. Later in Earth history, some cyanobacteria began to live within other living cells which were feeding on them. They weren't digested; they settled in their host and kept their solar-energy business going. Today, the descendants of this early symbiosis are the algae and the plants, both of which are food sources for other organisms and maintainers of our oxygen atmosphere. Cyanobacteria are still the most abundant organisms on our planet. They are found nearly everywhere—throughout the oceans, under thin layers of sand in deserts, and under the ice in Antarctica. They are even sought after as a special food. For years "blue-green algae" has been sold for high prices by individuals and in health food stores. People take "blue-green algae" because it is said to vitalize the body. Guess what? Blue-green algae is really cyanobacteria. Marketers changed the name because "bacteria" has a bad reputation. How wrong this notion is.

We could say now, with scientific backing, that life on Earth is sustained by the Sun. If it lives, it is either cyanobacteria or its descendants in the algae and plants—or it is feeding on one of these. It has been argued that there are ecosystems on our planet that are completely independent of the Sun. For example, the deep ocean volcanic vents discovered in 1977 are known to host communities of animals and bacteria that receive no sunlight whatsoever. Giant tube worms live there that have colonies of bacteria inside them that function like organs and metabolize the sulfur coming out of the vents. But on closer inspection, these organisms also depend on the dissolved oxygen and organic matter in the water, which come from the cyanobacteria and algae floating way above them near the surface.

Recently, some very strange bacterial life has been found deep within the Earth that apparently is disconnected from the Sun. Called SLiME (subsurface lithoautotrophic microbial ecosystem), these organisms must be using deep Earth gases to generate their energy. They grow extremely slowly and it appears that they are actually descended from surface organisms. But the jury is still out as to whether they derive some critical life energy from the Sun, indirectly.

The greatest accomplishment of life on Earth was to harness the Sun's energy. In the largest sense, we are exactly what astrology teaches—beings that are 100 percent vitalized by the Sun, though mostly indirectly. We feed on plants and animals that eat plants—our lives depend on eating. But let's not forget that we also need direct sunlight for vitamin D.

The Source of All Cycles

Astrology teaches that the Sun also gives us a sense of center, a kind of individual integrity. We do this by following the Sun as it makes time as we know it. Ancient astrologers knew that life followed the Sun in its movement through the day and through the year. Way back at about 150 AD, the greatest scientist of the ancient world, Ptolemy, had this to say about the Sun:

> For the Sun . . . is always in some way affecting everything on the Earth, not only by the changes that accompany the seasons of the year to bring about the generation of animals, the productiveness of plants, the flowing of the waters, and changes of bodies, but also by its daily revolutions furnishing heat, moisture, dryness . . . with its position relative to the zenith.
> —Ptolemy. *Tetrabiblios*, 1:2.

Ptolemy was speaking of how the motions of the Sun, as they appear to us from the Earth, create the day and the year. He was pointing to how the annual cycles of plants and the reproductive cycles of animals relate to the position of the Sun relative to the zenith—that is, how high in the sky the Sun is on any given day. Today we know that organisms do follow the Sun's cycles. In fact, they are so deeply embedded in them, and us, that life as we know it would not be very effective in navigating its environment without the Sun. In order to grow and reproduce, we (and other organisms) need to have some way of organizing all the different metabolic activities that go on within us. We can't be doing everything at once—some processes must occur before others begin, and some need to take place at regular intervals. How is all this accomplished? By tuning into the Sun, of course!

Circadian Rhythms

There are two major solar cycles that life has used to build its structures around—the cycle of the day and the cycle of the year. Today, daily cycles in organisms are called circadian cycles. A circadian cycle is a biological cycle that is about one day in length ("circa" means about and "dia" means day). Some of the first circadian cycles noted were in plants. During the course of the day, leaf movements, like the solar energy collectors that they are, track the movement of the Sun. Flowering is also regulated by Sun movements, and this allows plants to be available to insect pollinators at just the right time. Flower "clocks" are sometimes planted in which different types of flowers open in sequence throughout the course of the day. Circadian rhythms are found in nearly every kind of organism, including cyanobacteria. Size doesn't seem to matter when it comes to reading the Sun.

A good example of a circadian cycle is wakefulness and sleep. We do both everyday, but not at the same time. How do we know which one to do and when? Well, our ancestors were awake during daylight and slept at night. We still do that, although our modern lifestyle distorts this for many of us. One good example of how our attunement to the daily cycle is experienced is jet lag. When we travel a great distance quickly, our bodies can't make the adjustment right away and we must adjust to the new time zone—but this could take days. Other circadian cycles are continuously working in our bodies, raising and lowering hormone levels, shifting processes in organs, modulating blood pressure, and many other things that keep us going. All of these cycles are about twenty-four hours in length and they can run without us seeing the Sun. In fact, people working in mines or working night shifts are basically healthy, so circadian cycles are not immediately solar-dependent. But these cycles are very close to twenty-four hours, which obviously means they are based on the solar day, and they can be entrained or adjusted back to the solar day very easily. What has happened in life history is that living things have used the solar day to establish biological clocks, but they have also learned to let them run without any solar input—to a point. So we could say the Sun was brought into life as a kind of timer.

Photoperiodism

During the course of the year the length of daylight changes. For most of the globe, in summer the days are long and the nights are short—the reverse happens in winter. In the quote above, Ptolemy recognized that organisms followed the cycle of the year, which is shown not only by length of day, but also by the Sun's daily arc in the sky and its relation to the zenith. The higher the Sun gets in the sky, the longer the day. Animals use this constant day/night ratio to time breeding periods. Timing reproductive cycles with the Sun is critical—any animal that has offspring at a time of year when food is not available won't fare well at all. Plants use the changing day length for similar reasons: producing seeds in winter is hardly productive. Birds are able to use the Sun as a guide in navigation over long distances. In their annual migrations, some species of birds travel thousands of miles. They need to know when to leave on their long journeys and they need to know which direction to fly. Besides visual cues, it is now known that birds can use the location of the Sun, and magnetic field information, to reach their destinations. The measuring and use of the annual cycle in organisms is called photoperiodism. It is thought that humans are also sensitive to the annual cycle of the Sun and that SAD (seasonal affective disorder) is a condition that results from a lack of sunlight during the winter months.

Astrological Connections

I have often thought that the annual cycle of day-length is the physical factor behind the zodiac. When day and night are of equal length, the signs Aries and Libra begin. Cancer begins on the longest day, and Capricorn begins on the shortest. The cycle of day-length rises in the spring, peaks at the summer solstice, declines in autumn, and reaches its low point in Capricorn—at least in the northern hemisphere. We know that many organisms can track this constantly shifting balance between day and night length and then use it to time biological processes. It has been shown that births occurring at certain parts of the year will fare better than others. It may be that organisms track this day-length not as a continuous curve, but as a series of steps or stages. Each quarter of the year, that is, each season, is broken into three stages—which we call the zodiac signs. Each stage is a block of time that contains information that organisms know what to do with, and each stage makes its imprint on those born during it.

The Sun has many rhythms besides the very important daily and yearly cycles. Many correlations have been reported that link biological activity with the eleven-year sunspot cycle. Well-documented rhythms of about ten years, very close to the sunspot cycle, include crop yields, fish catches, and polar mammal population changes. Insect populations show very close correlations with the sunspot cycle and as such are regarded as sensitive climate monitors. Tent caterpillar populations peak predictably about two years before the peak of solar activity, and other insect populations appear to do the same. It has been suggested that these population increases are due to the increased warmth and ultraviolet radiation that follow the solar cycle. What is apparent is that life is so deeply linked to the Sun that it follows even the slow rise and fall of energy emanating from it.

Solar energy is ultimately what drives us on the physical level. Our bodies use "prepackaged" solar energy from plants, or from animals that eat plants, to stay alive. Our ability to navigate our environment successfully, to be in the right place at the right time, is due to our ability to make inner time from the Sun's movements. The Sun is our very vitality and our integrity, and it's hard to imagine living without it.

Astrological Real Estate
Sun Signs and Your Home

by Alice DeVille

Housing and related industries account for about 14 percent of our nation's gross domestic product. New households form at an annual rate of more than a million per year. The nationwide home ownership rate is expected to reach 70 percent by the year 2010. To meet housing demands, builders need to construct about 1.6 million new homes and apartments each year of this decade. Single-family and multi-family construction, plus remodeling expenditures, account for about $329 billion annually—equal to approximately 4 percent of the nation's total economic activity. For each one-point drop in mortgage rates, the average homebuyer can spend $20,000 to $30,000 more on a new home purchase.

The home-buying frenzy continues to dominate the real estate market with the planet Jupiter encouraging expansion and the purchase of big-ticket items like homes. The planet of real-estate investment, Saturn, favors significant gains and a desire for undertaking new responsibility. Americans invest in and earn more from their homes than they earn from savings accounts, IRAs, stocks, bonds, and other long-term investments. With interest rates at record lows, most individuals wanting to put down roots purchased a home during the last few years. Whether these home seekers were first-time buyers, empty nesters wanting to downsize, seniors looking for planned retirement communities, investors desirous of "flipping" properties for a quick profit, or homeowners wanting to cash in their accelerating equity for a move-up model or a vacation home, the planets have favored transactions in the real estate market. Home sellers and new home builders have realized record-breaking profits in their contract prices. Sellers receive multiple contract offers on their homes with buyers waiving standard contract clauses, such as home inspections, appraisals, and termite inspections, to make sure their bids are contingent-free.

Builders of new homes sell out of lots or, in the case of condominiums, units, before the construction begins. Waits of one to two years are the norm in these ultra-desirable developments. I work in the frantic northern Virginia real-estate market outside of Washington, DC, where you usually need an appointment just to visit the new home site. Your initial visit does not guarantee you a chance to bid on a property. Since demand is so high, some companies have a lottery and draw bids from an applicant pool of qualified buyers.

Resale properties are just as hot. Only grossly overpriced or very high-end properties linger on the market. The demand for property far outweighs the existing inventory. For every successful transaction, there are disappointed home seekers whose contracts were not as attractive to the home seller. Even with the help of a savvy real-estate agent, that very same buyer may have to bid on five or more properties before winning a contract. Home-buying fever comes with a sense of excitement that says "my dream house" is on the other end of the settlement table. When the money changes hands, the buyer wants to furnish or improve the new dwelling. In the first twelve months after purchasing an existing home, the average homeowner spends nearly $4,000 more on their home than their non-moving counterparts.

Easy As ABC

The home-buying process is a complex one with many rules and regulations driving the transaction. As a licensed Realtor, I care about customer service and keep my clients informed of each milestone. Recently I earned credentials as an Accredited Buyer Representative, which give me even more incentive to help buyers experience smooth transactions. TLC pays off, with satisfied buyers raving over results and giving referrals. Before you begin your search for the perfect home and meet with lenders, select a qualified real estate professional to guide you through the process.

If you were not among those who caught the recent house-hunting wave, this article will interest you. It offers pointers on planning your purchase, selling your existing home, meeting with lenders, finding out how much it will cost, and how to qualify for the mortgage loan. Using Sun-sign astrology, you'll learn tips for financing the home of your dreams along with guidance for keeping transactions stress-free.

A few key houses of the astrology chart relate to home buying and finances. The sign on the cusp of your Fourth House of home gives you insight into the type of residence that appeals to you. Planets that occupy that house strengthen your preferences for housing amenities and determine whether you are likely to be a long-time resident or a frequent mover. The Second House of income and resources indicates your prospects for having enough money to buy your home, and also describes lenders you seek. The Eighth House of money you owe indicates the loan you receive from the bank, its terms, and the mortgage company's assets and means of doing business with you.

While many planets play a role in the real-estate market, this article places less emphasis on them and more on the behavior of each Sun sign. As you prepare for the rewarding experience of buying a home, read the Sun sign segment that follows to get a feel for what works for you and what tendencies you will have to curb to be successful in your house-hunting venture. Keep your sense of humor as you review the stereotypes that depict characteristics of your sign. Review the process section and enjoy the "how-to" nature of the advice.

Aries

Like most fire signs, you have confidence that you can afford the home you desire. Regardless of what I recommend, you'll start looking for the perfect home before you know how much money you'll have from the sale of your current residence. If it weren't for the risks associated with buying without the professional services of a real-estate agent, you would race to the settlement table to close the deal in record time. Sellers see things differently and usually won't negotiate with buyers who have unsold residences. Put your present home on the market first to remove any contingencies that might delay settlement of your new purchase. Begin your new home search with the help of a competent buyer-agent. You'll be able to "show them the money" and enjoy stress-free negotiating, knowing that you have the cash it takes to buy your home of choice.

Taurus

Normally very lender savvy, you call five or more companies to check interest rates and terms. You won't want to pay more fees (loan discount points) than you have to, and will shop and compare more than most signs. Although ten-year ARMs (adjustable rate mortgages) with interest-only payments are popular with consumers, you are more likely to forego a lower payment in favor of a fixed rate, thirty-year loan with predictable payments and a reduction in principal. Don't forget that taxes and insurance rates rise and affect your future total payment. The type of loan you choose depends more on how long you intend to stay in the home. If this is your first home, you'll spend an average of five years in residence. Avoid loans that have a balloon payment due at the end of the term. You will have to pay the total balance when the ARM expires, normally in 1, 3, 5, 7, or up to 10 years. You may actually have more disposable income if you cut loose from your conservative mindset and take a closer look at creative loan programs. Think of what you can do with the extra $200-300 a month you will save on this low-interest loan. The savings could fund a convection oven, a weekend getaway, or a few gourmet meals.

Gemini

Who better than you likes the "lock and leave" convenience that condo living affords? Whether you are a working single or part of a childfree couple, a multi-unit complex could be the ultimate housing solution for you. With your energetic lifestyle and busy social calendar, you do not want to give up time and money to slave away at a weed-filled back yard or spend time maintaining expensive landscaping. Nix on the exterior painting and gutter cleaning—you would rather hire contractors and head for the beach while they beautify your surroundings. According to the National Association of Realtors, sales of condos have shattered records every year since 1997. What's stopping you from investing in your future? Those open green spaces, community pools, and gracious courtyards can be yours at an affordable price.

Cancer

Members of your security-loving sign intuitively understand how to stage a home for a results-oriented sale. When the moving bug hits, you pull out all the stops to make your home sparkle and shine. Introduce inviting aromas by baking cookies, using cinnamon aromatherapy, and arranging seasonal flowers to highlight your home's dramatic alcoves. Brightness sells, so light three out of four corners of every room and use "uplights" in large plants. Keep the fireplace burning in cooler seasons. Add mood music during open houses. Use restraint by not making decorations overly personal. You don't want prospective buyers to feel they are invading your private turf. Update tarnished doorknobs, turn on the porch light, dab vanilla on the chandelier and sweep off the welcome mat. The next "SOLD" sign on the block could be yours!

Leo

If applying for a mortgage is in your future, curb the tendency to run up credit card debt. Your impulsive nature finds it hard to pass up a sale, but too many cards with balances detract from your financial solvency. Say "no" to easy credit. Having too much credit is as bad as having no credit. Don't switch frequently from one credit card to another just to wipe out balances. This tendency adversely affects your credit scores. Make payments on time and especially make sure your mortgage check does not arrive after the late payment date that appears on the statement. By using credit wisely, you should have no trouble financing the castle of your dreams.

Virgo

Cost-cutting and thriftiness are associated with members of your sign. One expense you can't eliminate as a homeowner is hazard insurance. Due to the high volume of storms, floods, fires, and other natural disasters, home insurance rates have been on the rise. Your investment is worth protecting and you are required to provide proof of coverage at the time your loan settles. When you shop for insurance, be sure the replacement rate includes an inflation factor that protects your investment and all tangible goods. Increase your deductible and you will be able to save as much as 15 percent on your annual premium.

Libra

You adore collectibles and seldom want to part with the treasures accumulated over the years. This lovable trait means two things in the language of buying and selling homes. As a buyer, you look for abundant storage space, huge walk-in closets, and an oversized garage. Your significant other swears you will fill every nook and cranny. On the selling end? Your reputation as a pack rat surfaces when your real-estate agent suggests you de-clutter your living space to make your rooms look larger. Yes, you will have to rid your living room of most of the knick-knacks and hire a storage company to remove the excess furniture. But lighten up: eager buyers will give your home a "thumbs up" and come through with an attractive con-tract if your home makes a favorable first impression when they open the front door. Then spend some of your profit on built-in storage when you move to your new residence.

Scorpio

Tax deductions for mortgage interest, points, and local real-estate taxes reduce the cost of home ownership while the homeowner builds long-term equity in the investment. As the sign on the cusp of the solar Eighth House of mortgages, taxes, and investments, Scorpios recognize homeownership as a solid and sensible tax shelter. As equity builds, you can borrow on it for major expenses such as home improvement and cars. Home-related deductions make it worthwhile to itemize rather than to take the standard deduction on your return. If you are currently a homeowner, don't forget to apply all the deductions the tax law provides. Consult your tax advisor for answers to tax questions that apply to your particular property. If you are still renting, now is the time to buy so you can lower your tax bill next year.

Sagittarius

Members of your sign love the great outdoors and are usually attracted to a home based on its curb appeal. Add value to your residence by giving it a landscape makeover before you put it on the market. Be sure to plan ahead so the design flows and you keep to your budget. Focal points like fountains and birdbaths add visual appeal and help you center plantings around key spots. If you want a more established look for your garden, buy larger plants. Integrate plants with mulch bark beds, stepping-stone paths, and brick work. Add privacy by creating banks, building partial walls, or making visual screens using hedges, fences, or trees. Your home's new buyer will declare, "I found the most attractive home on the block. It was love at first sight."

Capricorn

Much as you treasure your own residence, you are always on the lookout for investment property. The idea of collecting above-market rents appeals to you, especially when the cash flow pays the mortgage and nets extra income. You don't care for the tedious job of managing the property and dealing with maintenance and repair issues. Another time-consuming task is obtaining extensive reference verification and credit checks for potential tenants. Why not hire a top-notch property management firm to take care of the messy details? These firms generally market your property assertively to attract solid tenants. Request leases of at least twelve months. Then relax, erase the worry lines from your forehead, and count your coins. Next year, when you sell the property for an appreciable gain, invest it in another successful venture. Your accountant will love you.

Aquarius

Contingencies represent contract conditions called "escape" or "kick-out" clauses that must be met within a specified time to close the home sale by the anticipated settlement date. The analytical members of your sign curl up with a real estate contract and pore over the document's legal loopholes—also known as contingencies. You don't want to be left holding the bag in case things don't work out. If conditions are not met, the party who benefits from the contingency may legally pull out of the sale. Among the most common contingencies that cancel a sale are the inability of the buyer to obtain financing by a specific date or sell an existing home whose proceeds are needed to close this sale, an appraised value that falls below the sales price, an unsatisfactory home inspection that uncovers structural or material defects, or a clouded title. Be sure you notify your real-estate agent as soon as you remove any pending contingency clauses and you'll get to the settlement table on time.

Pisces

A little planning goes a long way. Moving is one of the most stressful aspects of home buying. Once your sales contract has been ratified (all parties agree to the terms), the countdown to moving day begins. Your dead-on visualization helps you map out the location of every piece of furniture and pair of shoes in your new home. Start packing and contacting moving companies immediately to get cost estimates and to check availability for your big day. Many scams exist in the moving industry; get recommendations from trusted friends and real estate professionals. Check the reputation and integrity of moving companies with the Better Business Bureau before you hire them. If you base your decision on cost alone, you could find your furniture held hostage in some remote location for days or weeks. When it is finally delivered, you may be asked to pay excessively more than your contract price. Goods may be damaged or missing. Take away the illusion that all moving companies are created equal. You and your furnishings deserve a safe arrival. Happy landing!

For Further Reading

Riske, Kris Brandt. *Mapping Your Money: Understanding Your Financial Potential*. St. Paul: Llewellyn, 2005.

Your Soul's Purpose
Karma and Your Sign

by Anne Windsor

What can your Sun sign tell you about the meaning of life? Plenty. Just as the Sun is the center of our solar system, your Sun sign is the vibrant heart of your own life story. By investigating the nature of your Sun sign as well as your opposite sign, you can understand your strengths as well as the inevitable challenges that cross your path. So read on, check out your Sun sign, and apply these heavenly hints to get in tune with your soul's intention.

Sun in Aries

As an Aries, your soul purpose is to define your Self. Not exactly a short order—but the cosmic crew consistently helps you out by tempting you to rush headlong into the great unknown. While this life plan sounds impractical to your cautious Capricorn friends, it's just what the doctor ordered to help you overcome your past-life mistakes, take charge of your gifts and talents in this lifetime, and get out of your own way.

The heart and soul of every Aries is cut from the fabric of courage and nobility; that's why you look so good in uniform. Sure, you love to be loved, but the real thrill in life is to charge off to conquer the dragons that dare cross your path. But your "fight now, ask questions later" approach does find you jousting with the occasional windmill.

Libra is your opposite sign and points out the need for peace and tranquility. Use Libra's poise to grace your actions with logic and finesse—but if you're not quite sure what your marching orders are, it's Libra's indecision causing you to wander and waffle. It's up to you to triumph over those inner demons that subconsciously make you timid and tentative.

The key to tending the sacred Aries flame is to embrace your true-blue nature and circle your soul with courage. Be willing to take a risk, to break new ground, to make a path for others to follow. Reach for the biggest, the brightest, and the best without reservation or apology, and you will indeed embody the spirit of the conquering hero of your soul.

Sun in Taurus

Nickels, dimes, dollars, and diamonds: how do you measure up? You were born as a Taurus to do one thing: discover the value of your self and everything around you. Deep down is the need to have and to hold, to pursue and possess all for the sake of feeling secure. The quest for stability sometimes reels out of control when innocent wishes turn into unquenchable cravings, fueled by the fear of never "having" enough.

Taurus has a kinder, gentler side that tempts and entices you to step away from your "make a buck" existence and commune with nature. Sit a spell and watch the clouds go by. Breathe deep and listen as the rock-solid earth beneath you asks if your life is rich with pleasure as well as treasure.

Scorpio is your opposite sign and makes no bones about Taurus's blind ambition to "have it all." You can re-balance your life by adopting Scorpio's firm belief that if having something only feeds your hunger and not your soul, you should let it go and move on to greener pastures. Of course, if you stalwartly stand your ground and refuse to relinquish your possessions, you can be certain that you've been bitten by the dark side of Scorpio's obsession with power and control.

Eventually, in your own time, you happen upon the greatest prize of all: the reality that the purpose of life isn't just about having for the sake of having. Once you embrace this cosmic truth, your strength and tenacity propel you forward on an unstoppable quest to have the right stuff, the stuff that matters, and the stuff of which dreams are made.

Sun in Gemini

As a Gemini, your soul purpose is to delight in the ever-changing options and opportunities, choices and chances that await you on life's highways and byways. Rather than trying to plant your feet and pin down the secret to success, awaken your Gemini soul with a quick trip into the curious land of "what if." What if you didn't have to work full time? What if you finished that book you started to write when you were in college? What if you lived on the beach for a year? What if you really could have your cake and eat it too?

Sagittarius is your opposite sign and urges you to expand your mind and explore the big, wide world. Of course, those are noble pursuits, but if you find yourself stalled in search of the meaning of it all, you can rest assured you've been tainted by Sagittarius's pompous philosophy that everything has to make sense. But you don't need to buy into that singular view of life. As a Gemini, you can make peace with the fact that your life is like a day trip into the land of enigmas, paradoxes, and oxymorons. And that's a good thing.

Allow yourself to wonder and wander, pause and ponder as the world of possibilities dances in front of you. And as you hop, skip, and jump through the kaleidoscope landscape that your soul calls home, embrace Gemini's clever capacity to refresh your psyche with interesting insights and even more interesting questions. But if you expect to emerge from your time on the Gemini clock with the meaning of life, you'll be sorely disappointed. The Gemini twins giggle at the naïve simplicity of the idea, and hint that in asking the "what if" questions you have already started on a journey that is much more important than simply finding the answer.

Sun in Cancer

As a Cancer, your soul purpose is to put down some roots and surround yourself with loved ones. Learn to go with the flow of your softer, sensitive side and open up to your inner voice. Hone your instincts and act on your gut feelings. And while you don't need to take on house and home with the fervor of Martha Stewart, a few domestic talents will serve you well, especially in the wee hours of the morning when your best friend shows up on your doorstep to cry on your shoulder. That's when brewing a comforting cup of tea can make all the difference.

Of course, Cancer is not all about sugar plums and soccer moms. As a Cancer, you can apply your sensitivity and limitless imagination to almost anything you choose. What's the catch? Simply that you have to be in the right mood to do much of anything, so your life's work had better be something that makes you happy. Otherwise you'll find yourself sidestepping responsibility and being labeled as cranky, cantankerous, and ornery throughout your career.

Cool, emotionally remote Capricorn is your opposite, and goads you into setting the occasional boundary so that your friends and family respect you. But the minute your mood swings over towards cold and calculating, you know you've ventured too far into the cut-and-dried world of Capricorn. Then you know it's time to return to the gentle ebb and flow of emotions and intuition.

Since you have chosen to experience life through the lens of sentiment and sensitivity, you simply need to claim the power inherent in your compassionate nature. Use your emotion as a touchstone—a helpful guide to navigating through the maze of family and feelings, heart and soul.

Sun in Leo

Born into the lusty sign of Leo, your soul purpose is to pursue passion's promise in all that you do, whether it's writing the great American novel or creating a special rendezvous with your dream lover. Leo demands that you put your heart into every aspect of your existence and that you create a life to be proud of.

Your charismatic warmth and generous spirit easily make you the center of attention. Deep down, you love holding court and displaying your finer points in front of an adoring audience, but it's up to you as to what you do with all that popularity. In the land of Leo, your ego can either puff itself up with plenty of pretentious self-importance, or you can plow past your pride and access that part of you that is capable of noble humility, leadership, and ingenuity.

Aquarius is your opposite sign and offers a cool, breezy objectivity to offset your fiery passions. Use Aquarius's fascination for the future to define your goals and plans for the next week, month, and year. However, when you find yourself feeling cut off from the excitement of everyday life, then you have indeed taken a detour into Aquarius's penchant for disengaging when things get too dicey. Remember that, as a Leo, you thrive on the chaos of creation, so it's up to you to revive your life with inspiration and innovation.

As a Leo, your spirit reminds you that this lifetime is not a dress rehearsal. Rather, it is about mastering your self-expression so that you exude confidence and graciousness and inspire respect and loyalty. In order for your soul to take center stage you must honor the irrepressible enthusiasm that inflames your imagination and commands your inner light to shine.

Sun in Virgo

Being born a Virgo presents you with the perfect opportunity to create your own little island of perfection, to order your world according to your vision. You must balance the fight for flawlessness with real-world practicality, avoid obsession with the trivial tasks, and choose, instead, to dedicate your efforts toward making a difference.

Sure, anyone can talk big, but as a Virgo you actually follow up on those big words with even bigger actions and accomplishments. Virgo just loves that feeling that comes from a job well done and the sense of satisfaction that comes from creating order out of chaos. Of course, the devil is in the details, but it's up to you to recognize that sometimes a bit of bedlam is actually part of the divine order. Otherwise you'll live up to your fusspot, finicky reputation.

Dreamy Pisces is your opposite sign. You may scoff at Pisces's hopeful faith and innate idealism, pointing out that it's actually hard work that gets things done. However, a day trip to the enchanted land of Pisces every once in a while is a salve to your soul. Use the Pisces compassion and acceptance to acknowledge your strengths and imperfections. Just be wary of drifting along under the spell of Pisces for too long, or you'll find it harder and harder to deal with the real world.

It is your wholesome, helpful nature that is a gift to others, and it is crucial to acknowledge that your passionate devotion results in important contributions to the world around you. Take pride in your striving and make peace with your inner critic, realizing that it is this capacity to discern and distinguish that your soul longs to perfect in this lifetime.

Sun in Libra

According to the travel brochure from the lush land of Libra, you're nobody unless you book passage on the ship of dreams with your one and only. Yes, you are here to understand your relationship to the world and everyone in it. But you typically bend over backwards to force yourself to match your beloved's worldview rather than accepting the differences between the two of you. Not surprisingly, finding or becoming the perfect partner is not your soul purpose. Preserving your individuality, and seeking harmony and peace without sacrificing your self, are what your soul truly craves.

Once your illusions have been blasted to bits, it's easy to find refuge in Libra's second-favorite pastime of weighing the pros and cons of every issue before pronouncing judgment. Unfortunately, you won't see that life is passing you by while you mull over the rhetorical and the theoretical.

Your opposite sign is Aries, which gives you the occasional kick in the seat of the pants and insists that you do something, even if it's wrong. Your Aries shadow can turn love into a battlefield and create a mindset of confrontation and contention in even the most casual of interactions. The minute you tackle the convenience store clerk because she didn't smile at you is the minute you need to take a deep breath, relax, and resume your quest for peace and tranquility in Libra.

You've been blessed with a natural charm and grace as much to enhance your own being as to attract romantic relationships. As you move through your life, use Libra's unerring scales to balance your life and to make sure that you, your wants, and your needs are part of the equation. And if you decide to walk arm-in-arm with someone who honors you every step of the way, well, the heavens above couldn't be happier.

Sun in Scorpio

On a soul level, you have chosen this lifetime to master the deep, driving desire to create a longer, stronger link with the power that controls the cosmos. But first you have to exorcise the ghosts and goblins that haunt your soul and convert the monsters of your mind into powerful allies.

The dynamic, resourceful power that flows through you can singlehandedly work miracles, and you are quite familiar with chaos and upheaval as the messy but necessary processes of transformation. However, to truly become master and commander of your capacity to help and heal, you must hone your instinct and ability to read others' motives and emotions.

Your opposite sign is stable, secure Taurus. Lounging around Taurus's lush, plush pasturelands provides some much-needed peace and tranquility, and you can relax and release the resentment and obsessions that clutter your mind. In addition, Taurus can help you take stock of your possessions and grace your life with gratitude. Unfortunately, it's ever-so-easy to get stuck in the Taurus mud and spin your wheels, mistaking action for progress. Ultimately, it's up to you to extract yourself from the crushing comforts of Taurus and pursue the passions and perils of Scorpio's depths.

Claim your place as the most powerful sign of the zodiac. Make peace with the fact that the power streaming through you can either empower or destroy whoever and whatever you hold near and dear. At the end of the day it is this intimate awareness of life's sacred process that ultimately liberates your soul and sets the stage for an authentic life.

Sun in Sagittarius

Bigger, better, faster, stronger. This lifetime your optimistic soul has ventured into the "everything and more" store of Sagittarius. Somewhere along the "pursuit of plenty" your Sagittarian soul must answer two revealing questions: how much is enough; and how far are you willing to go to get it? Of course, as a Sagittarius you can overextend yourself and your resources with the best of them, but eventually you end up at the same truth that freedom-loving Sagittarius has been preaching for eons: you are a spiritual nomad; travel like one. Stop looking to fill yourself up with baubles and trinkets from the same old stores when your soul is craving the action, adventure, and exhilaration that comes only from beginning a new journey.

Your opposite sign is options-oriented Gemini. It's never a bad idea to make a quick pit stop at the Gemini garage before setting off toward parts unknown. Inform yourself, investigate your options, and make a few phone calls to let people know when and where you are headed. But don't tarry. Once you've decided on your course, stick with it. Otherwise Gemini's excessive array of alternatives will overwhelm your mind and scatter your intentions to the four winds. And if you find yourself buzzing around in circles, you need to pull out your compass and focus on traveling in one direction, one step at a time.

The secret to your soul's satisfaction is to recognize that the reason behind your wild exploits is to expand your understanding of who you are and who you are becoming. Be daring and bold and jump headlong into the great adventures that await you. Just remember to thank your lucky stars every night, no matter where you land.

Sun in Capricorn

As a Capricorn, your soul purpose is to take yourself seriously and to honor your own wisdom. You have a disciplined drive and ambition and easily take on additional responsibilities. Your innate efficiency can be a great boon to any project or organization, but it is just as important to ensure that your hard work pays off in your own life.

Organize your efforts so that you benefit as much as the next guy and create a solid plan for success.

While your flashy Leo friends may call you a stick-in-the-mud, your patient perseverance pays off in the long run. Your reserved nature masks a powerhouse of industrious innovation that is capable of founding and following through on massive projects.

Shy, sensitive Cancer is your opposite sign. Incorporating Cancer's empathy deepens your understanding of human nature and needs. Your innate patience and wisdom can benefit your interests as well as others', but you must be cautious of being used by others who play on your fears, or of using others' vulnerabilities against them. Draw upon your natural practicality to create appropriate boundaries to guide your personal and professional relationships.

As you march through life, conquering one project at a time, remember that life is not just about accomplishment. Make every day count, whether you meet with success or failure. Inwardly you will always keep an eye on the prize, but you must make time for what matters. Embrace the pragmatic philosophy of wise old Capricorn to face your fears, listen to your inner wisdom, do something worthwhile, and take personal responsibility for manifesting your dreams.

Sun in Aquarius

The cosmic wake-up call for an Aquarian soul is to reinvent yourself and to accept and expect the unexpected. You are rattled, restless, and ravenous for change, not just in your own life but in the lives of your fellow man. You're concerned with the future and fixed on the idea of grooving to the beat of a distant drummer. Draw on your inner confidence and conviction and talk about who you really are, what you want, and your quirky ideas about the future—despite the fact that the future is always unshaped and uncertain, dicey and downright dangerous. But that's the ultimate power of the unknown.

For Aquarius to work its radical wonders, it requires two things: space to spread out and a room with a view. Get away from it all, stand back, and peer at your life project from a different angle. Be impartial. Acknowledge what arouses your passions and motivates you to move toward your dreams.

Your opposite sign is proud, rowdy Leo. Use Leo's warmth to infuse your ideas and inventions with a magnetic zeal that inspires others to contribute to your cause. Unfortunately, Leo's ego and pride can eclipse your idealistic and unaffected nature. Listen to your inner voice and free yourself from the quicksand of self-importance.

It is a mystery how the same altruistic attitude that inspires you to dream also peppers your life with surprising twists and turns, dead ends, and detours. When the unexpected strikes, take a moment to gather your thoughts and re-design your strategy. Then, hold fast to the undeniable truth that when you keep on keeping on, when you hold the dream, it is then that your soul can truly be alive and liberated, now and in the future.

Sun in Pisces

As you thread your way through the labyrinth of life, your soul purpose is to honor your intuition and have faith in the power of your dreams. Your tender soul seeks tranquility, and yet your desire to help, to serve, and to sacrifice constantly draws you into the deep uncharted waters of personal relationships. It is there that your romantic nature seeks to combine with the divine as you navigate love's mists and myths in search of Heaven on Earth.

As a Pisces, you have an unshakable faith and can peer into the pitch-black abyss of human nature, knowing that there is an undeniable goodness at the heart of every soul. Your compassion and accepting nature enable you to connect with anyone and everyone, but no matter how poorly you are treated in response, your core beliefs are never tarnished. Even so, you must learn to grieve and mourn. You may have plenty of delays and disappointments, regrets and lamentations, but becoming a martyr simply robs you of your divinity.

Because you see the world as it could be, as it should be, you are an artist at heart. Give play to your imagination and allow your creative forces a free hand. The results will be a fascinating combination of realism and fantasy, whimsy and myth.

Vigilant Virgo is your opposite sign and offers a helping hand in terms of organizing your life and staying on track. Gentle Virgo guides you through the practical considerations of everyday tasks.

But Virgo's unrelenting focus on form will eventually debilitate your dreams and visions. Instead, give in to your Pisces muse who woos you to relax and go with the flow, to succumb to a little bit of fantasy, and to resolve and relinquish the regrets and misgivings that are littering your subconscious.

Finally, you must surrender to your inner light and listen to the silent whispers of the cosmos. Look inside and see, not what you are, but what you can be when you trust that you are exactly where you are meant to be, right here, right now.

For Further Reading

Clement, Stephanie Jean. *Charting Your Spiritual Path With Astrology*. St. Paul: Llewellyn, 2001.

Spiller, Jan. *Spiritual Astrology*. New York: Fireside, 1988.

A World in Flux
World Predictions for 2006

by Leeda Alleyn Pacotti

The world economy is in trouble. Countries in every quarter of the globe seek expected, but harder to find, power-generating resources to underwrite their national productivity. As symbolically portrayed and frequently stated in Frank Herbert's multi-volume saga of *Dune*, "The spice must flow!" On Earth now, "the spice" is our dwindling natural resources.

All the ways nations have learned to bolster their coffers are collapsing in on themselves. Whether through oil cartels, drug cartels, military takeovers, espionage of military secrets, pirating of intellectual properties, or any other of a myriad of unsavory financial and commercial tactics, these old ways are no longer serving the needs of humanity worldwide. In exploring the prevailing economics of 2006, leaders have forgotten an all-important ingredient of every national construct—the people who are "the country."

It Is a Depression
Since the early 1990s, the catchphrase has been the "new business

paradigm." Despite speculation of global conglomerates, no one really considered those at the bottom of the commercial pyramids, the workers who actually produce the goods and services sold by any company.

Although the United States began seeing major immigration problems from undocumented workers entering its borders several years ago, it shared this problem with another major power, China. Other countries, such as Kazakhstan, North Korea, and those in the midst of wars, experienced the reverse, or emigration. The peoples of the world are being forced to move away from their problems and seek better solutions. As they go, they take with them their intellectual force and sheer manpower.

Not surprisingly, those who immigrate are finding that the siren song of lucrative work simply is not true. Yes, some nations have plenty of low-paying jobs, but median-income employments are shrinking everywhere. As producers find that their remaining populations can no longer afford as many goods and services, they stave off costs by reducing employment positions. As less personal income is made, fewer goods and services are purchased. The continued reduction of jobs in all countries spirals downward into a global depression.

The Tightened Market

For most of 2006, Jupiter and Saturn are in an astrological square, which has its advent in December 2005. This aspect is well-known in astrological parlance to coincide with a depressed marketplace. Further, these two giant planets are poorly placed in extreme Scorpio and exuberant Leo. Jupiter's abundance for spending goes to outrageous tastes in Scorpio, while Saturn's conservative business instincts contract tighter, rather than flowering, during its transit through the sunny sign of Leo.

For those who believe technology is the new commercial messiah, Jupiter and Saturn also share poor aspects with Neptune, currently placed in Aquarius. Jupiter sends an astrological square to Neptune throughout the first eight months of the year, inflating the prices of technological products and stocks. As Jupiter ends this arrangement, Saturn rolls in with an opposition to Neptune, depressing that market for the remaining four months of the year.

Uranus, which rules computers and technological communications, trines Jupiter during the same period as Jupiter's aspect with Neptune. However, Uranus is ineffectively operating in Pisces, Neptune's sign. Uranus simply further inflates the technological markets with faddish gadgetry that is either impractical or has a planned, early obsolescence. This market character from Uranus is reinforced by a stressful inconjunct from Saturn, which tries desperately to jostle money from the buying public by improving the tried and worthless.

Not until late November, when Jupiter slips into its own sign of Sagittarius, will the markets all over the globe begin to experience an upswing. Jupiter will have moved away from these foreboding aspects, and Saturn will begin to trine Pluto, taking some edge off its remaining opposition to Neptune.

Boosting a Short-Term Economy

Although domestic spending and foreign investment are curtailed throughout most of 2006, the public is ready to buy, buy, and buy some more during the holiday season. Retailers need not stock high-ticket items or the latest fancy eye-catcher. The public wants to purchase in plenty, but its spending power is reserved for the basics, the practical, and the inexpensive.

Moderately priced housewares and decorative accessories are within reach. Nontechnological games, hobby supplies, and non-electric outdoor gear head the preferred lists for children. Classic clothing and mix-and-match wardrobes give surprise and surplus for working parents. Simple adornments spruce up existing apparel.

In short, to stoke ailing national economies, consumers want and need to be instilled with a sense of improving self-reliance. Should existing companies continue to disregard demands of the changing marketplace, expect a surge of local, inventive, and selectively networked small businesses willing to answer the call of despairing consumers—when, in a few years, Uranus plunges into Aries and the United States enjoys a fresh presidency.

Crazy Eight

Complicating the powerful astrological influences on economics is the numerology for the universal year 2006, which is an 8, indicating a year of material satisfaction. Usually, this numerological portent is read as business growth and a push into well-grounded finances. What seems a contradiction, though, is really misinterpretation.

Material satisfaction does not suggest that businesses or individuals plunge forth heedlessly to grab tightly held shares of the marketplace or wrangle for increasingly rare higher salaries. Instead, the emphasis is on satisfaction—an inner quality of personal need that cannot be measured in dollars and cents.

Defining satisfaction as pride in goods and services or as comfort in personal lifestyle, businesses and individuals have greater opportunities to work ingeniously with the astrological impacts of Jupiter and Saturn. Whether creating or expanding a business or securing a comfortable wage, Jupiter demands joy, while Saturn requires a stable foundation. In making business and employment decisions this year, applying energies toward the production of goods and services that are fun and fulfill innate talents answers the calls of these two largest and powerful planets. Those courageous souls who dare respond to the astrological urges and numerological force will find an old financial adage proven true: do what you love; the money will follow.

Making the Best of These Hard Times

Over the last decade, the cry of the marketplace has been globalization, promoted as the most innovative get-rich scheme of western history. Yet, this perspective ignores the fact that a global marketplace has been a reality for at least 2500 years, thanks to Alexander the Great, the Roman Empire, Marco Polo, and the audacious Portuguese and Spanish navigators. The search for raw materials and extraordinary goods has propelled nations throughout recorded history to thrust beyond known boundaries and seek new trade frontiers. Globalization just isn't a new thing.

What is new is the multinational corporation—that seemingly hard-shelled conglomeration with a defective core that reveals itself as inefficiencies in shipping and distribution of goods. Because these inefficiencies are so costly, multinationals purchase low-quality goods and low-wage services, and dress them up for consumption with advertising gloss, just to keep a profit margin and some form of shareholder benefit. However, the defect has started to run these businesses, as they move operations into economically poor countries, repress wages, and abandon a proven workforce at home, debilitating domestic incomes in their former stomping grounds.

Anyone who clings to a belief in multinational expansion will have a rough ride on the shifting financial swells of 2006. In fact, any form of get-rich-quick thinking is deluded. For those who believe they can make a fortune through the lottery or gambling, all bets are off. Those who think that preemptive strikes through commodities will save them need to wake up and smell the coffee. Stock players must step back from the market and take stock of themselves. Anyone sticking to hopes of a killing in real estate needs to get real.

All these attitudes speak to the fear that what any person really finds satisfying and joyful will never pay the bills. Every thing, activity, and valuation must then be measured by money—making a mockery of the real meaning of success, which is actually an accomplishment or an achievement measurable only by a sense of satisfaction or pleasure.

Here, we are led back to the numerological impact of 8: material satisfaction. Many people distracted by pipe dreams of fast wealth have opportunities this year to reassess their talents and resources to construct a more fulfilling career path. The changing state of domestic economic affairs gives some clues.

In contradiction to the multinational viewpoint or the mistaken idea of globalization is the manageable concept of localization. Local needs cannot be addressed by a multinational corporation, which creates a sales void for goods and services based on geographic or demographic needs. Regional specialties include needs specific to deserts, mountains, or shorelines, while demographic differentiations are produced from college towns or high retirement enclaves.

Nor will it matter whether the community or region is rural or urban. Although human needs of food, shelter, clothing, transportation, health, and entertainment are universal, such needs gain particular definition from the inhabitants of the area. Forms of decor and dress, for instance, are influenced by local occupations, such as farming, manufacturing, or professional services.

Specifically, food production is not well served by global distribution methods. Locally grown or produced foods yield more profit to the local farmer or producer, who typically can work on a small scale and needs a smaller base of consumers. Because everyone must eat, the typical raw-food producer needs about seventy households, which can be put on a weekly delivery contract. An excellent use of the continuing mutual reception between Uranus and Neptune suggests that hydroponic greenhouse produce or fresh-water shrimp—sold directly by local or regional contracts to select groceries, households, or restaurants—strikes a happy medium between innovation and water uses.

Ultimately, 2006 offers the chance to employ original thinking and refuse the cliches of sameness. This is the year to become reacquainted with personal talents and interests, observe the local landscape, and blend the two into an exceptional offering that addresses and meets the immediate needs of the individual and community.

Nations in Focus

Eclipses during late March and September influence the stability of certain nations, indicating potential changes in government, leadership, or economics. On March 29, a total solar eclipse carves a swath from central Asia through the eastern Mediterranean.

China: Although not affected directly by the eclipse, China's problems eerily echo those in the United States: border tensions, drug abuse, substantial rural unemployment, fuel shortages, and illegal immigration problems. Increasing its oil imports by 40 percent in 2004, China resolved border and immigration problems with Kazakhstan, which has abundant resources in oil, natural gas, and mining, just as the former Soviet republic resolved its own border issues with Russia. Throughout 2006, China experiences a number of slowdowns as its population attempts to reconcile an emerging international image of power and influence with domestic ills. In negotiations over oil, China encounters some cagey manipulations that put that market out of reach for a while. However, this Asian giant, which hosts the 2008 Summer Olympics, will not be deterred, although work on the Olympic venues slows down due to nuclear and other power shortages, affecting manufacture of construction materials.

Kazakhstan: Enviable Kazakhstan is blessed with low, rolling pasture land, enormous fossil fuel reserves, and wealthy deposits of minerals and metals. Of all the former Soviet republics, this nation has the potential for excellent international standing, with a solid diversity in agriculture, manufacturing, and services. The president understands how easily Kazakhstan can be plundered by other industrial nations, such as neighboring China and Russia. From January through August, the president opposes nuclear development and foreign demand for the country's oil reserves. During the March eclipse, which passes directly over the capital of Astana, the president is in danger during a national recreational event, possibly targeted for his opposition to foreign oil interests. Not a short-sighted man, he strongly pushes education for the Kazakh people, now that the effects of the emigration of technicians and scientists after the Soviet fall are showing. From September through December, the president staunchly withholds fossil-fuel reserves from all foreign negotiations. Fortunately, events during the spring have rallied the necessary cohesion of the Kazakh people, who support the president's stance and his efforts on their behalf to build a stable nation.

Russia: As the March eclipse makes its way through Asia, it traverses two southern regions of Russia—a portion bordering Mongolia, and the southeastern protrusion between the Black and Caspian Seas. With the eclipse, the cardinal points of Russia's progressed chart are activated, indicating a strong possibility of declared war. Certainly, the southern provinces have had their share of terrorism, leaving the Russian nation ready to march. Throughout the year, banking irregularities threaten domestic incomes with either a revaluation of the currency or a freeze on bank deposits. With the events of the preceding two years, more men have entered the military, which provides a guaranteed income. However, the Federal Assembly is reluctant to fund payroll increases for military service when that funding is desperately needed for social programs or to lay the foundation for a war machine.

Turkey: The March eclipse path passes close to the Turkish capital of Ankara. It's still all about oil for this nation, which controls tanker movement from the Black Sea to the Mediterranean. This eclipse could signal some foreign intervention and possible attacks in or near the capital. Otherwise, its influence disrupts and skews the 2007 presidential election by the National Assembly, suggesting reelection problems for the current president.

Benin, Togo, Ghana: These three independent African republics are sandwiched together between the civilly disrupted nations of Nigeria and Cote d'Ivoire. In late 2004, France invaded Cote d'Ivoire to protect its fuel interests after the obvious oil pipeline destructions in Nigeria during the previous summer. These small nations, collectively, are wealthy in gold, diamonds, timber, and arable land. During March, all three coastal capitals—Porto-Novo, Lomé, and Accra—are covered by the eclipse path. Each of these young nations has a multiplicity of human rights violations, a government removed from the farthest reaches of the nation, and financial irregularities compounded by money-laundering and drug trafficking. Of the three, Togo is most likely to lose its president through natural causes. Expect an invasion of Benin by Nigerian factions as well as a joint military operation between the British and French in Ghana.

Guiana: With a path tracing the southern Atlantic Ocean, the solar annular eclipse of September 22 nears its end, passing through the French territory of Guiana. With leadership vested in a foreign government, territories and protectorates experience strong and safe economics; Guiana is no stranger to international cooperation. This South American country maintains distinction as the launching site for communications satellites of the European Space Agency. After severe civil disruptions in central western Africa in late 2004, France placed itself in confrontation with Muslim factions. During 2006, that confrontation may be reactivated in Guiana. The appointed prefect is threatened by the eclipse, suggesting a direct assault on him within the coastal capital of Cayenne, possibly during a harvest or marketplace celebration or a recreational event. The satellite launch site at Kourou, twenty-five miles up the coast, offers a prime attack target, and European nations would be wise to increase their complements of military protection for that facility. Launchings scheduled from July through December prove fraught with problems.

United States: Factionalism and turmoil describe the national portrait. During January and February the president appears overly devoted to legislative issues, keeping the questioning press at bay with the "facts only." However, glowing statements about a robust, prospering economy are insubstantial, as an agitated public demands more social relief programs.

When the March 29 eclipse occurs, it will not pass through the United States, but the solar position activates progressed points. Another terror strike may be in the offing, aimed at a structure identified with the national character. The likely targets are a house of law, a church, or a college campus; specific buildings could be the U.S. Supreme Court, the Lincoln Memorial, the National Cathedral, St. Patrick's Catholic Church in New York, or a more prominent ivy-league campus. If this strike occurs, the national image is marred worldwide, and the president further isolates himself from the public and press, suffering more accusations of intelligence failures. At this point, the vice president may act more openly in administrative affairs, with the imprimatur of an absent president.

From March through December, the president busies himself with foreign negotiations, attempting some unusual, exclusive, or restrictive financial arrangements meant to bolster the U.S. economy. During the summer, the country experiences agricultural shortfalls due to high fuel prices and the cost of operating equipment. The nation suffers as a very stressed economy produces medical shortages in hospitals. Previous funding to military efforts inhibits Congressional solutions. Fortunately for the president and vice president, the American public remains resolute about any war effort, despite domestic setbacks and difficulties.

During September, Congress may make yet another war declaration, despite strain and agitation within the military rank and file. Unfortunately, the U.S. economy further tightens, and there is no assistance from foreign allies to underwrite war costs. Toward the end of the year an unusual and ominous silence pervades the administration.

For the last sixty-two years, the United States has wielded the saber of power, beginning with the invasion of Normandy. Yet astrological influences shaping the national image and that of the president have been difficult, culminating in the resignation of President Nixon. These distressing and confrontational aspects have required the American public and other nations to recognize and understand the fallibility of the presidency. With the last of these progressions occurring throughout the terms of President Bush, the United States is forced to develop an interactive leadership role with other nations. In another thirty years the American presidency will develop into an international example of matured leadership that is subtle and effective in championing both its own and other egalitarian causes. America's foremost politician will have learned to agree to disagree and reserve violent recourse as an ultimate last resort.

(This article was written in January 2005.)

Mundane Natalogy

Republic of Benin, December 1, 1990, 00:00:00 CET, Porto-Novo

People's Republic of China, December 4, 1982, 00:00:00 AWST, Beijing

Republic of Ghana, April 28, 1992, 00:00:00 UT, Accra

Department of Guiana (French Territory), 00:00:00 AST, Cayenne

Republic of Kazakhstan, August 30, 1995, 00:00:00 USZ5, Astana

Russian Federation, December 24, 1983, 00:00:00 BGT, Moscow

Togolese Republic, September 27, 1992, 00:00:00 UT, Lomé

Republic of Turkey, November 7, 1982, 00:00:00 BAT, Ankara

United States of America, March 4, 1789, 12:13:12 am LMT, New York City

About the Authors

Bernie Ashman has a degree in political science with a focus on international politics. In addition to his career as a social worker, he has been a practicing astrologer for over twenty-five years. He is the author of several books, including *Astrological Games People Play*, *Roadmap to Your Future*, and *SignMates*.

Stephanie Clement, Ph.D., has been practicing astrology for over thirty years. She has published numerous articles and has written several books, including *Power of the Midheaven*, *Mapping Your Birthchart*, and *Mapping Your Family Relationships*.

Alice DeVille is an internationally known astrologer specializing in relationships, real estate, government affairs, and spiritual development. She has conducted more than 140 workshops and seminars related to astrological, Feng Shui, metaphysical, and business themes.

Sasha Fenton now has 120 books to her credit, and she is still writing! Her knowledge is based on years of work as a consultant and teacher, but she says that she is an enthusiastic student, as there is still so much for her to learn.

Dorothy Oja is a certified astrological professional and career astrologer offering complete astrological consulting through her practice, MINDWORKS. She specializes in individual and relationship analysis as well as electional work.

Leeda Alleyn Pacotti practices as a naturopathic physician, nutritional counselor, and master herbalist. A former legal analyst in anti-trust and international law, she enjoys poking a finger in political machinations of all sorts.

Bruce Scofield has been practicing astrology for over thirty-five years and maintains a private practice in western Massachusetts. He is the author of several books on astrology, including *The Circuitry of the Self: Astrology and the Developmental Model*, *Users Guide to Astrology*, and *Day-Signs: Native American Astrology from Ancient Mexico*.

Anne Windsor is a professionally certified astrologer from Salt Lake City, Utah. She conducts astrology classes and seminars throughout Utah and has lectured at national astrological conferences since 1996. She is the author of Llewellyn's *2006 Daily Planetary Guide*.

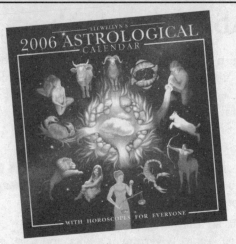

The Most Popular Astrological Calendar in the World

A must for everyone who wants to plan 2006 wisely, with an amazing amount of astrological data laid out on forty pages. Colorful, contemporary art by Mia Bosna kicks off each month, and monthly horoscopes by Carole Schwalm include the most rewarding and challenging dates for each sign. You'll find major daily aspects and planetary sign changes in addition to the Moon's sign, phase, and void-of-course times. As always, there is a table of retrograde periods and ephemerides for each month. This year's calendar also includes an article about travel planning for 2006 by Bruce Scofield.

LLEWELLYN'S ASTROLOGICAL CALENDAR 2006

40 pp. • 12 x 12 • 12 full-color paintings
0-7387-0147-5 • U.S. $12.99 Can. $17.50
To order call 1-877-NEW-WRLD

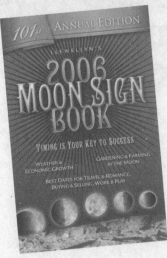

Best-selling Guide to Successful Living Since 1905!

A best-selling guide to successful living since 1905, no other book on the market tops the *Moon Sign Book* in supplying useful tips for daily success. Get weather forecasts for eight U.S. zones year round; economic forecasts; tips on planting; best hunting and fishing dates; and timing tips for personal and financial decisions. Plus, there are special articles on topics that affect us all. This year's features include: "Here Comes the Bride" by Leeda Alleyn Pacotti; "Moon Plants" by Janice Sharkey; "Finding Money by the Moon" by Natori Moore; "Quickie Gourmet Meals" by Dan Brawner; "Fashion and the Moon" by Terry Lamb; and more!